Letting Go

OF WHAT'S HOLDING YOU BACK

Maximize Your Happiness in Work, Love, and Life

Letting Go

✳ OF WHAT'S HOLDING YOU BACK ✳

Maximize Your Happiness in Work, Love, and Life

WAYNE M. SOTILE, PH.D.
and MARY O. SOTILE, M.A.

STEWART, TABORI & CHANG
NEW YORK

Published in 2007 by Stewart, Tabori & Chang
An imprint of Harry N. Abrams, Inc.

Library of Congress Cataloging-in-Publication Data:

Sotile, Wayne M., 1951-
   Letting go of what's holding you back : maximize your happiness in work, love, and life /
Wayne M. Sotile and Mary O. Sotile.
      p. cm.
   ISBN 978-1-58479-578-0
   1. Happiness. I. Sotile, Mary O. II. Title.

BF575.H27S68 2007
158--dc22

2007008207

EDITOR: Pamela Cannon
COVER, BOOK DESIGN AND COMPOSITION by Michelle Farinella Design
PRODUCTION MANAGER: Tina Cameron

The text of this book was composed in Janson Text.

Printed and bound in the United States of America
10 9 8 7 6 5 4 3 2 1

harry n. abrams, inc.
a subsidiary of La Martinière Groupe

115 West 18th Street
New York, NY 10011
www.hnabooks.com

DEDICATION

We dedicate this book to all the people in our
lives who provide the moments of caring
connection that keep us thriving.

CONTENTS

What's Holding You Back?

꙳

"Life is about love and work."

Sigmund Freud

꙳

In our careers as counselors, consultants, and speakers we have learned that most people can be happier, more productive, more contented, more self-confident, and more satisfied with life. If you're like most of the thousands of patients we have counseled or the tens of thousands from throughout the world who have attended our seminars, you probably can relate to this statement: "Well, I would be happier if only . . . " Do any of these reasons sound familiar?

- I would be happier if only I could get a promotion.
- I would be happier if only I could lose some weight and get more comfortable with my body.
- I would be happier if only my family would do what I ask of them.
- I would be happier if only I didn't have this health problem that I didn't deserve to get.
- I would be happier if only I had come from a different background and had the advantages other people had growing up.

What all these "if only" statements have in common is that they are major life events or factors, many of which are not controllable. Whether we're working with top-tier salespeople or executives, overworked professionals, couples interested in marriage enrichment, harried homemakers, or patients recovering from an unwanted illness, it seems that everyone is waiting to thrive, and most are waiting for some major thing in their life to change in order to thrive.

This is one of the most common ways we sabotage our own success. We focus on the big things that we cannot change overnight, if at all. Or we think in ways that keep us experiencing the glass as half-empty, rather than half-full. We live in the future or the past and, in the process, miss the present. Sometimes we allow our if-only statements to lower our expectations, essentially fulfilling our own self-limiting view that we can try as hard as we can but we'll never make it to the level of success that others achieve.

Alternatively we may let our if-only thinking stop us from appreciating and celebrating the goodness of the lives we do have.

The major life events that happen to us are important. In some cases, past events have so traumatized us that a great deal of psychological treatment and hard emotional work is necessary to get beyond the damage. It's also true that if something very difficult is going on in the present, it can shape the lenses through which we view the world. Dealing with a major illness or loss certainly has an impact on our happiness. But in the long run, happiness is affected only slightly by these big factors. Throughout this book we will share with you key points from research showing that, *over time, it is not the big things that matter most; it is the little things that account for the difference in long-term resilience and well-being.* We want to help you learn to let go of what's holding you back from appreciating the little things in your day that can lift you up— even for a moment. Do this, and you will start to thrive. In the pages that follow, we will teach you to counter those inevitable hassles that are a part of life with "daily uplifts."

Uplifts are essentially moments of caring connection with other people, with nature, with god, with your deepest authentic self, with anything that makes you feel nurtured or cared about. An uplift can be as simple as a pat on the back, a beautiful flower or piece of music, a moment of excellence at work, a smile, a prayer, a deep breath, or a moment of mindfulness and appreciation of your own worth and goodness.

Research has shown that boosting your "daily uplift" factor can make the difference between thriving and just getting on, even during difficult times. Too many people sabotage this simple strategy for maximizing their happiness in work, love, and life. They habitually discount what's good about their work, family, and life; they learn to ignore signs that they are holding back; and they live as though they are doomed to follow a script filled with others' expectations and directions, rather than their own decisions about who they want to be and what kind of life they want to live. This book will walk you through a process for evaluating whether you are holding back in any of these ways, and will provide you with the tools and techniques to let go.

First, we will elaborate on exactly why your happiness matters and help you to diagnose whether you are holding back in ways that may be dangerous to your health and well-being. Next, with facts about what truly healthy work/life balance is all about, we will dispel the myth of the balanced life. Gaining or reclaiming passionate involvement in good work, overcoming "work ambivalence," and becoming a true hero to the people you love and work with complete the foundation of our letting-go program. Next, we will walk you through the steps involved in changing for good, from the inside out, and help you to clarify your authentic self. Common-sense lessons from the best research on resilience will show you how you can move through difficult times and come out stronger because of the experience. Then, we will help you to evaluate the "fencing" that outlines your life territory. After reporting cutting-edge news about stress, we will explain why you should not fear it and how you can manage your stress reactions. Finally, we will provide you with twenty-two specific strategies for countering daily hassles with uplifts.

You Get to Choose

Just as we do with clients who come to us for counseling, we invite you to strike a deal with us. We promise to do our part in helping you transform your life, and we ask that you commit to doing your part. This means that you have to be realistic about the work that faces you. As you will see in the pages to come, part of what holds most people back is their eagerness to buy into a quick-fix mentality. The truth for most of us is that no one will rescue us; our past won't change; we won't win the lottery; and no perfect mentor, lover, or friend will erase our insecurities or heal our psychological wounds. Instead, it's up to you to take charge of yourself and your life. Change takes considerable effort over long periods of time, and only you can do the work it will take to make your life better.

This doesn't mean that you're doomed to years of miserable effort before you see the light at the end of the tunnel. On the contrary, most people start feeling better as soon as they commit to making a change.

It's not initiating change that's difficult; it's maintaining the effort behind it. It has been said that, in any area of life, successful people make a habit of doing things that people who fail don't like to do.

We want you to maximize your happiness in work, love, and life. To do so, you must learn to recognize and then eliminate or effectively manage the psychological issues that short-circuit everybody else.

The information in this book will give you a template for thriving in all areas of your life. We will provide you with detailed self-improvement information, including the psychological factors, skills, and concepts our patients and consulting clients have found to be most helpful in transforming their lives, families, and work teams. We will provide you with a set of coping tools that you can use to repair what's broken in your life and to help you let go of what's holding you back.

Let's get started.

✳

CHAPTER 1

Happiness Matters

"Is the life you are living worth what
you are giving up to have it?"

Jim Loher and Tony Schwartz, The Power of Full Engagement[1]

HOW HAPPY ARE YOU?

Check the one statement below that best describes how you usually feel.[2]

- ○ 10. Extremely happy (feeling ecstatic, joyous, fantastic)
- ○ 9. Very happy (feeling really good, elated)
- ○ 8. Pretty happy (spirits high, feeling good)
- ○ 7. Mildly happy (feeling fairly good and somewhat cheerful)
- ○ 6. Slightly happy (just a bit above neutral)
- ○ 5. Neutral (not particularly happy or unhappy)
- ○ 4. Slightly unhappy (just a bit below neutral)
- ○ 3. Mildly unhappy (just a bit low)
- ○ 2. Pretty unhappy (somewhat "blue," spirits down)
- ○ 1. Very unhappy (depressed, spirits very low)
- ○ 0. Extremely unhappy (utterly depressed, completely down)

We have given this test to thousands of people in our seminars and private psychotherapy practice, and researchers have administered it to groups of people from around the world. Regardless of race, culture, or class, most people rate themselves as a 7 on the happiness scale. Thus 7 is considered average.[3]

So, what's wrong with being average? Here's what's wrong: Every 7 we've known longs to be a 10. But most underestimate their potential and overestimate which characteristics and behaviors they would have to change in order to be as happy as possible, in other words a 10.

We have written this book to help you let go of what's holding you back from thriving. You will see that the keys to moving from an average 7 to a thriving 10 are accessible, attainable, and sometimes very simple.

Your Happiness Matters

There is nothing more crucial to your well-being and resilience in work, relationships, and life in general than your happiness. When happiness is high, all other indicators of well-being are likely to be high as well. In short, you are thriving.

Webster's defines to "thrive" as to "grow vigorously, becoming increasingly healthier; to advance successfully; to prosper outstandingly; to flourish despite difficult circumstances, to achieve progress and growth toward one's own goals." This is exactly what 10s are doing; they don't just experience life, they thrive on it!

To put it simply, 10s have it all. They out-produce, out-perform, and make more money than other people, and they are more satisfied in their jobs or careers. If your manager is a thriver, he or she is easier to work with and better able to recruit and retain key employees. Those thriving 10s are also more likely to enjoy a satisfying personal life, to have more rewarding romantic relationships and friendships, and to have a more enjoyable family life.

Studies show that happier people tend to be healthier, recover more quickly when illness strikes, and live longer overall. Conversely, compared to their unhealthy peers, healthy people are more likely to be happy. But the connections don't stop there. It's also true that happy people are more likely to stay healthy. That's because happier people tend to take better care of themselves and to enjoy the health boosts that accompany positive emotions (more about this later).

To help illustrate this point, let's consider the health consequences of a few conditions that could be considered the opposite of happiness: depression, anger, loneliness and isolation, and conflict with loved ones.

Depression is now recognized as a risk factor for developing a major illness. Even mild long-term depression can increase the risk of early death after developing a serious disease.[4] A recent study of 285 heart attack patients by Johns Hopkins University found that those who were even minimally depressed had a five times greater risk of dying after a heart attack than those who were not depressed.[5] As the patient's level of depression rose, their risk of dying rose. Those patients who were highly depressed were ten times more likely to die after a heart attack.

Studies have also revealed that loss of human companionship, chronic loneliness, and social isolation increase the risk of virtually every major disease including cancer, pneumonia, heart disease, and mental illness.[6]

Recent research has shown that harboring intense hostility may increase the risk of major illnesses, like heart disease, more than other risk factors, such as cholesterol and smoking.[7]

Relationship distress also increases the odds of major illness striking. Married people who are unhappy with their mates are far more likely to struggle with physical illness than those who are happily married.[8]

Most recently, researchers discovered that people with coronary heart disease who tended to experience negative feelings were at considerably elevated risk of heart attack and death. Patients who chronically struggled with negative emotions and who tended to hold back self-expression in order to avoid possible negative reactions from others tripled their risk of needing bypass surgery or of having a new cardiac event like a heart attack.[9] This psychological pattern of struggling was more predictive of complications and death than were the major physical risk factors or stress.

The benefits of being happy do not stop with better health. Healthy, happy people are also the ones most likely to thrive at work, regardless of the industry they work in. And people who like their work are far more likely to remain healthy and happy.

In addition, these healthy, happy people who are thriving at work are the very same people who report the highest levels of satisfaction with their personal lives.

Fair or not, it is typically the case that people who thrive in one arena—love, work, self-care—tend to thrive in all areas. Happiness is the epitome of positive emotion, and thriving people exude happiness. Their positive emotion is contagious and serves as a bridge that connects high performance across arenas.

Likewise, unhappiness in one major arena of your life can permeate other arenas and affect the lives of those around you. If you are dissatisfied in one of your roles, you're unlikely to thrive in the others for long. For example, if you're unhappy in your career, and you spread your negative emotions around your workplace, you will erode your work team's cohesiveness and your own productivity. Soon, the negative emotions that start at work will follow you home, straining your most important relationships.

Are You Holding Back?

The good news is that you can become a thriver. You just need to find the right path for yourself and begin to let go of the things that are holding you back. This isn't, however, as simple as it sounds.

While we long to live more fulfilling lives, to contribute more to the happiness of people who matter to us, and to feel greater inner peace along the way, we continue to struggle with the same old demons that sap our energies, blunt our joy, and leave us quietly wondering, "is this all there is?" This kind of holding back keeps us from celebrating what is good about our lives—our work, our relationships, our families, and ourselves.

Sometimes the ways in which we hold ourselves back are apparent to anyone who is looking. Events like job losses, divorces, or alcohol-related incidents indicate to the world that something is wrong. Other times the signs of holding back are more subtle. You may be the only one aware of emotional exhaustion in your job or sadness and disappointment in your marriage or regular self-medication with alcohol or drugs.

Whether or not they have reached the point of being obvious to others, negative emotions are the enemies of success, happiness, and health. Take the following quiz to see how you might be holding on to negative emotions that are holding you back.

HOW TO TELL IF YOU'RE HOLDING BACK

Check all of the statements that apply to you:

○ I make note of what I don't get done more often than I pause to celebrate what I've accomplished.

○ I'm more likely to notice or to comment on what's wrong in a relationship than I'm likely to compliment another person or express appreciation to the people I love or work with.

○ I can't get through the day without feeling exhausted or getting irritated over something that happened.

○ When I stand before a mirror, I automatically look at the parts of my body that bother me the most.

○ More often than not while I'm working, I daydream about wanting to be someplace else.

○ When I'm not working, I often feel restless or guilty about what I'm not getting done at work.

○ I fantasize often about working someplace else or in another profession.

○ I spend a lot of time feeling bored and have a "take it or leave it" attitude about some major aspect of my life (work, marriage, friendships).

○ I spend so much time fantasizing about how things might be better or less stressful for me that I don't fully enjoy what's going on in my life *right now*.

○ Most days I dread getting out of bed.

○ Most days include doing things I hate doing.

○ It seems that no matter what I achieve, I think I should have or could have done better.

○ I pursue a goal as if there might be a scarcity of whatever it is I am after and I'll get short-changed unless I compete relentlessly.

○ I don't tell people who matter to me often enough exactly what it is about them that I cherish.

○ I feel bad about unsolved problems in my marriage or important relationship.

○ I feel guilty about what is not getting done when I'm trying to have fun.

○ I feel ashamed of my family background or carry emotional wounds as a result of the way I was raised.

○ Un-soothed feelings from past hurts still haunt me.

○ I often revisit memories of people who have hurt or disappointed me.

○ I feel guilty for wanting more than I have.

○ I often wish my life was more like someone else's who I admire.

○ I've stopped learning new things that excite me.

○ I'm growing more cynical and skeptical.

○ I sometimes worry about what might happen to me if I continue to climb the ladder of success.

○ I feel that my life is too stressful.

○ It seems to me that other people have better work/life balance than I do.

○ I don't tell other people what I truly think, feel, need, or want because I don't trust how they might respond.

○ I hold back at work from doing things I know would improve my productivity.

○ I frequently wish I took better care of my health.

○ I try to improve myself, but more often than not, I backslide into old, unwanted habits.

○ I can't remember the last time I had a creative thought.

○ I experience emotional pain, but do nothing to change the situation.

How many of these did you check?

Whether you are showing big symptoms of nonthriving or are simply aware that you are somewhere short of being a 10, the information in this book will help you to pinpoint the factors, both obvious and subtle, that contribute to the way you feel. Later in the book we will show you how to let go of these negative emotions using our new paradigms for work/life balance, stress management, personal change management, and for thriving at work and home.

The Flip-Side of the Coin

Let's say that right now you are among the not so happy, not so healthy, job-dissatisfied, and so on. Perhaps you checked more than a few of the symptoms of holding back we listed above. In order to start letting go and thriving, you must begin by understanding that symptoms contain important wisdom about your life. Often, the way we suffer offers clues about what we need to do to feel better. This is most obvious when it comes to symptoms that signal physical threat or danger. For example, as your hand approaches an open flame, you notice the "symptom" of your skin getting hotter, and an internal alarm signals you to do the healthy thing: *Move away from the flame!*

When it comes to our psychological symptoms, however, we don't always respond so wisely. Many of us have learned to ignore psychological signs of impending danger. Instead of making health-enhancing adjustments, we just go numb and continue doing what's hurting us, to an even more intense degree. We even fool ourselves into thinking that our ability to go numb is a sign of strength. This is the psychological equivalent of holding your hand over a flame, bearing through the pain, and then convincing yourself that the smell of your burning flesh is not burning flesh at all, but rather the sweet smell of success! In other words, we mistake our pain for evidence of success, when in fact it is signaling impending danger.

Holding Back Comes in Many Flavors

Let's take a more detailed look at the symptoms that we referred to earlier, including unchecked worry and anxiety; chronic struggles with depression; unchecked anger, hostility, or cynicism; isolation and loneliness; and chronic marriage or family tensions and conflict; as well as burnout, a malady that inflicts great professional, emotional, health, relationship, and economic consequences. As we said above, many people are living with the frustration of trying hard but never feeling that they really make it to their goals. Others hold themselves back by clinging to unrealistic fears—of stress, success, failure, rejection, or love. Some of us can't enjoy the present because we're holding on to unforgiven hurts and have a cynical, skeptical attitude stemming from when we've been double-crossed in the past. Here are a few examples of how these issues have shown up in the lives of our clients.

"I'm doing pretty well in my career, and I guess I shouldn't complain. But I look at those guys who earn the biggest bucks and wonder, why not me? What's holding me back from taking the next step? Sometimes I feel like I've already risen above my upbringing, and I almost feel guilty for wanting more." **—John, insurance salesperson**

"I'm sick and tired of battling with myself. My 'demons' are wearing me out! I am not living the way I want to live. I binge eat. I drink too much and exercise too little. And I worry that my 'social smoking' is becoming a habit. I'm tired of waking up feeling guilty for what I did or did not do the day before. Why am I sabotaging myself like this?" **—Karen, 36-year-old banking vice president**

"I know what I need to change. My problem is sticking with it once I begin changing. I go through the same old pattern, again and again. I commit to turning over a new leaf, and I feel better immediately. This high lasts a few weeks, at most. Then I start to struggle with a vague sense of unease, like I'm faking it; not being my 'real' self.

*Sooner than later, I'm back to my old ways. I'm stuck in a pattern of getting nowhere." —***Fredo, battling personal and job problems**

*"By most standards we have a great marriage. No major problems or dramas. But I sometimes worry that our spark is fading. Maybe this is as good as marriage gets. But I don't want to become one of those dreadful couples you see having a silent dinner together. Is it realistic to expect that we can keep our flame alive?" —***Walter, married 15 years**

"I worked harder than anyone I know to get here, and now I seem to resent what has come with my success. I'm avoiding going into the office. I dread returning phone calls to the very clients I've worked so hard to get. And the people who report to me act like they're afraid of me.

    *"I know that my behavior is the main problem in our office, but I can't figure out what I need to do to get back on track and start enjoying my work again." —***Jerry, business executive**

Different psychological habits are keeping each of these people from thriving and functioning at their highest capacity. John's tendency to "try hard, but not make it" beyond certain levels of success and happiness is keeping him down. Karen's own shame is sabotaging her efforts to change. Fredo's confusion about the psychology of changing shuts down his best efforts. And Walter is lacking a realistic yardstick for measuring the success of his marriage. Jerry has already moved into the dangerous condition of burnout.

Burnout

Life is about love and work, and burnout can affect us in both areas. Burnout can be caused by holding back, and holding back can result from burnout. Either way you are in trouble.

    The nearly 5,000 studies about burnout that have been published suggest that you are suffering from burnout if you show any combination of the following symptoms.[10]

Emotional exhaustion is signaled by lost passion for your work or in your relationships. In fact, when you're suffering from burnout, you show signs of resenting the routine demands that come with the roles you have chosen, and you no longer "bounce back" with a sense of rejuvenation after taking time off from work or after engaging in activities with loved ones.

At work, emotional exhaustion may sound something like this: "What?! Another customer wants me to return a call? Another patient wants my advice? I've got to attend another meeting? I'm sick of this." It's as though you own a restaurant, yet find yourself grousing, "Oh no! Here come more hungry people, expecting me to feed them."

Signs of emotional exhaustion can also surface at home: "Not another 'talk'! I've been working hard all day. I don't feel like talking." Or "Another birthday party? You must be kidding. We went to your sister's birthday party last year. How many birthdays is she going to celebrate?"

Depersonalization means that you have hardened emotionally, and you're behaving callously toward others. Maybe you haven't lost your compassion, but you're acting like you don't care. You're so numb or lost in your busyness that you don't take time to do the simple things that make people feel cared about, like making eye contact. You ignore (or don't even notice) the nuances during conversations: the tear in her eye, or the sigh in his voice. You just keep steamrolling ahead.

A diminished sense of personal achievement haunts a person who is burning out. You start to question whether you really are making a difference at home and/or at work. You might find yourself thinking something like this: "All I do is try to take care of everyone else's needs, but I feel like I'm failing everywhere. My family says I work too much. My colleagues say I don't work enough. I'm not so sure that this is worth it."

Your performance starts to slip as your memory, concentration, and attention lapse, especially during the later stages of a demanding workday. You approach problems rigidly, relying on over-learned ways of thinking and behaving. Work-related mistakes increase in frequency.

Physical wear-down leads to poor health behaviors, and the wear-and-tear of your chronic stress leads to health problems.

Emotional distress spreads, and you get caught in an unfortunate feedback loop: You take work frustrations home, and your irritability, worry, or anger contaminate your home life. Then tensions from home follow you into your workplace, fueling inappropriate workplace behaviors. Soon, you feel misunderstood in both arenas.

What Happens Next?

This scenario is bad enough, but it can get worse. Burnout leaves us feeling out of control of the stresses in our lives, and this kind of high-demand, low-control situation is dangerous to our health and emotional well-being.

Stress is not inherently dangerous. In fact, stress that is challenging and over which we have some degree of control is a good thing—it is energizing, exciting, fulfilling, and increases our self-esteem. For example, surgeons experience this kind of energizing stress when they are performing life-saving procedures for which they are expertly trained. It is the kind of stress that an athlete feels when the competition is at hand and they have prepared diligently in anticipation of it.

Stress that is highly demanding and over which we feel little control, on the other hand, is toxic. It makes us afraid and causes us to start holding back. This creates psychological paralysis that leads to further burnout. Another A-causes-B-and-B-causes-A circle. There's more to be concerned about here. Living in a state of burnout increases your chances of suffering one or more of five psychological conditions we call The Big Bad 5.

The Big Bad 5

- Unchecked worry and anxiety
- Chronic struggles with depression
- Unchecked anger, hostility, or cynicism
- Isolation and loneliness
- Chronic marriage or family tensions and conflict

In his book *Thriving with Heart Disease*, Wayne called attention to the fact that each of these conditions is a risk factor for major chronic diseases, unnecessary suffering, and early death.[11]

Each of the Big Bad 5 psychological conditions fuels the others. For example, if you constantly worry about your life being too stressful (or about anything else, for that matter), you'll suffer an increased risk of becoming depressed. And if you stay stuck in depression, you'll likely grow irritable, avoid other people, and start to struggle in your family relationships—which will add fuel to your chronic worrying, depression, irritability, and so on.

We're not saying that we believe that all physical illness is caused by psychological factors. In fact, we fear that sometimes those in our profession inadvertently promote a new-age guilt that leads people to feel ashamed that they are sick, as though they have failed at the task of maintaining excellent health. Rather, we're simply trying to underscore a truth that has been confirmed by scientific research: The five psychological factors we are discussing do interact with physical factors in causing or curing illness. Ignoring the psychological puts us at risk of losing both our health and our happiness.

Nor are we saying that all psychological suffering leads to physical illness. Anxiety, anger, loneliness, irritability, and family squabbling are all part of the human condition. But each of these experiences is only normal up to a point. When any of these conditions characterize most of your days, you are in danger of encountering a cascade of negative outcomes across the various arenas of your life. We caution you against accepting as normal a chronic struggle with any of these five dangerous psychological conditions. Let's look more closely at each of them.

Unchecked Worry and Anxiety

According to the National Institute of Mental Health (NIMH), more than 23 million Americans suffer from some form of anxiety disorder. We're not talking here about a passing worry. We're referring to the pain that comes with unremitting worries or full-blown anxiety or panic attacks.

If any of the following are true for you, you might be worrying too much.

- I'm full of fears that I can't get out of my mind.
- I feel like something terrible is going to happen.
- I worry excessively about what might go wrong.
- I have difficulty unplugging from my worries and simply enjoying myself.
- I feel I have no control over what happens to me.
- No matter what I'm doing, my worries are constantly in my head.
- One of the first things I think about when I wake up each morning is what I've got to worry about.

Any of these symptoms may signal that you're stuck in a worry habit that can hurt your health, happiness, and productivity. Especially dangerous is the sort of chronic worrying that comes with panic and anxiety disorders, phobias, and stress disorders.

Chronic Struggles with Depression

Between 10 and 14 million Americans, and more than 100 million people worldwide suffer from depression.[12] Depression is among the most common conditions that bring people to seek medical care for aches and pains, but studies have shown that physicians do not adequately detect or treat 40 to 60 percent of cases of depression.[13] And most people who are depressed don't seek any help for what ails them. In fact, less than one fourth of those who are depressed receive treatment.[14]

The costs we incur because of this problem are staggering. In the American workplace alone, lost productivity due to depression amounts to an estimated $44 billion per year, not including disability payments or costs related to treatment.[15] It is estimated that by the year 2020 major depression will become the second leading cause of disability worldwide (second only to heart disease).[16]

Depression is now recognized as a risk factor for developing a major illness, and as we have already mentioned, even mild, long-term depression increases the risk of early death after developing a serious disease.[17]

Are You Depressed?

We're not talking here about a blue mood that passes. The kind of depression that you need to be concerned about is signaled by changes in your normal mood, thinking, bodily functions, and behavior that last more than three or four weeks.[18]

Mood in depression can be sad, worried, angry, or irritable. Depressed people lose interest in things that typically would bring them pleasure. Many complain of high levels of fear that something terrible is going to happen, and feelings of hopelessness and helplessness may get so strong that thoughts of suicide creep in.

Depressed thinking takes the form of negative thoughts, especially about yourself and your situation. Depressed people have difficulty seeing anything good about themselves, their past, or their future. Their thoughts fill with mental images and "self-talk" that convinces them that their lives will never be the same again. Many have difficulties with concentration and memory, and making decisions can be very difficult.

Bodily functions are also affected by depression. Some people lose their appetite and lose weight when depressed. For others, the change that signals depression is an increased appetite; they gain weight in reaction to the fact that they overeat in an effort to soothe their emotional pain.

Depression can also interfere with sleep. Again, the changes here can be in two directions. Most depressed people have difficulty falling asleep or staying asleep, or they wake up earlier than they do when they are not depressed and then can't get back to sleep. Others, however, react to depression by oversleeping. In either case, depression is usually signaled by fatigue and lack of energy, regardless of how much you sleep.

Other body changes that come with depression might be loss of sexual interest, dry mouth, constipation, or unexplained pains in different parts of the body.

Behavior changes related to depression interfere with your ability to carry out your everyday activities. You may sit stewing in guilt and anxiety about all that you "should" do, but simply lack the energy and focus to get started.

The checklist below can help you to "diagnose" yourself. Read through these obvious and subtle signs of depression[19] and check any that apply to you.

- ○ On most days, I feel hopeless and disinterested in activities that I typically find to be stimulating and enjoyable.
- ○ I seem to have lost interest in activities that I normally find to be pleasurable.
- ○ I have much less sex drive than usual.
- ○ I feel indifferent and passive about my problems.
- ○ In recent weeks, my appetite patterns have changed markedly, and my weight has changed significantly (gained or lost).
- ○ My sleep patterns have changed in one or more of these ways: insomnia (difficulty falling asleep), disrupted sleep (difficulty staying asleep), or sleeping more hours than normal.
- ○ I have much nervous energy.

○ My muscles feel weak.

○ I feel unusually fatigued, like I'm "stuck" and I have no energy to do anything about it.

○ I feel inadequate and guilty.

○ I am having difficulty thinking, concentrating, remembering, or making decisions.

○ I am preoccupied with thoughts of death or suicide.

If you checked any five of these symptoms, and if you have been feeling this way more often than not for the past several weeks, you may be suffering from clinical depression. This is the sort of depression that is dangerous to your health, and it requires medical attention and professional help.

Medical Causes of Depression

Both anxiety and depressive symptoms can stem from alcohol abuse, personality disorders, sleep apnea, or other medical problems. And certain medications taken for various physical ailments may have side effects that cause or complicate anxiety or depression. Be sure to consult your physician about any of these concerns.

Unchecked Anger, Hostility, or Cynicism

In their book *Anger Kills*, authors Redford and Virginia Williams state that for the chronically hostile person, "getting angry is like taking a small dose of some slow-acting poison—arsenic, for example—every day of your life."[20] So does this mean that anger can kill you? Recent research has shown that high hostility may be associated with major illnesses like heart disease more than even high cholesterol and smoking.[21] Mismanaging anger will not only make you unhealthy and unhappy, it will also poison relationships with those around you. Consider how mismanaged anger can affect your relationships at work.

Check any of the following that apply to your behavior in your job:

○ I'm sometimes verbally abusive to others at work.

○ I yell or scream at others if they disagree with me or in order to get them to do their jobs.

○ I use derogatory names when referring to coworkers.

○ I use aggressive eye contact when dealing with a worker who has upset me.

○ I use threats of job loss to intimidate the people who report to me.

○ I humiliate others in front of their coworkers.

A recent study suggests that if you are guilty of any of these workplace bullying behaviors, it is likely that you're costing your company money. The study documented that abused subordinates may seek revenge by not helping coworkers and by speaking unfavorably about the organization to outsiders. [22] In fact, a poorly delivered criticism from a superior in front of peers is one of the reasons white-collar workers give most frequently for experiencing conflict on the job. And a 2006 British survey of 2,330 workers found that bad bosses—rather than heavy workloads, unreasonable clients, or a high-pressure environment—caused most worker anxiety and stress. Nearly 60 percent of those polled said they had looked for another job simply because of their boss.[23]

And if you are the *target* of these kinds of hostile acts by a superior or colleague at work, your health is also at risk. Toxic work environments, where demand is high and an employee's control over how the job is done is low, create relationship tensions that have been found to be bad for employee physical and mental health.[24] (We offer guidelines for evaluating your work environment in Chapter 3.)

How do you know if you're at risk? A landmark study of mind-body connections determined that if any of the following apply to you, you're at risk of suffering from dangerous levels of anger, hostility, or cynicism:[25]

○ I tend to be a perfectionist (I have trouble accepting that I am or another person is good enough).

○ I am excessively competitive.

○ My main pleasure comes from work.

○ I have difficulty relaxing.

○ I am suspicious and guarded in dealing with others.

○ I tend to think that other people cannot be trusted to be competent (to know what they are doing).

○ I tend to do and think several things at once.

○ I constantly make note of what irritates me.

○ I'm always rushing.

○ I'm constantly aware of time—that there is not enough of it.

○ I am told that I am self-focused.

○ I tend to be a poor listener.

○ I tend to interrupt others when they are speaking because I can "see" the point they are making and I want them to get on with it.

○ I am easily angered, especially if I am not in control of a situation (like getting caught in a long line or a traffic jam).

○ I am often frustrated with others' poor performance.

○ I like to be in control of what others do.

○ I tend to give others my advice and my opinion, even when they do not ask for it.

○ I'm constantly tapping my feet, fidgeting, or acting nervous.

○ I drive and act aggressively. I try to dominate others.

Failure to control any of these tendencies can fuel free-floating hostility—the sort of "on alert" physical and psychological state that strains your body, ruins your relationships, and erodes your happiness.

Isolation and Loneliness

The health risks of chronic loneliness and social isolation, including cancer, pneumonia, heart disease, and mental illness, were noted earlier. We also know that the opposite of loneliness or social isolation—supportive relationships—boosts health, happiness, and productivity. In fact, research across industries has shown that when coworkers interact supportively with each other throughout the workday, everyone benefits from boosted productivity, commitment to the company, and stress resilience.[26]

When assessing your support factor, recognize that social support comes in many forms. How are you doing in each of the following areas?

Tangible support has to do with whether you have the help you need to face your daily challenges at work and home.

At work: Do you have the information, tools, and support systems you need to get your work done?

In your personal life: Do you have access to people who can help you to meet the demands of your daily life? How about during especially challenging times, like when you are sick or without basic resources; do you have people you can call to help you out?

Affection support comes when others show you love and affection, make you feel wanted, and generally remind you that you are cared for.

At work: Do you feel that your coworkers like you? What about your superiors? Do you get your fair share of recognition and expressions of appreciation for what you contribute to your company? Do you consider any of your coworkers to be among your true friends?

In your personal life: Do you get your fair share of hugs or other acts of affection? Do you speak often enough with friends and loved ones who matter most to you? Do loved ones and friends ask how you are doing in a way that feels soothing to you? Do they do this often enough to satisfy you?

Positive social interaction means you have someone to have a good time with, to get together with for relaxation and fun.

At work: Do you enjoy interacting with the people at work—your clients, customers, or coworkers? If you were to tape record a typical day in your workplace, would a listener hear a lot of laughter, compliments, and pleasant conversation?

In your personal life: Are you satisfied with how often you get together to share a fun time or a relaxed evening with a loved one or friend? When you're in the mood for doing something fun with another person, do you know people that you feel comfortable calling? Do others reach out to you frequently enough with invitations to do fun things?

Emotional support comes when you have someone to listen and offer helpful advice when you need to talk, confide something, or share private worries and fears.

At work: Do you have a mentor you trust enough to confide in? Do you feel that the powers that be in your workplace care about your concerns? If you are upset about a problem at work, is there a person available to speak to?

In your personal life: Do you have someone you trust enough to confide in? Do you have a supportive loved one or friend whose advice you value? Is there someone you can count on to understand and not criticize you?

Chronic Marriage or Family Tensions and Conflict

Nothing feels better than getting along with loved ones, and few things are more toxic than when tensions fester in these same relationships. Conflict with loved ones super-charges your body's stress response. Perhaps this is why people in high-conflict marriages are more likely to get sick than are people in happier marriages.[27]

But the repercussions of unresolved family problems don't stop there. Research shows that marriage and family conflict can also significantly affect workplace behaviors. For example, lack of family support for work stress is a primary cause of career burnout. Even more remarkable are the findings of studies of workplace violence. One study analyzed nearly 1,000 cases of enacted or threatened workplace violence recorded in human resource records for a number of Fortune 500 companies during the 1980s and 1990s.[28] The researchers found that in only 6 percent of cases were job issues identified as the primary cause for threats or acts of violence, but in fully 74 percent the perpetrator had been involved in a domestic dispute the night before the incident. The study concluded that many disrupters enter the workplace with the attitude, "I might have to put up with all of this grief at home, but I'll be damned if I'll tolerate anything from you people at work."

There is no universally accepted checklist for assessing marriage and family health. However, most experts in the field would agree on some general characteristics of effective families. Healthy families provide love and affection for family members, as well as protection and comfort in times of stress. There is a clear boundary between parents and children and mutual acceptance that final authority rests with the parent or parents. Members of healthy families keep aware of each other's life events, and they are effective in confronting and dealing with whatever problems come their way. These families maintain rituals of connection, which create continuity as family members feel a part of previous generations and of generations to come.

If the family is headed by an intact marriage or other committed relationship, the health of that relationship will impact the overall functioning of the family. Psychologists Scott Stanley and Howard Markman of the University of Denver, two respected marital researchers, devised a useful way to assess the status of your marriage or committed relationship in the area of communication and conflict. The Relationship Dynamics Scale is based on their thirty years of research on communication and conflict management patterns that predict if a relationship is headed for trouble.

RELATIONSHIP DYNAMICS SCALE[29]

Answer each of the following questions in terms of your relationship with your "mate" if married, or your "partner" if dating or engaged. We recommend that you answer these questions by yourself (not with your partner).

Use the following 3-point scale to rate how often you and your mate or partner experience the following:

1 = Almost never   2 = Once in a while   3 = Frequently

__ Little arguments escalate into ugly fights with accusations, criticism, name-calling, and bringing up past hurts.

__ My partner criticizes my opinions, feelings, or desires.

__ My partner seems to view my words or actions more negatively than I mean them to be.

__ When we have a problem to solve, it seems like we are on opposite teams.

__ I hold back from telling my partner what I really think and feel.

__ I feel lonely in this relationship.

__ When we argue, one of us withdraws—that is, doesn't want to talk about it any more or leaves the scene

Add your scores: __

A nationwide survey found that the average score on this scale was 11. Higher scores mean that your relationship may need improvement.

Interpretations

A score of 7–11 suggests that your relationship is probably in good or even great shape at this time. It's like you are traveling along and have come to a green light. There is no need to stop, but now is a great time to work on making your relationship all it can be.

A score of 12–16 suggests that your relationship is coming to a "yellow light." You need to be cautious. While you may be happy now in your relationship, your score reveals warning signs of patterns you don't want to worsen. Take action to protect and improve your relationship. Spending time to strengthen your relationship now could be the best thing you could do for your future together.

A score of 17–21 suggests that your relationship is approaching a red light. Stop, and think about where the two of you are headed. Your score indicates the presence of patterns that could put your relationship at significant risk. You may be heading for trouble—or already be there. If so, don't despair. Help is on the way!

CLOSING THOUGHTS

Remember that no checklist can truly capture the quality of your life or predict your future. We presented these rating scales to call your attention to any signs that you might be at risk of psychological threats to your health and well-being. For many of us, responding to these checklists reveals that we are in distress and that it's time to start working on getting ourselves to the next levels of happiness, health, and productivity.

CHAPTER 2

❧ Rethinking the Balanced Life ❧

"At work, you think of the children you have left at home.
At home, you think of the work you've left unfinished....
Your heart is rent."

Golda Meir

Most people we counsel are searching for a more balanced life. In fact, discontentment about work/life balance is one of the most pervasive forms of holding back we encounter. The problem is, few seem to understand exactly what balance means in contemporary life. Guidelines used by prior generations are outdated, and most contemporary notions of balance hinge on new-age guilt about working hard. This contrasts with contemporary data suggesting that passionate involvement in good work is a key ingredient in any formula for thriving—a topic we will explore in detail in our next chapter. In this chapter, we want to emphasize the fact that life balance is not a static or constant state. It's a dynamic, ever-changing process that involves repeatedly changing where you choose to focus your passions and energies and how you choose to spend your time during a given day, week, or month. Resilient people never get balanced and stay that way. Rather, they regularly switch their focus from one life arena to another—work, family, physical self, intimate relationship, mind, and spirit. In the truest sense, balance is like walking across a stream on rocks: you constantly counter-balance by adjusting your stance. The trick is to make sure that you don't neglect any one area for so long that it becomes a weak link that causes you to lose your balance altogether.

The information in this chapter will help you to rethink your life balance. Start by identifying the areas that are the shakiest parts of your life foundation.

Is Your Foundation Solid?

When the going gets rough, resilient people return to the fundamentals. This applies to athletic teams trying to recoup after a poor performance, to couples who bounce back after rocky times, to loyal work teams shaken by unwanted changes, and to every individual who battled back from a career setback, a lost love, or an unwanted medical diagnosis.

Returning to the fundamentals means different things to different people, but, for everyone, it involves bolstering an aspect of life that has been neglected. To elaborate this point, we will draw on two sets of experiences that at first glance seem unrelated: our experience counseling patients who have chronic illnesses and our experience consulting with business leaders who are having trouble motivating their employees. As you will see, both experiences teach the same lesson. Let's begin with people dealing with a major, chronic illness. Every day, people outlive textbook predictions about their illnesses by healing their lives in some essential way. A major lesson from the mind/body research on these remarkable medical patients is that they respond to their diagnosis as a wake-up call to attend to what is ailing them emotionally, not just physically. Some reconnect with estranged loved ones. Others find peace spiritually. Still others start having more fun, decide to finally engage passionately in their work, travel, or enroll in classes to learn something new.

The content varies, but the life-sustaining themes of these resilient patients' reactions are similar: They take responsibility for doing something about fortifying their overall life foundation by bolstering any life arena that is suffering. They start living more fully, focusing on areas that are important but that they've been neglecting. The resilient person faced with his or her mortality isn't satisfied to keep up a "business as usual" way of living. Instead, they assess, reevaluate, and reflect; then they adjust what is out of balance. They notice the life areas that have been neglected, assess their relative value, and then change in ways that bring them more in line with their authentic selves. They don't do more of what they are already doing well, and sometimes to excess. Instead, they create more balance by counter-balancing: They get busy repairing the damage that has come from neglecting important aspects of their lives.

One part of our work is consulting with corporate and business leaders who want to motivate employees to higher levels of performance. These experiences have convinced us that business leaders too often try to motivate with the carrot-and-stick approach. They alternate between threatening penalties for poor performance ("We will hit you with this stick if you don't perform better!") and dangling "carrots," like pay bonuses, fancy trips, and other prizes as rewards for meeting corporate production or sales goals.

These strategies do work to motivate many employees, especially those who are already focused on career performance. The puzzle is how often these same incentive programs fail to motivate certain employees. What's driving the relatively low performers, and why don't they get motivated to avoid the penalties or earn the "carrots"? And why do some proven high performers level off in production and fail to take advantage of the clear shot they have at even higher levels of career success? What's holding these people back?

The answers almost always lie in the fact that the performance incentives offered don't ameliorate what's broken in the life of the seemingly unmotivated employee. To put it simply, a trip to Hawaii won't solve a sales agent's guilt about her drinking, a production bonus won't resolve anyone's marriage problems, and the threat of a demotion won't motivate someone who is wracked with guilt over some deeply personal issue.

Thriving Across Life Arenas

Employees who are failing to thrive most often need whole-person mentoring and management, not a carrot or a stick. They will have to get better in their lives before they can get better at their work. Translation: They have to build up the weakest parts of the most important aspects of their lives. In this way they create a more solid and balanced foundation, one that is strong enough to allow for growth, across their life arenas.

Soon, we will ask you to assess your overall life balance with a tool we developed to evaluate yourself in seven areas—work, health, family (including children and extended family), friends, intimate partner or spouse, spiritual life, and intellectual growth—and get a graphic indication of where you need to work to solidify your foundation. But first, we want to give you two case examples of what we will be asking you to do.

The Case of Jerry

Jerry was a college professor who came to us for career counseling. He had been offered his dream-come-true career opportunity—a departmental chairmanship at a prestigious university, the culmination of his academic ambitions. He sought counseling to help him better understand the mixed feelings he was having about accepting this dream job.

Jerry's confusion about what was bothering him lifted when we had him evaluate his overall levels of functioning across his various life arenas using our Foundation Assessment Graph. Here's how he rated himself:

Jerry's Foundation Assessment Graph							
I'm thriving! Let me teach you what I know.							X
I'm doing great here. Being good at this is part of my identity.	X			X			
I'm fulfilled and pleased with my outcomes here.		X					
I'm doing fairly well most of the time.							
I'm doing fairly well about half the time.			X				
I'm maintaining, but this area needs work.						X	
I'm suffering and struggling to survive.					X		
	Work	Health	Family	Friends	Intimate Partner	Spiritual Life	Intellectual Growth

Jerry's self-ratings suggested that an exciting new job would not fix what was broken in his life. Rather, he would more likely find the inner peace he longed for by taking responsibility for building up the weakest aspects of his life foundation. For Jerry, this meant working on his marriage, rather than floundering in unsolved conflicts that were holding him and his wife back; improving his relationships with his two children; reconnecting with his estranged brother; and resolving spiritual questioning that had begun to surface for him during recent years.

The Case of Alice

Alice's struggles typified those of many men and women we counsel these days. She and her husband had worked hard to create a great marriage and family life, she had a very supportive network of close friends, and she was generally pleased with her spiritual life and her health habits. Her work as a realtor allowed her enough scheduling flexibility to continue in her role as primary caregiver for her family.

On the surface, Alice had what she described as a very balanced life, yet she was haunted by the fact that she often felt melancholy and irritable.

Alice was surprised by her disproportionately low levels of fulfillment in her work and intellectual areas, compared to all other aspects of her life. As she looked at her graphic representation of the true sources of her discontent, she had an important insight: "The truth is, I am a low producer at work, and I don't like the feeling of not trying my best there. Before we had kids, I was always considered a high performer—in school, in my early career training, and in my previous job. Once I became a mother, I put my career so far down my list of priorities that I've neglected it. And when I 'checked out' from my career, I also stopped learning and growing, intellectually. I love my family life; I don't want that to change. But I have to admit that I miss being intellectually challenged and being considered a high performer at work.

I've always assumed that taking the reins off my career interests would lead to my compromising my family life."

Alice's Foundation Assessment Graph							
I'm thriving! Let me teach you what I know.			X				
I'm doing great here. Being good at this is part of my identity.		X		X	X		
I'm fulfilled and pleased with my outcomes here.						X	
I'm doing fairly well most of the time.							
I'm doing fairly well about half the time.							
I'm maintaining, but this area needs work.	X						X
I'm suffering and struggling to survive.							
	Work	Health	Family	Friends	Intimate Partner	Spiritual Life	Intellectual Growth

Alice's concerns about what would happen to her family if she re-engaged in her career and intellectual pursuits are understandable. Indeed, if she approached reigniting her work and intellectual life with the same all-or-nothing strategy she used when she became a mother and decided to focus so exclusively on that role, she'll just suffer a variation of the pain she's already enduring: foundation imbalance.

Just as was the case for Jerry, the true challenge for Alice was to focus her energies on repairing the neglected parts of her life foundation. To feel better, she needed to take the risk of rethinking balance, this time bearing in mind our concept that *our lowest stage of fulfillment across important life arenas will hold us back from reaching our true potential in other arenas.* Put another way, low-level functioning in any major life arena will cause "imbalance" in your psychological foundation, and this weakened foundation will not tolerate the "weight" of continued growth in any other arenas. In this sense, if Alice continues to hold herself back from pursuing her bliss at work and other intellectual stimulation, her enjoyment of her family life will begin to suffer.

It Takes Courage

Unfortunately, when we are distressed about under-functioning in one life arena, it's human nature to go where the warmth and good feelings are: we tend to play to our strong hand, and do more of what we already do well. Instead, we encourage you to accept that you aren't likely to get better in areas where you are suffering by neglecting them more. Jerry's marriage won't be improved by his grabbing yet another career "prize." Instead, he needs to make amends with his wife and brother, and spend more time with his kids. And Alice's boredom and discontent won't be soothed by going to yet another one of her kids' ballgames or spending more time with her wonderful husband. She needs to get to work igniting her career and stimulating her intellect.

Life Foundation Assessment

In the diagram on the following page, place an "X" in the box that best describes your level of functioning for each of the life arenas described at the bottom of the diagram.

Your Foundation Assessment Graph							
I'm thriving! Let me teach you what I know.							
I'm doing great here. Being good at this is part of my identity.							
I'm fulfilled and pleased with my outcomes here.							
I'm doing fairly well most of the time.							
I'm doing fairly well about half the time.							
I'm maintaining, but this area needs work.							
I'm suffering and struggling to survive.							
	Work	Health	Family	Friends	Intimate Partner	Spiritual Life	Intellectual Growth

Now shade each column up to and including the boxes in which you placed your Xs. You now have a graph of your life balance. Pay particular attention to your lowest levels of functioning. Unless you improve these areas, growth in the other areas of your life will be held back.

Make Peace with the Need to Balance

So where do you need to focus to create a stronger foundation in your life? Don't ignore the obvious: Improving your least actualized areas is where the action is. Focusing on the weak areas will strengthen your foundation and create an environment for thriving. Then will you find balance and never have to worry about being out of balance again? The answer is a resounding no. Balance is a process, not a product; a journey, not a destination.

Consider adopting what preeminent work/family expert Rosalind Chait

Barnett of Brandeis University calls the "expansionist theory" of work/family balance: juggling work and family is stressful, but "having multiple roles actually produces a net gain. Even though you expend energy, you get back psychological, monetary and other rewards."[1] Living a full life will keep you busy and make you tired, but it will also leave you much more satisfied than someone who is holding back and living a less than fully engaged life.

Fight the Right Fight

Before we proceed with offering specific suggestions about how to achieve balance, we want to issue a caution. Too often, we find people frustrated in their efforts to create better balance because they fail to complete the process. Most of us assume that better balance will come if we manage to set aside time to do those things that our busyness otherwise keeps us from doing. This is only half right. Once "captured," the time that is earmarked then needs to be spent mindfully and congruently engaged in what you are doing. So often we sabotage our own hard-won efforts to create better balance by getting caught in the emotional triad of anxiety, guilt, and anger. No matter where we are— work or home, for example—and how much we might be enjoying it there, we contaminate our experience by feeling anxious and guilty about where we are not. Eventually, all this anxiety and guilt wears us down, and we settle into feeling just plain angry about never feeling good.

Firewall It!

Don't confuse a "life balance" problem of the sort that involves chronically neglecting some aspect of your life with the problem of too seldom engaging congruently in what you are doing at the moment. Recent research shows that a lack of engagement leads to psychological and family suffering.

Interviews with 1,300 working men and women conducted in 1998 and 2001 in upstate New York found that those who regularly used cell phones or pagers experienced an increase in psychological distress and a decrease in family satisfaction, compared to those who used these devices less often.[2] For both genders, the distress was attributed to "spillover"—the seepage of work concerns into home life, and vice versa. Compared to men, women suffered more spillover of home concerns into work.

Sometimes, what it takes to achieve satisfying work/life balance is counter-intuitive: to achieve better balance, it's sometimes necessary to be less available to work or home concerns for specific periods of time.

So firewall your life! When you are working, focus on and enjoy your work. And, when possible, protect your time off from work by screening your calls and limiting the times you're available via paging or email. If it's impossible to do this fully, read on.

It may be that the crumbliest link in your foundation has to do with self-care. If that is the case, your biggest challenge may be learning to say no to what your other family members want—not forever; just for the few minutes or hours you need to take better care of yourself.

Life coach Dan Sullivan recommends that you plan three sorts of days: Buffer, Focus, and Free.[3] Buffer Days are devoted to taking care of all the "stuff" that has to get done in order to maintain your life and work and to keep you from feeling cluttered and otherwise disorganized. Declaring a Buffer Day allows you to feel good about what you've gotten done, rather than wondering "where did the day go?!"

A Free Day is just that: a 24-hour period completely free from work-related problem solving, communication, and action. While most of us might think of this sort of recess as a reward for hard work, Sullivan proposes that enjoying free days "is a necessary precondition for achieving success and optimum productivity."

That productivity comes on Focus Days, when you commit 80 percent of your time to focus on an important project or endeavor. The remaining

20 percent of the day is left open to respond to legitimate emergencies or to do small amounts of Buffer activity.

If you are to remain a high performer in any area of your life, you have to regularly take breaks from that arena and allow your energies to rejuvenate. When you are passionately, fully engaged in your job, for example, you can come home, sated from the satisfying stint of good work you have done, and passionately, fully engage in your home life, relaxation, or other arena of value to you. Thriving in these other areas further fuels you so that you return to work with renewed energy, focus, and passion.

Learn to schedule and control the contaminations. Let people at work know well in advance that you will soon be relatively unavailable (that is you will be taking what used to be called v-a-c-a-t-i-o-n!), and that they have to get you while they can, if they need something from you.

Then set your email and voice mail at work to notify people you are on vacation and give them a contact who can handle things in your absence. In our experience, most people will honor, even admire, your ability to do this.

Whether it's an evening or weekend at home or an extended vacation, set specific, limited times that you'll check with the office. Do it. Get it off your mind. Then go have some fun.

Similarly, we urge you to get over the new age guilt-trip that says enjoying work means that your family is suffering. Remember: The worst thing you can do to your loved ones is to stay mired in feeling miserable about your life.

At Minimum, Manage the Contamination

We promised at the outset of this book that we would be realistic and practical. So, let's tell the truth: We know that it's close to impossible to achieve 100 percent firewall between work and family. The next time little Johnny calls you at work, you're going to take the call because—who knows?—maybe this time it'll really be something important and urgent, and, if you weren't available because you were following our sage advice, you might end up in the Bad Parents' Hall of Shame.

And we know *for sure* that most of you are not going to just say no to all pages, emails, and phone calls from work when you're at home. Even though most of those calls might be some Big Johnny Who Ought to Know Better asking for your help with something that's clearly his responsibility, you're going to take the call, just to make sure that the office is not falling apart in your absence.

You're not alone with this dilemma. In a landmark survey of 21,501 married couples from 50 states conducted in the late 1990s by family scholar David Olson and colleagues, 82 percent of couples endorsed this item: "I wish my partner had more time and energy for recreation with me." [4]

For anyone in a committed relationship, regularly *making* time to play together is certainly a necessary work/life balance strategy. But, again, making time may be necessary, but it's not sufficient. You must also bring your attention, energy, and enthusiasm to the party.

A poll released in 2005 by Travelocity estimated that 40 percent of travelers check their work email while on vacation and 33 percent take their mobile phones to stay connected with employers, employees, or clients. [5] Interestingly, one third of workers claimed that *not* checking in while on vacation was more stressful than the actual work. A study conducted by America Online in 2000 found that 47 percent of its subscribers took their laptops on vacation, and 26 percent continued to check their email every day during their time away. [6]

We know from personal experience that it can be foolhardy (or disastrous to your career) to not return a call to a key client, a demanding boss, or an under-functioning colleague. Or that volunteer committee or Little League team you coach may, indeed, need communication during your vacation. We also know that a relatively small amount of checking in and keeping up with work while on vacation can pay dividends in limiting the mountain of work you'll have to do once your vacation is over.

A healthy work/life balance does not imply that you never allow work/home spillover. Rather, the point is to take control of the process. Decide how much is enough spillover from one arena when your goal is to be passionately focused on another.

Is "Blending" the Best?

Author Barbara Glanz urges us to "*recognize* where you are in your life today, accept that this is where you need to be right now, and then begin to *think creatively* about how to BLEND other aspects of your life into the one that is dominant." [7] Here are some of her practical suggestions for what she calls "blending" our various life roles.

- Invite family to help with work projects. And not just the kids; don't forget parents or other elders.

- Take family members to conferences with you.

- Videotape your workplace, include greetings from co-workers, and watch the video with your family.

- Display your family pictures and family artwork in your work space.

- Work at home occasionally so that your family can see what you do.

- Hold family meetings when everyone shares what they did that was good at their "work" that day.

- Help your children develop and maintain a positive attitude about work.

- Explain what you do in language they can understand.

- Point out benefits that come to them from your working.

- Resist the temptation to always blame your crankiness or tiredness on work.

- Let them know that work can be stimulating, uplifting, and satisfying.

- Invite colleagues to your home.

When work takes you away from home:
- Leave surprise notes for your loved ones under pillows, in sock drawers, in briefcases. And communicate with your family in creative ways from work or on the road.
- Leave voice-mail and email messages.
- Buy two identical books written at your child's age level. Schedule "reading time" by phone each night.
- Remember special events and phone immediately to hear the details.
- Send postcards from every place you travel.

Manage Your Time

People who enjoy the best work/life balance are those who are most effective at managing their time. Here are some tips for managing your time in a way that will offer you a better balance.[8]

Spend time planning and organizing. Make time each day and week to get organized, both at home and work. Doing so can ultimately save you time. Using time to think and plan is time well-spent. In fact, if you fail to take time for planning, you are, in effect, planning to fail.

Set goals. Within each of your major life arenas, what do you want to maintain, to change, to add, to do less of? Set goals that are specific, measurable, realistic, and achievable. Your optimum goals are those that cause you to "stretch" but not "break" as you strive for achievement.

Prioritize. We recommend that, every three months, you take time to prioritize your balancing goals for the next quarter. Approaching balance in this way will match the realities of your life more closely than any vague notion of "living a more balanced life." Be realistic about the fact that exceptionally busy times at work and home require disproportionate amounts of your time and energy. Taking care of the demands that come with these busy seasons is part of your overall balancing act. The other part is then prioritizing counter-balancing strategies. Once the busy season at work or the family wedding is over, your next quarter's priority should shift your attention to another area of your life's foundation.

Use a to-do list. In our age of constant interruptions and never-ending pulls on our time and energy, a thoughtfully constructed to-do list can serve as a beacon that directs you through the busy storm of the day. In addition, a completed list is gratifying documentation of exactly how you spent the preceding day or week. The trick is to continually update your list, noticing any pattern in what you don't get done and, more important, *noticing what you do get done and feeling good about it.*

Be flexible. At the same time, a nod toward realism insists that you allow time for interruptions and distractions. Time-management experts often suggest planning for just 50 percent or less of your time. With only 50 percent of your time planned, you will have the flexibility to handle interruptions and the unplanned "emergency."

Delegate. Work on those tasks that you alone can do. Otherwise, delegate them.

Eliminate. If it doesn't have positive long-term consequences in an important area of your life, delegate it or eliminate it. Say no to what is truly unimportant in your life.

Avoid being a perfectionist. Paying unnecessary attention to detail can be a form of procrastination. Learn to recognize when "good enough" truly is enough, and save your perfectionism for life-or-death issues.

Reward yourself. Even for small successes, make sure to celebrate the achievement of your goals.

Fine-Tune Your Partnership

Collaborating with each other in ways that show respect for each other's contributions is a survival skill for modern families.

Share responsibility. There's a big difference between "helping out" and truly partnering with your mate to share responsibility for raising your children and running a household, or for earning money to support the lifestyle you've chosen. The push for more balance is coming not only from women who are embracing their work, but also from men who are tired of the solo-wage-earner role and want to spend more time and energy bolstering other aspects of their lives.

As of the early 2000s, the percentage of single-earner married couples had dropped to less than 25 percent, from a 1940 level of 66 percent. The Employment Policy Foundation's Center for Work and Family Balance estimates that, by 2030, a mere 17 percent of couples will reflect the single-earner arrangement.

This major change in roles requires that we develop new concepts and unprecedented levels of sophistication in our ways of thinking about and discussing with each other the ever-changing balancing act. One sign of the importance of this issue is the very fact that the Ackerman Institute for the Family in New York has a special Center for Time, Work, and the Family. Center director Peter Fraenkel, Ph.D., underscores the importance of couples spending time honestly discussing their beliefs about gender roles and devising and revising plans for sharing responsibilities.

Perhaps even more important than agreeing on the details of your role divisions is conveying to each other that your respective contributions are of equal value to your life together. Burnout in the partnership can be fueled by real or perceived lack of appreciation for all that you do. Don't forget to honor each other.

Don't "wait until" for too long. Don't wait until all of your stress is over before connecting with your loved ones: "I'll spend quiet time with my spouse as soon as this big project is over . . . or I'm less preoccupied . . . or I've caught up on my sleep." Instead, nourish your relationships while you are waiting for those other things to happen. A night off can be as simple as ordering in pizza—and agreeing not to think about cooking, laundry, bills, the office, or any difficult subjects all evening.

Schedule it! What sort of system or gadget or device do you use to keep yourself organized? Use it to help keep you connected with your loved ones. Create a "join-your-family" reminder. Whether in your Treo, Day Timer, or voice messaging, remind yourself to stop, look, listen, and connect with your loved ones.

Carve out couple time. Whether it's an evening off each week, a full day on the weekend, or a several-day period each month (or all of the above!), protect time to connect with your loved one. Your "couple time" doesn't have to be that elaborate. The point is to protect time to be together on a regular basis, and then show up with your hair combed and your teeth brushed! Don't give your partner your life's leftovers. Regularly dish up to this most important person in your life the best you have to offer.

Protect your communication-generating rituals. Most couples don't refer to it this way, but their "communication-generating rituals" are the lifestyle habits they develop that keep them connected. This might mean taking a walk together several times a week, or sitting together for a few minutes after dinner, before the evening rush of activities, or sharing a soak in a hot tub a couple of times a week. Whatever the form, the point is that these are precious times when you pay exquisite attention to each other. Protect those rituals; they can help keep you together.

Continue to get to know each other. Every week, learn something new about your partner. If you are not learning something new about each other, you are not paying close enough attention.

Hang in there! It's never too early or too late to make your marriage better. Studies show that, just as good marriages go bad, bad marriages can "go good." One study showed that five years after reporting high levels of marital unhappiness, 86 percent of continuously married couples that stayed married now called their marriage either "very happy" or "quite happy."[9]

Don't Forget a Balanced Life for the Children!

Experts today encourage parents to resist the "hyper-parenting model" that drives so many families.[10] Children who are taught that they have to choose a limited number of extracurricular activities each semester will grow familiar with the notion of balance in their lives.

And don't forget that your behavior is scripting your child's notions about balance. When was the last time your morning family conversation sounded like this:

Dad or Mom: "I am so excited! I am looking forward to my day. I have a lot of great things waiting for me today. I've got a busy schedule filled with what I love to do!"

Too often parents live in ways that convey to their children the message, "This is what being a grown-up is like, kid: You get to choose between being stressed, anxious, guilty, angry, frazzled, fatigued, irritable, and fed up. Now, if you study hard, you will get to grow up and become like me."

A few sobering questions can help you to evaluate the psychological environment you are creating for your children.

- Do you drive your children with life-scripting messages to "hurry up," "be perfect," and "get more aggressive"?

- Would your children and your family be better off with fewer activities, less "stuff," and calmer parents?

- Do you teach your children to fear "wasting time" and enjoying life?
- Do you maintain contact with your children by keeping up with who they know, what they do, what they like, and what they worry about?
- Are you creating family rituals that teach children to protect time for loved ones, even in a busy life?
- Are you teaching your children to be loyal to loved ones?
- Are you honest about the effects that your life is having on your children?
- Are you doing your fair share of the mundane, everyday parenting tasks?

We know from experience that most of us parents feel compelled to constantly monitor, prod, coach, and direct children. We do so out of concern about their well-being. We want them to learn the right things and make good choices, so they can be safe and happy. But don't forget the other set of life lessons you want to teach your children, those that compelled you to pick up this book: how to avoid or correct those things that might otherwise hold them back from thriving.

Teach your children well. Show them how to juxtapose working with playing. Make a point of showing them the joyful, playful, tolerant, accepting parts of yourself at least as often as you show them the part of you that's about monitoring and shaping their manners, work ethic, social life, activities, and so on.

If You Are Single

In many ways, balance is more difficult for someone who lives alone. For one thing, you won't have another person there, either encouraging or nagging you to take better care of yourself. You also won't have anyone to help shop, cook, clean, or otherwise run your home . . . unless you get help. And this is our point: Even more than for couples, single people need to partner with others. When possible, hire others to do the tasks that can be delegated. Make it a priority to develop and nurture support systems with friends or relatives that can help you with your balance challenges and support and encourage you to make healthy self-care choices.

We have special compassion for people living alone whose needs for balance get discounted by others. Work colleagues and extended family members alike can sometimes be insensitive to the fact that holidays, weekends, and special occasions are just as important to people living alone as they are to those who live with life partners and/or their families. A recent survey by Hudson, a global human resource consulting corporation, found that 34 percent of unmarried workers were unhappy with their work/life balance as compared with 18 percent of married workers.[11] The importance of this finding is underscored by the fact that 43 percent of the U.S. workforce is unmarried.

Thomas F. Coleman, executive director of Unmarried America and an advocate for singles' rights, encourages unmarried workers to be wary of employers whose family-friendly policies exclude single people. Expect and demand the same benefits as married colleagues or those who are working parents. If you don't remember that your life outside of work is just as valuable as the personal lives of married workers or those raising children, your employer and colleagues won't either.

CLOSING THOUGHTS

We hope that the information in this chapter has stirred you to think about life balance in new ways. Even more, we hope that you will begin to experiment with new approaches to your balancing act. As you do so, remember that healthy change always feels awkward, at least at first. Clarify your formula for balance at this moment in this stage of your life, and then dare to enjoy what you are doing right now! That's what letting go of what's holding you back is truly all about.

CHAPTER 3

Good Work!

"Your work is to discover your work and then
with all your heart to give yourself to it."[1]

Buddha

If you had enough money to live as comfortably as you would like for the rest of your life, would you continue to work? If your answer is yes, you've got a lot of company. Surveys conducted from the 1970s [2] through the early 2000s [3] have found that approximately 70 percent of people from around the world state they would continue to work, even if they had financial independence. In fact, only 28.5 percent claim they'd quit working altogether. And these findings hold across all professions!

You might consider this information surprising, since complaining about work seems to have become one of our biggest international pastimes. Studies show that a large percentage of workers in industrialized nations express openly negative feelings about their jobs.[4] Workers of all ages and in all job categories claim that they spend too much time working and that they don't play enough.[5]

Who Feels Most Overworked?

In the U.S., 37 percent of baby boomers surveyed in 2005 said they feel chronically overworked, while only 28 percent of employees in other age groups placed themselves in that category.[6] More than half of 1,003 employees in all age groups surveyed by the Families and Work Institute in New York reported feeling overwhelmed at some time in the past month by how much work they had to complete.

We also complain that we are stressed by our work. The truth of this is born out by Metropolitan Life Insurance Company estimates that an average of one million American workers are absent on any given day, largely due to stress disorders.[7] Across the industrialized world, studies show that work stress is increasing rapidly every year.[8]

What Employees Say Stresses Them Most [9]	

- *Changes at work*
- *Staff cuts*
- *Excessive workload*
- *Concerns about management's ability to lead successfully*
- *Anxiety about future job security, income, and retirement*
- *Boredom and lack of challenge in their job responsibilities*
- *Insufficient recognition and unfair pay for high performance*
- *Difficulty getting along with coworkers*
- *Workplace bullying*

So we complain about work, yet we claim that we would keep right on working, even if we could afford to quit. Most of us are stuck in chronic work ambivalence: We are attracted to working, but we convince ourselves that we don't want to do it. And this work ambivalence is one of the most powerful factors holding us back from thriving.

In this chapter, we challenge you to resolve your work ambivalence. We will ask you to consider what might be holding you back from celebrating and enjoying this huge and hugely important part of your life, a part that, on average, consumes one-third of your waking hours throughout your adulthood. And we will show how you can make good work part of your formula for thriving.

Do You Have "Work Ambivalence"?

In the early 1970s, pioneering researcher Mihaly Csikszentmihalyi created a method for measuring thriving that uses a pager or programmable watch to signal people to fill out a journal they carry with them. Signals programmed to go off at random times cue the person to write down where she is, what she is doing, what she is thinking about, and who she is with, and then rate her state of consciousness at the moment on various numerical scales—how happy she is, how much she is concentrating, how strongly she is motivated, how high her self-esteem is, and so on. This method, called Experience Sampling Method (ESM), allowed researchers to examine what sorts of activities are associated with a person's mood and level of self-esteem.

Using this technique, Csikszentmihalyi and his colleagues have researched the factors associated with *flow*, finding that this optimal psychological state occurs when five conditions are present:

- You are dealing with a task that has a clear and present purpose that you understand distinctly.

- You receive immediate feedback on how well you are doing.

- You concentrate supremely on the task at hand as other concerns are temporarily suspended.

- As you do this task, you experience a sense of growth and being part of some greater endeavor.

- When engaged in this task, you lose awareness of the passage of time.

More than 200,000 pages of data collected from more than 6,000 respondents worldwide make it clear why most people would continue to work, even if they didn't have to: *Adults experience far more moments of flow when they are on the job than during free time.*[10] That's because work is more likely to place you in a high-challenge, high-skill situation; require you to be creative and to concentrate; lead to at least momentary satisfaction with your accomplishments; and have a clear set of goals and rules of performance. Much of the rest of life lacks these elements.

Now back to the notion of work ambivalence. Here is a fascinating fact from Dr. Csikszentmihalyi's work that helps explain our high levels of reported dissatisfaction with work: When they are at work, people endorse the thought "I wish I was doing something else" more than at any other time of the day. Go figure.

It seems that we have a chronic ambivalence about work. When we are engaged in doing it, we love it. Yet most of us think we'd enjoy doing just about anything else more than we enjoy working.

Our counseling experiences over the past 30 years have suggested that a major perpetrator of this work ambivalence is the misapplication of well-intended urgings to strive for work/family balance. The problem is that, in our efforts to create life balance, we seem to have thrown the proverbial baby out with the bathwater. Failing to thrive in your work—no matter how much you might enjoy your time off or how many of your kids' ballgames you attend—is a mistake that will come back to haunt you and your loved ones.

Research has underscored the importance of avoiding this trap. In 2003, we surveyed a national sample of physicians' spouses and demonstrated that, short of working 90+ hour workweeks, the actual number of hours busy physicians worked did not affect their mates' levels of marital happiness. Rather, it was the physician's *mood upon returning home after a long day's work* that most powerfully predicted their spouse's marital happiness. Specifically, spouses' marital satisfaction scores dipped when their physician mates came home stressed, preoccupied, distressed, worried, or angry about work or too exhausted to participate in home life.[11]

In a survey, more than 1,000 third- through twelfth-grade children were asked, "If you were granted one wish to change the way that your mother's/your father's work affects your life, what would that wish be?"[12] The researchers also asked a representative group of more than 600 parents to guess what their child's response would be. (What would you say if asked the same question?) Fifty-six percent of the parents assumed that their children would wish for more of their time.

Here was the surprise: Only 10 percent of the children wished for more time with their mothers and only 15 percent for more time with their fathers. More than any other response, children stated they wished their parents would be less stressed and less tired when they were home. Interestingly, only 2 percent of parents guessed that their children would wish to reduce parental stress and fatigue.

Get Engaged

More than a great vacation, people need great work. According to the Gallup Management Group, people who thrive are *engaged* when they are at work. These are the people who work with passion and feel a profound connection to their company. Needless to say, these are the most innovative and productive employees, and their organizations benefit from their superior work performance. But recent research has found that the engaged also are most likely to believe that their work contributes positively to both their physical and mental health. In fact, 62 percent of engaged workers feel their work lives positively affect their physical health and 78 percent of engaged workers feel their work lives benefit them psychologically.[13]

Conversely, not being engaged is guaranteed to keep you from thriving. The *not-engaged* employees are those who have essentially "checked out"; they're sleepwalking through their workday, putting time—not energy or passion—into their work. Only 39 percent of the not-engaged feel their work lives positively affect their physical health, and just under half (48 percent) of the not-engaged say their work lives benefit them mentally.

The *actively disengaged* employees are a risk to themselves and others. These are the folks who are unhappy at work and are busy acting out their unhappiness and undermining what their engaged coworkers accomplish. More than half of these activity-disengaged employees say they think their work lives are having a negative effect on both their physical health

(54 percent) and their psychological well-being (51 percent). And the misery of the actively disengaged isn't confined to the workplace. More than half (51 percent) of the actively disengaged employees stated in a recent Gallup Organization survey that they had three or more days in the past month when work stress caused them to behave poorly with family or friends, compared to 35 percent of the not-engaged and just 18 percent of engaged employees.

Overcoming Work Ambivalence

Maybe you're one of those lucky people who are thriving in their work: your job demands match your talents and values; you receive a fair wage; and you are able to work creatively with people you like. If so, celebrate your good work! It is, indeed, one of the most important and precious aspects of your life. It is to be cherished and protected.

But if you aren't among this celebratory group, it's time to fix what's holding you back about work. We challenge you to honestly answer five questions:

1. Is your work toxic?
2. Is your lack of skills or poor attitude toward work holding you back?
3. What's right about your job and your company?
4. Do you have a work-friendly family?
5. What do you think about work?

Question 1: Is Your Work Toxic?

When it's bad, work can be really bad. In fact, a truly toxic work environment is dangerous to your health. We're not referring here to work that is simply demanding. Under the right circumstances, we thrive with high-demand work. The problem is not working hard; the culprit that can turn even the best work sour is when it seems like we have little control over how we do the work. Let us elaborate.

Beware of high-demand/low-control work. Researchers have observed for a long time that people who hate their jobs seem to suffer bad health consequences. Recent research suggests a possible reason why. Researchers in Germany found that the level of cortisol, the hormone necessary for the functioning of almost every one of our body parts, is higher among people who report high levels of stress at work than in those who don't.[14] In the discussion of stress in Chapter 9 we will explain in depth why too much cortisol can be dangerous.

The question remains, exactly what type of work stress is toxic? A famous study of nearly two thousand Swedish workers showed that work that could be described as highly demanding and that prevented workers from having any say in the pace or control over the process of the work (low-control) significantly elevated workers' risk of developing heart disease.[15] Other researchers have shown that so-called toxic work—that is, work that could be described as high-demand/low-control—raises blood pressure and increases death rates from various causes. In fact, low perceived job control was significantly related to developing heart problems in 68 percent of scientific studies that examined this connection.[16]

In addition to posing health risks, a toxic work environment also degrades our performance and attacks our self-esteem. A fascinating study demonstrated this last point. In this study, a group of people was given complex puzzles to solve and a proofreading chore. They were exposed randomly to a loud, distracting noise. Individuals in one group were simply told to work at the task. Each person in the other group was provided with a button to turn off the noise. The group with the "off" switch solved five times the number of puzzles as their cohorts and made a tiny fraction of the number of proofreading errors. The kicker: ". . . none of the subjects in the off switch group ever used the switch. The mere knowledge that one can exert control made a difference."[17]

Across industries, toxic work environments share certain characteristics. Use the following checklist to evaluate your work environment. Check any of the following statements that apply to you or your work.

__ I worry that I might lose my job.

__ I lie awake at night with anxiety about my work.

__ I just don't believe in what I'm doing at work anymore.

__ At the end of a workday, I'm so worn out I don't have energy to participate in activities in my family or home life.

__ My job requires me to do the same things over and over.

__ I don't have freedom to decide what I do and when I do it on my job.

__ My job requires that I work fast.

__ My job requires me to work very hard.

__ I am required to complete excessive amounts of work.

__ I don't have enough time to get my job done.

__ My job does not require me to learn new things.

__ My job does not allow me to be creative.

__ Many of my best talents are not used in my job.

__ I have a difficult boss.

__ I am often required to work overtime, particularly at the last minute.

__ I don't have a clear understanding of what's expected of me at work.

__ I face conflicting demands at work (sometimes, to please one superior I have to do something that displeases another superior).

__ I am asked to do things at work that exceed my ability or training.

__ My job does not afford me with reasonable opportunities for progressing in my career.

__ In my job, there seems to be little relationship between working hard and getting rewarded.

__ My workplace is a stressful interpersonal environment.

__ I'm afraid of or intimidated by my boss.

__ My manager/supervisor criticizes people openly in front of others.

__ Our workplace is filled with "Us versus Them" distinctions.

__ In my workplace, colleagues discredit each other.

__ Abusive or abrasive behaviors are tolerated here: shouting, cursing, citicizing, or anger outbursts.

__ My supervisor "punishes" with the silent treatment.

__ If you make a mistake, you're likely to get "the look."

__ Snubbing or ignoring people is commonplace here.

__ Insults and put-downs happen often.

__ Our work team seems to be all about blaming, discrediting, or discounting others.

__ Physical threats are tolerated in my workplace.

There is no absolute scoring system for this checklist. The point should be self-evident: If you checked more than a few of the items listed above, you've got a toxic job. Toxic work is filled with what management experts call "dissatisfiers." When they are present, factors like unfair or unclear policies, unfair or critical administrators, poor supervision, interpersonal tensions, lousy working conditions, and inadequate pay creates so much dissatisfaction that motivation for the job withers.[18]

If your job is filled with toxic factors, do something about it. It's impossible to thrive in dangerous life territory, and you won't feel better until you find a way to either detoxify your work or get another job. But before you tell your boss "I quit!" consider the following question.

Question 2: Is Your Lack of Skills or Poor Attitude Toward Work Holding You Back?

Sometimes, quitting your job won't fix what's broken in your life. Perhaps your work itself is not your major problem. Perhaps the real problem is some combination of the way you approach your work and the way your family responds to the demands that come with your job. Let's be realistic: If you've got a lousy attitude, low levels of competency in the skills required to do the job, and/or lack of family support for working hard, changing jobs won't fix what's broken.

Whether you change jobs or stay put, take responsibility for safeguarding what management gurus call the "satisfiers."[19] These are the factors that insure lasting career happiness, that promote feelings of esteem and satisfaction with work. Satisfiers include feelings of achievement, recognition of your good efforts, a high sense of meaning about your work, assuming increasing levels of responsibility, and enjoying the corresponding sense of growing in your career that comes with these factors. In a nutshell, boosting your satisfiers requires that you take responsibility for doing what you can to become engaged in your work.

How's Your Job? [20]

What percentage of your job is work *(drudgery)?* _____%

What percentage of your job is play *(enjoyment)?* _____%

What percentage of your job is hell *(pain and torture, regardless of the source)?*_____%

Total: 100%

Interpretations

How much drudgery is too much depends on your personal work ethic.

Less than 20 percent enjoyment: *You have a job problem.*

More than 20 percent hell: *You have a job problem.*

Rethinking Work Stress

"I make more money than I thought I would, but I don't feel much joy about what I'm doing. I've lost my passion for this."

"I'm secure—once you get this many established accounts, just renewing old business will suffice to secure your future with the company. But I don't feel very good about how I'm doing."

These comments from two of our clients highlight an important point about work stress. We tend to think about work stress in a very limited way. Everyone knows that too much pressure or too many conflicts or deadlines can create stress overload. These are stresses caused by external factors that aren't under your direct control.

But the other forms of work stress come from *within*. Not having the skills necessary to do a good job is an immediate roadblock. But it is also true that boredom, lack of meaning or job satisfaction, or apathy about your work or career can create a form of stress that comes from being under-stimulated or under-challenged.

We believe that no one joins a team with the intention of sitting on the bench. Everyone starts out wanting to be on the first string. Some state openly their intention to go for it, and they do. They do what it takes to win the trip awarded for top sales figures, to get noticed and promoted, to enter upper management. But many others gradually settle into patterns that hold them back from excelling at work, then justify their mid- or low-level performance with rationalizations and excuses.

Here's what we've learned when career coaching members of this latter group: To a person, they did not start to enjoy their lives more until they did something to reignite their pride in their work. Failing to feel good about your work puts a ceiling on how good you will feel in general. For most people, boosting work passion necessitates learning new skills and undergoing an attitude makeover about work. We'll say more about work attitudes later in this chapter. First, let's focus on your skills.

When your skills match the demands that face you, thriving is possible. Low skills, on the other hand, will dim your enthusiasm about any job. One way to determine whether you need to devote yourself to improving your skills or learning new ones in order to derive greater fulfillment from work is to note where you fall on the diagram below.[21]

If you placed yourself in any quadrant other than thriving, instead of suffering or assuming that only a new job will cure your misery, we encourage you to commit yourself to learning something new about your job or applying yourself in some new way to the work at hand. If you already have a high level of required skills, perhaps you need to explore new ways to apply these skills at work. On the other hand, if your misery stems from low skills in areas crucial to high job performance, you need to get busy learning what you need to know to improve your performance.

What keeps you from being eager to learn new skills for your job? This kind of learning is a big energy booster. In his book *Flipping the Switch*, author and consultant John G. Miller warns of the roadblocks that hold us back from going after energy-boosting learning:[22]

- *The exception mentality:* "Let's hold others accountable, but not me!"
- *Negative expectations:* "I figured that consultant had nothing worth hearing to offer, and he didn't."
- *Entitlement thinking:* "I should be given a pass on having to comply with these new policies, given all the changes I've been through with this company."
- *The experience trap:* "I've already learned all I need to know."
- *Exclusion:* "Those other people—the ones that work in another division, or another profession, or are different from me/us in some way—don't have anything to say worth listening to."

Question 3: What's Right About Your Job and Your Company?

A recent study that polled 40,000 employees in medium and large companies across the United States and Canada about their attitudes toward their work and their workplaces found that the vast majority of people have a very strong work ethic and remain committed to helping their companies succeed. Fully 78 percent said they're personally motivated to help their company succeed, and an equal number agreed they are willing to put in extra effort, beyond what's normally required in their jobs, to make that happen. Just over three-quarters (77 percent) said they really care about the future of their company, while 70 percent said they're proud to work for their company, and 61 percent agreed their company is a good place to work.[23]

Such observations might at first seem to contradict the fact that so many of us are dissatisfied and stressed by our jobs. But don't be confused; there is no contradiction. When we are engaged, most of us love to work. Just as in romance, when we first start out, most of us love being in love.

In both work and love, the crucial question is this: *Once the bloom of infatuation withers, what are you going to do next?* Beware of a tendency that has wrecked more careers (and romances) than any other: When the hard times come, we tend to settle into the habit of selectively perceiving what is *wrong* with our relationship or job and ignore all that is *right*.

We'll have much to say later about evaluating marriage and other relationships. Here, we want to encourage you to evaluate your job and your company using two checklists we administer routinely to any client considering making a major career change.

How to Know If You Have a Good Job[24]

Check any of the following that apply to your job:

__My work is varied, challenging, and meaningful.

__I have opportunities to make decisions.

__I receive feedback regularly.

__I learn new things.

__My colleagues and I show each other mutual support and respect.

__My job offers me room to grow professionally.

__I am compensated fairly.

__My superiors show me respect.

__My company honors my personal life.

How to Know If You're Working for the Right Company

Check any of the following that apply to your organization:

__We sell products and/or provide services that are relevant to our culture's needs.

__We sell products or services that match my values.

__Our mother organization has market savvy that looks to the future and provides career and company security.

__My company is deeply rooted enough to withstand market volatility.

__My company is financially secure.

__My company pays me a good, competitive wage.

_My company has visionary leaders who are interested in learning about emerging markets.

_My company is flexible enough to change.

_My company is committed to controlled, targeted, strategic growth (as opposed to "Ready. Fire! Oh, what have we done?" sorts of change).

_My company is customer-oriented.

_My company encourages broadening and deepening of my relationships with my customers or clients.

_My company facilitates my daily work by providing me with necessary tools, technology, and support systems.

_My company shows respect for my personal life.

_My company demonstrates interest in my professional development.

_My company invests time, energy, and money in my lifetime learning.

_My company is a positive interpersonal culture.

_My company epitomizes collaboration and collegiality.

_I am proud to be associated with my company's brand or service.

If you checked more than half the items on these two lists, maybe your job is not your problem. Most people would readily trade places with anyone who has work that could be described by even half of these items. If this applies to you, perhaps you need to identify and fix what's really causing your pain. Start by examining your family's attitudes toward your hard work.

Question 4: Do You Have a Work-Friendly Family?

Most people arrive for our life-coaching sessions assuming that our advice will be some version of "You've got to stop and smell the roses." About half the time, we do, indeed, offer some version of this bit of common sense (which is not so commonly practiced).

The other half of our clients are surprised when we tell them something quite different. Usually, that surprising message goes something like this: "It seems that the problem is not that you're working too much but that, as a family, you aren't supportive enough of each others' hard work." Families today who are concerned about work/life balance should know what contemporary research has taught us about this important topic. In a nutshell, this research has shown that, for both men and women, it is often not their work but their family's lack of support of their work that causes them distress.

Researcher Michael R. Frone of the State University of New York analyzed data from 2,700 men and women who were employed and either married or the parent of a child 18 years old or younger.[25] Those whose work problems interfered with family life were 3 times more likely to have a mood disorder, such as depression; 2.5 times more likely to have an anxiety disorder; and twice as likely to have a substance dependence disorder than those without conflicts.

The amazing news from this study came when the researchers examined the flip side of the issue. That is, what happened *when family problems interfered with work?* Respondents who indicated this sort of stress were 30 times more likely to have a mood disorder, 9.5 times more likely to have anxiety disorders, and 11 times more likely to have a substance abuse problem than those who received family support for their hard work.

We do not encourage or endorse work addiction. It is true that long work hours and success tend to go hand-in-hand. But working hard and being work addicted are not the same thing. The major difference between abusive (or addictive) work and healthy (or constructive) work is the degree to which excessive work interferes with physical health, personal happiness, or intimate and social relationships. Soon, we will give you guidelines for determining whether you suffer from work addiction.

For now we would like to focus on correcting any misconceptions you and your family have about what you should support and what you should encourage each other to change. It pays to know that you do a loved one a huge service when you support and encourage his or her working hard at good work.

Of course, it's also crucial to remember that your family is much more likely to support your work if it makes you happy. So often, our families witness only our fatigue, worry, frustration, or negative gossip about our work and the people we work with. When was the last time you showed your family your enthusiasm, joy, pride, or appreciation about your work? This takes us to our final question.

Question 5: What Do You Think About Your Work?

No matter how good your job or how supportive your family, your own attitude will ultimately determine your feelings about your work. Two factors are key here: Learning how to dive in and love working; and recognizing when it's time to stop, switch channels, and enjoy other aspects of your life.

Learn to Love Your Work!

Resolving work ambivalence starts with reminding yourself that working hard does not mean the end of good times; it is a crucial part of living a good life. Working hard on something you believe in is good for your physical and emotional health and it's good for your family. Remember that even though working sometimes precludes your doing other things that are enjoyable and important in your overall value system, your hard work is a crucial ingredient in a recipe for a successful and happy life. Just as when cooking a delicious stew, each important ingredient has to be applied in the correct proportions, one at a time. Accept that working hard is one of the ingredients in a good life. Next, stop waiting to find the perfect job before you start enjoying yourself at work. Instead, find something interesting and challenging about what you've got right before you. Getting engaged in your work—rather than spending time engaged in fantasizing about a job you don't have—creates a no-lose proposition. Maybe your renewed engagement will bump up your progress within your current company. If so, great! Just by becoming engaged, you've created a "new" job that you enjoy more than the old one.

But even if that doesn't happen, getting more engaged in the job you've got might lead you to develop new skills that will increase your marketability. Plus, as we've already discussed, engaged workers are happier and healthier than their non-engaged colleagues.

Choosing to enjoy the work of the day is one way of shifting from a victim's mentality (low perceived control) into an in-charge mentality. And this applies both to work for pay and to the work involved in running a family or a household. Research has proven that when work is perceived to be more voluntary than mandatory, people are more likely to enjoy it. This argues for learning to shrink the difference between "I have to" and "I want to."[26] Whether it's calling on a new client, seeing another patient, or changing another diaper, the people who will do best at their work and enjoy themselves along the way are the ones who see the work as something that they *want* to do because doing it matches their commitment to a higher and deeper purpose in their life.

Learn to think of work as play. Notice what you enjoy about it. And remind yourself that the parts of work you do not enjoy are necessary aspects of the larger whole. Put another way, it pays to remember that getting through the hard stuff is a way to get to the fun. For example, any golfer knows that practicing on the driving range can be grueling. But repetition of the fundamentals, while sometimes boring, is the only way to get your skills to the point that you have fun on the course.

In a similar vein, a client of ours who is a professional football player explained, "Training camp and practice are like torture. But I just keep my eye on the prize: There is nothing like the feeling of playing on Sunday."

One final example: We travel approximately 150 times a year to speaking and consulting engagements. We realized some years ago that the traveling is our hardest work; the speaking and consulting are the fun. We work at finding ways to make the travel more meaningful and pleasurable. The time spent traveling takes on a new meaning when we use it to get our writing and behind-the-scenes work done. When we do it right, rather than feeling we have "lost" days commuting and sitting in airports and planes, by trip's end, we enjoy a sense of satisfaction about the work that we completed along the journey.

We also try to counter the toxic aspects of traveling with multiple uplifts. In the truest of terms, traveling is toxic work—it is a high-demand/low-control endeavor. (We can attest to fact that the only people who think traveling a lot is glamorous are people who don't travel much.) Our mood, energy level, productivity, and sense of well-being are all directly tied to how diligent we are about countering the toxic parts of traveling with special uplifts. We protect ourselves from wear-down by controlling what we can, even during an uncontrollable trip. For example, when we travel, we both read for pleasure things we don't otherwise take the time to read, make it a point to enjoy the new foods and sights that come with the trip, or otherwise give ourselves permission to engage in special forms of "recess" that help to break the monotony of traveling.

The point of each of these examples is to demonstrate that high performance requires that you find creative ways to make peace with working hard at even the most undesirable, hard-work aspects of your job.

What's Good About the Worst Parts of Your Work?

On a blank sheet of paper, list several things you do not enjoy about your job, leaving several inches of space between each item. This list might include certain tasks like making morning rounds, writing reports, doing performance reviews, or dealing with certain people.

Next, beneath each of your items, write at least three things that you enjoy and value that come with doing this task or dealing with the person listed.

Example

I dread calling on John Doe.

1. I enjoy traveling to Mr. Doe's city.
2. The physical surroundings of Mr. Doe's offices are first-class, and I enjoy being there.
3. I like interacting with Mr. Doe's office staff. They are very friendly and helpful.
4. Keeping Mr. Doe satisfied leads to my boss showing me appreciation in ways that I value.

What If I Just Don't Want To?

Low work performance can be an indirect way of making a statement. One insurance agent we worked with put it this way: "I don't like my boss. I don't want to win a sales competition that helps him to look good in the eyes of his superiors. Plus, why would I want to win the trip to Europe the company is offering as an award for high sales figures when it would mean I'd have to travel with him, someone I don't even like?"

Be honest: Are you avoiding dealing directly with some negative aspect of your work? If so, is your indirect way of dealing with this discontent holding you back from thriving in your work? Everyone has something or someone at work they're less than thrilled about. Find a way to deal directly with what or who is the problem without sabotaging your daily enjoyment of your work and your desire to earn your place on the "A" team.

This means taking responsibility for managing yourself. Experiment with pretending that this is the only job you will have for the rest of your life.

What could you do to make it more interesting, challenging, rewarding, and enjoyable? Examine your own attitude, and avoid blaming, complaining, or denying responsibility.

When Too Much of a Good Thing Hurts

By now it's no doubt clear that we believe in the value of working hard. However, we return to our caution that workaholism can ruin even the most well-constructed life. The challenge is to become one of those healthy and happy people who work hard and also enjoy social and leisure activities, hobbies, and personal and family time. Work addicts get lost in a compulsion to work that severely imbalances their lives and blunts their ability to enjoy their work.

Work addicts work for the sake of working. They are in constant pursuit of the temporary "fix" that comes from the feelings of esteem and accomplishment that working hard brings. Many numb themselves from painful feelings by escaping into work and busyness. But overwork can never fill their emptiness, and their perfectionism leaves them feeling that nothing is ever good enough. They get lost in the belief that another accomplishment will make them complete. Keeping their work dependency a secret from concerned observers is the *sine qua non* of the work addict.

Do any of these symptoms of work addiction describe you?[27]

Hurrying and staying busy. Are you haunted by a constant sense of time urgency, always struggling against the limits of time?

Need to control. Does an obsessive need to control keep you from asking for help or delegating responsibilities to others?

Perfectionism. Do you micro-manage others and fail to discriminate important from unimportant details?

Difficulty with relationships. Does your excessive working chronically interfere with your intimate relationships, close friendships, and collegiality with peers? Do you secretly feel inept and helpless in relationships? Do you forget, ignore, or minimize important family rituals and celebrations?

Work binges. Do you regularly binge for days on a project until it is finished, driven by your self-imposed early deadlines, not mandatory time frames?

Secretiveness. Do you conceal your work binges from friends and family, sneaking work when you get a chance?

Difficulty relaxing and having fun. Do you feel restless and have trouble turning off the nagging voice in your head when you try to relax and unwind?

Brownouts. Does your mental preoccupation with work keep you from noticing or remembering? Do friends complain that you ask the same questions or tell the same stories several times?

Impatience and irritability. Do you purposely arrive late for appointments, in order to insure that you will not waste time waiting?

Self-inadequacy. Do your work accomplishments only give you a temporary high, with no achievement ever feeling like it is enough?

Self-neglect. Do you engage in emotional and/or physical self-neglect in order to keep working?

We encourage you to pause whenever you notice yourself engaging in one of these behaviors. Ask yourself, "Is it really necessary for me to act this way right now? What might I do to switch channels, bear through my awkwardness about relaxing, and pause a bit?" Remind yourself that relaxing helps you rejuvenate and return to working hard, this time with greater efficiency.

❄

CLOSING THOUGHTS

We trust that our point that levels of overall life satisfaction and job satisfaction are strongly correlated is now clear. But there's one more association that's worth noting here: Research has shown that the impact that life satisfaction has on your ability to like your job is stronger than is the contribution of job satisfaction to your overall level of life satisfaction.[28] In other words, learn to like your life, and it's far more likely that you'll find something to like about your job.

CHAPTER 4

Becoming a Hero

"A hero is someone who creates safe spaces for other people."

Wayne and Mary Sotile

In our workshops and keynotes, one question comes up more than any other: "If you were limited to offering us only one piece of advice about how to thrive, what would it be?"

Our answer is always the same: Without question, the best investment of your time, energy, and money is to use caring interactions to make your relationships better. Caring interactions with others is *the* primary key to staying happy, healthy, and high-performing.

The Power of Caring Connections

The power of caring connections has been demonstrated in research on marriage and family life, career and customer satisfaction, behavior change, and emotional and physical health.

Marriage and Family Life

The quality of parent-child interactions correlates with later measures of adolescents' and young adults' levels of emotional health, cognitive ability, life stress, social competence, and health behaviors. Specifically, children are more likely to grow into healthy, happy, and productive adolescents and young adults when parents express warmth, closeness, and affection; convey confidence in the child; and show friendship and support (as opposed to harshness or criticism) when the child faces problems.[1]

Marital research also underscores the power of uplifting interactions in countering the inevitable hassles that come throughout any couple's journey together. Researcher John Gottman, Ph.D., and colleagues counted the number of positive and negative interactions during 15-minute conversations of 700 newlywed couples. Ten years later, the ratio of positive to negative interactions predicted divorce with a 94 percent accuracy, with the magic ratio being five or more positive exchanges for every negative exchange.[2]

In the Workplace

Spreading good cheer in your workplace pays dividends on multiple levels. And failing to do so can be risky.

In a study of customer satisfaction, the Gallup Organization reported that the best of nearly 5,000 customer service representatives evaluated—those who generate high customer satisfaction and customer loyalty—have, on average, six positive interactions for every negative one, based on post-contact interviews with customers.[3] The worst 10 percent of customer service reps, on the other hand, have only three positive for every four negative encounters.

Why is this important? The attitudes and behaviors of staff can cost the average business between 15 and 30 percent of its gross revenues. In fact, 67 percent of people who stop patronizing a business do so because an indifferent employee treated them poorly. Researchers claim that 96 percent of dissatisfied customers never complain about rude or discourteous service. But 91 percent of those dissatisfied customers will never buy from that business again, and you can bet that 100 percent of these dissatisfied customers will tell their "horror stories" to at least nine other people to discourage them from patronizing the business.[4]

Even medical outcomes can be affected by employee behaviors. Healthcare research has shown that positive, interdisciplinary teamwork fuels cheerful attitudes in medical staff, which correlate with higher levels of patient satisfaction, greater patient adherence to medical advice, and increases in patients' abilities to cope with their illnesses.[5]

In case you're not yet sold on just how good for business caring behaviors can be . . .

- Nine out of ten people say they are more productive when they are around positive people and that they want to be around more positive people.[6]
- Members of work groups characterized by positive teamwork cope

better, and report higher levels of job satisfaction, less strain, and improved scores on measures of mental health.[7]

- In the eyes of the people they supervise, showing more warmth and fondness toward subordinates is *the* factor that most clearly distinguishes the highest-performing managers from those in the bottom 25 percent.[8]

In Times of Change

Whether your goal is to eat more healthfully, manage your temper, stop smoking, curb drug or alcohol use, exercise more, get regular medical check-ups, wear your seat belt, curb workaholic behaviors, or get more sleep, one factor can increase your odds of succeeding: engaging in supportive, nurturing, and encouraging interactions with people who care about you. Knowing that others are pulling for you—rather than shaming, blaming, or criticizing you—can help motivate you to stick with your commitment and change for good.[9]

For Your Health

We have known for nearly 30 years now that people with caring relationships live longer than those who are isolated or who live in conflict with others. Compared to their lonely or bickering neighbors, people who manage to stay caringly connected to others take better care of themselves, report less stress and depression, show more resilience when they do get sick, and are more likely to engage in virtually every form of positive emotional management described in this book.[10]

Miles to Go

Positive relationships clearly make a difference. Yet we continue to struggle. In the United Sates, the lifetime divorce rate hovers near 50 percent. And

Gallup research on 4.5 million employees in 112 countries indicated that fewer than 50 percent of employees feel strongly that they have a supervisor at work who cares about them as a person.[11] Less than one in every three feels strongly that they have someone at work who encourages their development. In fact, 65 percent of Americans reported receiving no recognition for good work in the last year.[12]

It's tempting to put the onus for changing on the shoulders of others. But rather than floundering in this passive state of waiting, we challenge you to take the lead in seeding both your home and your workplace with positive interactions. This is our most important guideline for letting go of what's holding you back: Both the end result of and the best way to stay the course when letting go is to be a hero for others.

In our terms, *a hero is someone who creates safe spaces for others.* In this chapter, we will give you guidelines for being a hero by building caring relationships with others at home and at work. We'll describe psychological and behavioral tools that you can use to shape friendship, communication, and intimacy at home and collaboration and collegiality in the workplace.

Be Generous and Be Gracious

Who did you think of when you first read our definition that a hero is someone who creates safe spaces for other people? How would you describe this person to another?

We have asked this question to corporate and lay audiences around the globe, and the thousands of answers we have gotten have taught us a great deal. Real-life heroes are seldom described as people who have accomplished great feats by society's standards. Rather, the people mentioned most often are grandparents, parents, teachers, coaches, mentors, or special friends who "always pulled for me" or who "believed in me when others didn't" or who were "there for me during a dark passage in my life, when others went away."

My (Wayne's) own experience is a case in point. I was fortunate enough to have seen each of my four grandparents almost daily throughout my childhood. This was not only because we all lived in the same small South Louisiana town of Donaldsonville, but also because my parents were relentless about their commitment to the value of family. "Go see your grandparents today, they might not be here tomorrow." My siblings and I agree to this day that this admonition from our parents, which we grew up hearing, remains one of the most valued gifts they gave to us.

My grandparents had very little formal education, even less money, and they were quite unsophisticated. Yet, amid my very abundant life, it continues to be true that I think of each of my grandparents many times a day, every day of my life. The reason gets to an important point about thriving: Virtually every memory I have of my grandparents follows the same theme: They were always so *nice* to me. In a nutshell, they were generous and gracious in their treatment of me. Here's an example of what I mean.

My grandfather Sotile once said to me, "They should have given you that trophy." "What trophy?" I asked. "For scoring the most points in that basketball tournament," he replied.

"I only scored 5 points," I said through my shame and embarrassment. "Lou Frey scored 112 points; he won the trophy."

My grandfather looked me in the eyes, leaned forward, and said softly, "They still could have figured a way to give you the trophy."

I've told this story thousands of times, and, still, when I do, it brings tears to my eyes and a warmth to my heart. You see, as I stood there, vulnerable and ashamed for having, in my eyes, "failed" one of those masculinity tests life puts in your path, my grandfather eased up to my exposed heart and wrote a message that resonates with me to this day: "I love *you*, and I believe in *you*. You deserve a trophy for who you *are*. You're my grandson. You're a member of my team."

I could tell you similar stories about each of my grandparents. But suffice it to say that being around my grandparents was like being in a sacred space created by their generosity and graciousness.

And this is the best advice we have to offer you: Be generous and be gracious. That's how people around the world describe their real-life heroes. Be a hero for the ones you love and the ones you work with. Generously offer others what they need in order to feel safe in your presence, even if it's awkward for you to offer that sort of compliment, attention, affirmation, forgiveness, or (if appropriate) affection. And graciously respond to what they offer you, even if their "gift" is not your first choice. Doing so regularly will ensure two things: You will become a source of resilience for others, and, in the process of creating a caring connection, your own resilience will be boosted.

Practice Empathy

What does it take to become one of those real-life heroes others refer to with statements like these: "No matter what's going on, she always seems interested only in you." Or, "He doesn't always agree with me, but I know that he understands me and respects me."

One thing such people have in common is that when you interact with them, you feel their *empathy*. Empathy is the capacity to participate in another's feelings, actions, or ideas.

Practice tuning into others' experiences. When you interact with others, practice listening and reflecting back what you hear and what you sense with your "third ear." Heroic people resist the temptation to judge others or to discount them. Rather, they jump to inquisitiveness. When you are surprised or bothered or disappointed in another person's behavior, ask, "What is this person's experience right now? What do they need more or less of from me *right now* that might make a difference for them? Regardless of how they are acting, what is this person needing, wanting, or feeling right now?" You won't know all the answers. The point is that heroes are empathic, and they show that empathy by asking questions that help clarify the inner and underlying experiences of the people they interact with.

Commit to getting to know each of your colleagues or loved ones as a person. Regularly update your information about them by asking about their thoughts, experiences, dreams, concerns, and reactions to what is happening, both at work and at home. And avoid making assumptions about people based on race, ethnicity, gender, culture, socioeconomic status, or even past encounters. In short, become culturally competent.

Develop Cultural Competence

Cultural competence is the ability to understand and work with people whose beliefs, values, and histories are significantly different from your own. In our culturally diverse world, failing to pay attention to cultural differences can lead to alienation and poor outcomes.

In some cases, cultural competence requires language skills. More often, it requires an attitude of curiosity, tolerance, and warmth that will lead you to convey acceptance as you acquire specific knowledge about other people.

Think of cultural competence as a broad term that applies to your dealings with people who are different from you in any way. Whether you agree with them or not, convey a desire to understand people from different generations, of different genders, and from different walks of life—both at home and at work.

Think "Dot-to-Dot"

The best way to insure resilience in any relationship is to orchestrate many *mini-moments* of positive connection with others throughout each day. Psychologist Peter Fraenkel recommends an approach that's reminiscent of children's connect-the-dots puzzles, where you draw lines from one number to the next, until a picture is completed.[13] Here's our version of Dr. Fraenkel's great idea, which can be applied to relationships with both family and coworkers.

Get two sheets of paper. Think of a relationship you want to improve. While bearing in mind our definition that heroes create safe spaces for others by being generous and gracious to them, make two lists of all the fun, pleasurable, or endearing things you could do for the other person *in thirty seconds or less*. The first list should contain things you can do when you are together. The second should contain things you can do when you are physically apart (by using email, cell phone, fax, etc.). Examples might include referring to the other person with a pet name, giving a pat on the back or hug (if appropriate), complimenting or praising the person, or leaving a surprise note that expresses your appreciation, admiration, thanks, or love.

Next, commit to doing ten, thirty-second (or less) heroic acts for that person every day for the next month. Spread these moments of caring connection out through the day. For couples and family members, Dr. Fraenkel recommends that you do a few in the morning before leaving for work, a few when you are apart, and a few more at the end of the day. By spreading these acts out, you can create what he calls "arcs of pleasure and connection" with each other throughout the day. Staying connected in these ways helps to counterbalance the effects of disconnection that come with your busy schedules.

Give People What Makes Them Feel Good

Have you ever been surprised or shocked to discover that a loved one or colleague you thought knew how positively you felt about them actually felt unsupported, criticized, or unloved by you? This sometimes happens when we give attention or affection of the sort we like to receive without making the effort to discover what the other person would most value receiving.

Give people what makes them feel good, and do it at work and at home.

Speak Their Language

Do you know what acts of love or affection the people who are most important to you most appreciate receiving? In *The Five Love Languages: How to Express Heartfelt Commitment to Your Mate*,[14] author Gary Chapman offers a wealth of practical advice about how to discover your respective "love languages." With just a little creativity, his concepts can be appropriately applied to work relationships as well as those with your family.

LOVE LANGUAGES

Take our modification of Dr. Chapman's 30-second Love Languages test.[15]

At Home

First, read through the statements below and write your initials next to the description that most applies to you. Next, think of each of your key loved ones as you read through the list again, and write their initials next to the statement that you think most applies to each of them, respectively.

 __I feel especially loved when people express how grateful they are for me, and for the simple, everyday things I do.

 __I feel especially loved when a person gives me undivided attention and spends time alone with me.

 __I feel especially loved by someone who brings me gifts and other tangible expressions of love.

 __I feel especially loved when someone pitches in to help me, perhaps by running errands or taking on my household chores.

 __I feel especially loved when a person expresses feelings for me through physical contact.

Next, ask your loved ones to complete this same exercise. Finally, discuss your ratings, and let what you find out impact your behavior moving forward.

At Work

In a recent *Industry Week* survey and the International Workplace Values Survey of 1,200 people in 18 countries, more than two-thirds expressed an interest in feeling a greater sense of belonging in the workplace.[16] To help your colleagues and coworkers know that you value them, you must interact with them in a "language" they understand and convey familiarity with them as people. Here are some tools for accomplishing both of these tasks.

First, we recommend that you use our modification of Dr. Chapman's test to evaluate what it takes to show appreciation for colleagues. Read through the statements below, and write your initials next to the description that most applies to you in your workplace. Next, think of each of your key coworkers as you read through the list again, and write their initials next to the statement that you think most applies to each of them, respectively.

__I feel especially valued and appreciated at work when people express how grateful they are for me, and for the simple, everyday things I do.

__I feel especially valued and appreciated at work when a person gives me undivided attention and spends time alone with me.

__I feel especially valued at work when someone brings me gifts and other tangible expressions of appreciation.

__I feel especially valued and appreciated at work when someone pitches in to help me in tangible ways.

__I feel especially valued and appreciated at work when a person expresses positive feelings for me through appropriate physical contact, like a pat on the back or a heartfelt handshake.

Next, ask your coworkers to complete this same exercise, and then discuss your ratings and use what you find out here to shape your future behavior.

We too often work with managers and business leaders who are trying to boost the morale and productivity of their work teams while skipping the very first step in being an effective team member or leader: getting to know the *people* who are on your team. At minimum, you should be able to provide the information that follows for each of your team members.[17]

What Do I Know About _____? A Checklist

Name of spouse or significant other

Number of children (if any)

Hobbies

Favorite lunchtime topic of conversation

Career goals

A current personal concern

Types of recognition or praise this person likes best
  (public, private, written, verbal, or other)

What drives this person?

  __The need to get along

  __The need to be appreciated

  __The need to get rich

  __The need to win

  __The need to get it done

  __The need to please others

  __The need to rebel against authority

What has this person accomplished in their past that has yielded the greatest sense of pride and satisfaction?

What would they like to be famous for?

Which aspect of their work do they most love to do?

What do they do well?

Which skill or talent has been responsible for most of their success and happiness in life, up until now?

What's easy for them to learn?

What do they love to learn about?

What is their career dream?

What do you most appreciate about this colleague?

Have you made this obvious?   __Yes __No

If so, how? When?

When will you do so again?

How?

Ten Principles of Employee Recognition[18]

1. Recognition really matters—to people, performance, and your organization.

2. The most powerful form of recognition is your attention. Greet employees, calling them by name. Listen to them, show interest in what they do and who they are. Ask questions and convey respect for the individual.

3. Compensation is important, but it is not an effective recognition method. Employees view compensation as a right. They view recognition as a gift.

4. Give rewards that have symbolic value. Good recognition methods are immediate, flexible, and they can occur anytime.

5. Link recognition to performance. Clearly pinpoint the behavior that triggered the recognition.

6. Recognize positive behaviors as soon as possible.

7. Make it personal. Give recognition through direct contact with the recipient.

8. Don't create winners and losers. Make everyone eligible for recognition, and don't neglect people who work to support the "winners."

9. Get everyone involved. Solicit employee feedback to assess and improve your system.

10. Use many sources of recognition. Combine informal and formal, planned and spontaneous, serious and whimsical, traditional and novel, simple and effortful types of recognition.

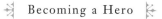
Accept that if the people important to you at work and home don't seem to be appreciating your way of expressing your positive regard for them, then it's up to you to change your style. The meaning of your communication is the response you are getting. If you're not getting the response you'd like, change your style of communicating, until you do.

Ask for Feedback from Others

Think of your most important relationships at home and work, and of the many things you do for and give to those people. What do you think each of them values most about you? If they could change you in any way, what changes would they ask for?

At Work

What do your colleagues, staff, and coworkers think of you?

What are their expectations about your role and their roles?

Do they see you as part of their problem, or a source of solutions to their problems?

Are you considered a source of information or aggravation?

Are you their safe space, or do they fear your criticism?

Consultant and web author Wendy Leebov suggests a very useful tool for soliciting input from the people you manage.[19] Give it to your staff to gain information that can be invaluable to you as you consider making changes in your work life.

My Manager . . .	Report Card				
	A	B	C	D	E
1. Has made an effort to get to know me and show respect for who I am.					
2. Makes job expectations clear to me.					
3. Communicates thoroughly and often so I feel in the loop.					
4. Gives me honest, regular feedback about my performance					
5. Shows respect for my life outside of work.					
6. Shows flexibility to help me manage the many facets of my life.					
7. Encourages me to express my concerns and shows responsiveness.					
8. Helps coworkers get along, so we have harmony within our team.					
9. Helps me feel appreciated.					
10. Advocates for what we need; removes barriers.					
11. Finds ways to help us lighten up and have fun.					
12. Provides learning opportunities; helps me grow.					
My suggestions:					

At Home

We'll bet that we share something important with any of you who, like us, have children: We agonize regularly about what it means to be good parents. Our daughters, Rebecca and Julia, are the two biggest blessings in our life, and we have been committed from the outset of our family to be their "safe spaces."

At different stages of life, this challenge has presented itself in different forms: Should we send them to private or public schools? How many extra-curricular activities are enough to enrich them but not too much to over-stress them? How lenient or strict should we be about curfews, friendships, and how they spend their time?

As they grew older, the content changed, but the process—our concern about whether we were giving them the right "stuff," tangibly and psycholog-ically—remained: How adamant should we be about insisting that they be present at family gatherings, even if this meant they would miss something they really wanted to do with friends? How should we react to plans they were making about how to spend their summers during their college years? Should we be supportive or not about life-shaping decisions they are making that frighten us more than them?

Rebecca is now 28 years old, and Julia is 26. They are old enough and candid enough to speak with insight about what it's been like to be our daughters. Their comments are enlightening and sometimes surprising—both in good and difficult ways. What our daughters have taught us about what has mattered most to them in our relationships is a lesson worth passing on, one that applies to all relationships. The essence of Julia and Rebecca's message is best expressed in a few excerpts from cards they have written to us on special occasions:

From Julia: "Thank you for loving each other so much and for giving Rebecca and me to each other."

"Thanks for creating a home that feels warmer and safer than anywhere else in the world."

From Rebecca: "Thank you for always making whatever I am excited about seem so much more important to you than anything else."

"Thank you for how it has always felt, deep down inside me, whenever I hear you laughing."

"Thank you for how it still feels whenever I see the two of you dancing together."

Our daughters are educated, sophisticated young women who have traveled the world. Yet, what they count among their most valued treasures are the feelings of safety, joy, and love that stem from our family life, and the small things that make them happy.

We encourage you to ask your loved ones what they most appreciate about you. Find out, too, which specific things you could change that would make them feel even safer and more loved in your relationship. And update your understanding of their dreams, regrets, wishes, and goals. Remember, each of you is a growing, developing, changing person. Stay abreast of the latest and most important "news" about the people who are most important to you.

Support Each Other's Efforts to Change

Anyone who is trying to change feels vulnerable. And whether they ask for it or not, your support is important to them. Research has taught us what does and doesn't work when supporting someone who is trying to change. Whether at work or home, bear in mind these guidelines when dealing with others during changing times.[20]

Do	Don't
Remind the other person of the benefits of changing	Nag about the dangers of not changing
Participate in the change	Shun the other person as they try to change
Discuss what's happening	Remain silent about the change
Compliment	Criticize
Notice what the other person does right	Ignore the other person
Encourage	Complain
Suggest	Lecture
Share information relevant to the change	Compete by withholding information that might be helpful
Respect your differences	Expect everyone to be the same
Listen	Talk and lecture incessantly
Reassure	Dwell on the worst-case scenario of what might happen if the change doesn't "stick"
Sympathize	Pretend you know what it feels like if you don't
Recognize that changing is difficult	Insist that this should be easy

Beware of the Superachiever Paradox

In Chapter 1 we asked you to evaluate whether you suffer from dangerous levels of anger, hostility, or cynicism. The set of coping behaviors associated with this is called Type A behavior pattern. Research shows that more than 70 percent of us develop some elements of this pattern which, left unchecked, may interfere with our caring connections with others.

It is ironic that one of the biggest impediments to success and happiness is how we act toward others while striving for success. Mismanaged Type A coping weakens your best resource for managing stress: your relationships.

We call it the *superachiever paradox* and it results from striving so hard to achieve perfection that you become psychologically rigid, ignoring your own needs and those of the people around you as your driven lifestyle takes you further and further into emotional deprivation, relationship tensions, and burnout. Keep in mind that superachievers aren't all CEOs and top-level executives. Some of the most stressed superachievers we know are busy moms and dads trying to achieve the perfect family, young workers trying to find the right career path, or the scores of people struggling to keep their lives on track while going through unwanted changes.

The signs of this superachiever paradox are everywhere. Our culture values achievement, yet we also espouse a commitment to balance. We have become a nation of spirituality-seeking, workaholic, stimulation addicts who suffer new age guilt over our failure to achieve that mythical, perfectly balanced life. Talk about a paradox! Nearly 80 percent of successful people say they regret how their family relationships suffered as they pursued their career goals. We pay lip service to the value of simplifying, downsizing our lifestyles, and reclaiming our time and our family relationships, yet our behaviors don't reflect these values.

The superachiever paradox will hold you back because of how it impacts your relationships with other people.

- If you are constantly *in a hurry*, your connections with loved ones will be impaired.
- If you are constantly *doing more than one thing at a time*, others will feel that you never fully attend to them.
- If you are *impatient*, others will feel anxious when around you.
- If you are a *perfectionist*, your criticism will alienate others.
- If you repeatedly show *irritation and hostility*, others will feel wounded, not nurtured, by you.
- If you are *controlling* in your interactions, others will stop self-disclosing to you, fearing another unwanted lecture.

- If you are excessively *competitive*, others will avoid spending time with you for fear of being put one-down in your relationship.

Here are suggestions for managing Type A coping:

Notice how your behavior affects people around you. Be alert to the ways you use high-intensity coping skills when they aren't really needed—and could even be hurtful. For example, accuracy is important when you're fulfilling a large order from an important customer or if you're a surgeon operating on a patient. But correcting your partner's grammar or drawing attention to other small mistakes is most likely going to make him feel hurt, inadequate, and resentful, without much, if any, positive payoff.

Beware of another common offender: a chronic sense of urgency. Moving fast may make us more productive, but it also makes us less sensitive to others. People are kinder and more generous when they're relaxed and taking their time. When we're rushing at breakneck speed, others become like blurs in our peripheral vision. We ignore the effect we're having on them.

It's tempting to justify impatience by telling ourselves, "This is just how I act when I'm in a hurry. The *real me* is more loving, and everyone knows that." But the person your family, colleagues, and customers see every day *is* the real you.

When you arrive at home or work, pause for a few seconds before going inside. Remind yourself, "No superhumans live here." The people you love are not perfect and you should not expect them to be. Enter their presence mindful of the effect your reactions to their imperfections has on them.

Be honest about your own coping style. Research has shown that, while high performers tend to honestly and accurately evaluate their coping styles in work settings, they are notorious for underestimating the effects of their high-powered styles on family relationships. If you think this may apply to you, start by listening to yourself as you deal with your loved ones. Ask for feedback from them regarding your way of relating to them. You might even tape record an evening's conversation with your family, and then listen to the tape with an ear toward noticing your own communication style. Become aware of how your coping habits affect your relationships.

Be helpful to each other as you try to modify your coping habits. It helps to know that the fuel for misguided high-powered coping is usually deeply felt insecurity or anxiety; not haughtiness, power, or inflated self-worth. As you attempt to change these reactions, be nurturing, not blaming or shaming of each other.

Practice becoming a better environmental engineer. Create experiments that allow you to practice new behaviors. For example, if you want to curb Type A coping habits, force yourself to drive slowly while listening to soft music. Seek out the longest line at a check-out counter, and use the time spent in the line to think pleasant thoughts about your past, present, or future. Limit the number of things you do at once: turn off the radio or television for fifteen minutes, close all reading material, and simply sit and talk with a loved one. Practice doing nothing for fifteen-minute stints in order to get more familiar with slowing your pace.[21]

Curb Your Anger and Manage Conflict

No matter how many positive strategies you use to strengthen your relationships, periodic conflicts are inevitable. The good news is that the presence of conflict does not differentiate healthy from unhealthy relationships. Every couple, family, or work team that lasts beyond the infatuation stage squabbles at times. The key is to control your steps in the squabbling. That is, manage your own anger and the interactions that go on as you are dealing with conflict.

Accept that conflicts will happen, and view them as opportunities. Beware the myth of naturalism that goes like this: "If we love or work together, we're supposed to just get along naturally." Accept that any relationship is constantly charting new territory as the people in the relationship keep growing, and that disagreements and conflicts are inevitable. Don't react to these difficult times as though you're being double-crossed by the other person; accept that this is part of your relationship journey together. Try to see conflict as an opportunity to deepen your mutual understanding, trust, and respect. It all depends on how you handle it.

Strike when the iron is warm, not hot. Express what's bothering you either before you reach the boiling point or once you've cooled down a bit. Accept that neither expressing nor suppressing works in the long run, since both will cause your anger to fester and damage your relationships.

When you get angry, slow down. Curbing aggressive, hurried behaviors—the very behaviors that are fueled by anger—is the single most effective anger management strategy. Slow your rate of speech, your response time, even your pace of movement. If you curb aggression, your anger will subside.

After an anger slip-up, apologize. Everyone has at least an occasional grumpy day. But people who manage anger and conflict well make it a habit to quickly clean up any emotional residue left in relationships after they get angry. "I'm sorry" are amazingly powerful words; say them often.

Acknowledge high-risk situations or relationships, and get prepared. When you know you are going to have a difficult conversation with someone or that you will be in a meeting or social gathering with someone who tends to irritate you, prepare for it. Relax and visualize yourself remaining calm as you enter the situation or dialogue. Once there, privately repeat your calming practices. If possible, try to distract yourself from focusing on the irritating person or the specific things that person does that irritate you. Do anything reasonable to disrupt both the physical and emotional aspects of an anger reaction. Take deep breaths. Pray, meditate, or simply focus on the task at hand. Do what it takes to control yourself, even though you cannot control the other person or situation.

Manage your thoughts. Anger is fueled by thoughts that justify outrage. It helps if you can substitute compassionate or empathic thoughts for ideas that someone is purposely acting incompetent or inflammatory. (This is admittedly very difficult to do in a moment of anger.) So take a deep breath and walk away until you are calmer and can manage your thoughts.

Separate the person from the problem, and be respectful of the person. No matter how serious the issue is that is distressing you, show respect for the other person. Use phrases like, "I'm sorry we're having this problem. I do value our relationship, and I want us to get beyond this." And never show contempt by using sarcasm, cynicism, mockery, or hostile humor.[22]

Be specific. Discuss what is bothering you in specific terms. Don't be vague or depend on innuendo. Specify exactly what the problem is and what sorts of solutions or changes you are requesting, and explain why this change would work better.

Stay on topic. When a person receives feedback that upsets them, it's not unusual for them to switch the topic to something about the behavior of the giver of the unwanted news (that would be you!). Remember that receiving unwanted feedback is embarrassing, and striking back is a natural reaction. Try not to get defensive and do not give in to the pull to switch topics—at least not yet. Acknowledge that your own behavior is, indeed, a legitimate topic, but one that deserves its own conversation. Offer to schedule a follow-up meeting to discuss anyone's concerns with your own behavior and stay focused on the fact that your colleague's behavior is the topic of the current discussion.

Look to the future. Avoid thinking or speaking in terms of forevermore. Let the other person know that you are looking forward to getting beyond this conflict or disagreement.

Finish it. Emotionally disengaging in the midst of a discussion is unfair fighting. If you are too upset to respond sensibly, call a time out with the promise of re-engaging at a specified time. It might sound like this: "I'm sorry, but I would like to take a break to gather my thoughts and calm down a bit. I promise that I will remain engaged until we've resolved this, but right now I need a break. Can we agree to continue this discussion tomorrow morning at 9:30?"

Don't mess with the repair attempts. By "repair attempts," marital therapists mean two things. One definition, from the research of John Gottman, is anything that helps cool down an otherwise escalating argument. Here we're referring to things like using humor (appropriately), affection, statements of agreement, softening your tone of voice, and so on.

The other form of repair is of the shaking-hands or kissing-and-making-up variety. Once the tension from your conflict has soothed, one of you will eventually make a move to reconnect more comfortably. That "repair attempt" might come in the form of an opening to chitchat, an overt apology, or a sympathetic look.

Here's the point: Failing to respond to a repair attempt is an unfair and hurtful way of restirring the fight or of getting back at the person for having had conflict with you in the first place. Do this too often, and you will damage the soul of your relationship.

Practice Collaboration and Collegiality

To be a hero at work, become an ambassador of collaboration and collegiality. The five guidelines we will offer for doing this combine our best insights with those of leading authors in the field of business leadership.[23] These guidelines are:

1. Make attending to relationships a part of everyone's job description.
2. Be a positive participant in relationship-building opportunities.
3. Show that you care about your teammates.
4. Take responsibility.
5. Show humility.

⋇

How to Manage an Angry Colleague

- *Don't wait too long before confronting your colleague.*

- *Do it in person. Don't gossip. Go directly to the person of concern, and never give negative feedback through a memo or email.*

- *Do it in private. Inept criticism delivered in front of staff or peers is a collaboration killer.*

- *Be definitive, but never blame or shame. Be clear that inappropriate management of anger is unacceptable and damaging to you and to your organization, but also let colleagues know that you value and respect them.*

- *If one-on-one discussion doesn't work, do it as a group. Include colleagues or staff who are willing to speak up about how your colleague's behaviors are damaging and what he or she needs to change.*

- *Do not debate. Your colleague will probably feel that his or her anger is justified. That's not the point. The point is that, regardless of the legitimacy of his or her underlying issues, inappropriately expressing anger is unacceptable.*

Make attending to relationships a part of everyone's job description. Every member of your organization should be charged with the responsibility of relationship building. This will set the groundwork for making your workplace a positive interpersonal culture, one that commits to giving each other the benefit of the doubt, refusing to participate in gossip or coalitions within your team, and including all members in your information flow and decision-making processes. Encourage colleagues who may be having difficulty with each other to meet and discuss their concerns, and model verbalizing insights from the perspective of others, particularly those team members whose opinions may differ from your own. Expressing and showing respect for individual differences in training and methods of getting things done is one of the most powerful ways to promote collaboration and collegiality. Freely exchange information and help within your team, and acknowledge your common vision, mission, and business purpose.

Be a positive participant in relationship-building opportunities. Spending time with colleagues and conducting yourself appropriately is the way to strengthen your relationships. Stage and participate in office events like retreats, holiday celebrations, or casual social gatherings that bring your families together. Traditions like this can deepen your collegial relationships and will mature your organization. They also create opportunities to expand your perspectives of each other. Learn to see each other not only as work colleagues, but also as people—each with loved ones, interests, and abilities outside your work. This also makes it more likely that when you have conflict with each other in the workplace, you will respond to each other as individuals worthy of mutual positive regard, rather than as adversaries.

Hold regular, focused meetings that include all principals on your team, and use the following ground rules during the meetings:

- No whining.
- Leave your title at the door.
- Everyone speaks for himself.
- Do not interrupt the speaker.
- No sidebar conversations. If you have something to say, say it to the group.
- Be specific regarding concerns.
- Remember that the purpose of this discussion is to identify work-related problems in order to move forward together, not to place blame.
- Let statements lead to requests for change.
- If confused, paraphrase and ask for clarification.
- Everyone should contribute at least one worthwhile idea.
- Expect to have to work to implement ideas that surface in the meeting.

Show that you care about your teammates. Show that you are proud to be a member of your organization and team. Speak positively about the work of the people in your group and of your organization as a whole. Verbalize optimism about the future, speaking in terms of "we" rather than creating "us-and-them" distinctions. Focus on common purposes and don't get sidetracked by differences in the details or personalities. And openly praise and express appreciation to coworkers, giving others credit for their good work and modeling how to offer feedback or criticisms constructively. Don't forget to let others know when you are enjoying yourself. Show passion for what you do, and celebrate team victories and the accomplishments of your teammates.

Take responsibility. Be honest about the effects that your actions have on others. Never make excuses or blame others when things go wrong. Rather than wasting time trying to find ways to cut corners, try to find ways to accomplish more and show initiative to take on responsibilities above and beyond your stated job. Manage yourself, your time, and your work commitments, and don't assume the role of martyr who works harder than everyone else in your organization. Stay curious. Expanding your skills and knowledge is one way to constantly rejuvenate your interest in and passion for your work.

Show humility. Self-centeredness is a malignancy that, left unchecked, can ruin the best of teams. Acknowledge your interdependence with other individuals and departments by openly requesting help from colleagues within the organization. Admit your own shortcomings and mistakes.

Openly solicit the opinions and input of others, and do so in front of your group of colleagues. Ask for help and express appreciation when you get it. Regularly admit, "I'm not good at this—could you help me out?" and express appreciation to those whose talents are different than your own.

When conflicts occur, apologize quickly and sincerely. And always respect organizational structures and roles and don't use them in undermining ways. Never act like you are the exception to the rules that govern the group.

If You Are an Employer, Shape a Family-Friendly Workplace

A survey conducted in 2005 asked two-income couples about work/life balance strategies.[24] One finding should serve as a heads-up for employers interested in shaping a work environment that keeps employees engaged. Employees from all levels of corporate America indicated that they worked harder and felt more loyal toward employers in a workplace that was flexible and allowed them some autonomy when it came to work/life balance. And, when at work, they tended to focus and get work done efficiently.

- Shape a family-friendly workplace.[25] Help to organize "Bring Your Family to Work" days that allow families to come to learn more about your company and what their relatives do. For every dollar spent on family resource programs such as on-site childcare, companies yield more than $2 on direct-cost savings generated by lower absenteeism, lower healthcare costs, and improved performance.
- Offer work/life retreats for your employees.
- Offer special recognition for spouses and family.
- After a big project is completed, send something to employees' homes to say "thank you" for the extra time they had to spend at work.
- Send family gifts at holidays.
- Honor the spouses or significant others of employees.
- Recognize children and spouse accomplishments.
- Use employees' families and children in your company ads.
- When recruiting, be sensitive to the fact that relocating is stressful for families. Help your new employee's family integrate into your community by offering help finding doctors, churches, schools, and housing.
- Don't forget to honor the needs of single employees. For example, just because they aren't married doesn't mean holidays are not important to them.

Lighten Up!

Who would you say is your all-time best friend? We'll bet you that the person you just pictured or named is someone who makes you laugh. We gravitate toward people who appeal to our wit and sense of humor, and we remain committed to those who make us feel safe enough to come out and play. The value of "slack time" and playfulness in the workplace has been well documented in studies of productivity, employee retention, and worker satisfaction.

Forgive and Seek Forgiveness

Because there are no perfect people, there are no perfect relationships or work teams. An overarching characteristic of thriving families and teams of colleagues is their ability to seek and grant forgiveness, over and over again. This requires four things: apologize effectively, ask for forgiveness, work on forgiving others, and forgive yourself.

Apologize Effectively

In their book *The Five Languages of Apology*, Gary Chapman, Ph.D., and Jennifer Thomas, Ph.D., offer practical insight into the languages of apologizing and forgiveness. Use the following checklist from their work to clarify what works best for you when it comes to apologizing and forgiving.

___I am able to accept an apology from someone who expresses regret simply by saying, "I'm sorry."

___When I am offered an apology, I long to hear the words "I was wrong."

___I find an apology most sincere when the person who has wronged me takes action to make it right.

___I find an apology most sincere when it is followed by a promise to change, with the offending person saying, "I'll try not to do that again."

___I find an apology most sincere when the other party places great importance on asking for my forgiveness.

Be honest about what sort of apology is most likely to get you in a forgiving mood, and find out the same information about loved ones and coworkers.

Effective apologies also convey to the other person that you have insight about how and why your behavior hurt them. An effective apology goes beyond a simple "I'm sorry." An apology that is far more likely to lead to acceptance and forgiving sounds more like this: "I am sincerely sorry for what I said. I know that my words hurt you, and that the way I acted probably stirred bad memories about the way things used to be in our relationship. I want you to know that I take very seriously the fact that I do not have the right to hurt you like that, and I promise you that I will try my hardest never to do that again."

Ask for Forgiveness

Apologizing is not enough. You should also ask for forgiveness. This is best done by stating that your relationship matters, and then making your request: "Our relationship is truly important to me. I am asking you to please forgive me."

Work on Forgiving Others

Forgiving people who have hurt you is one of the ultimate steps in letting go of what's holding you back. Of course, it's a lot easier to think about forgiving and to write about forgiving than it is to forgive. We're not talking here about those superficial things we sometimes do, when we say the words "I forgive you" just to get an argument over with. We're talking about soul-level, true forgiveness. There is a spiritual quality to this. Forgiving is the equivalent of letting go of the ember of hurt that was unfairly placed in your hands.

True forgiving is a deep, emotional letting go of pain; it's a spiritual uplift; and you deserve it. It also takes work. Try to forgive someone who has hurt you one day at a time, accepting the degree that you can forgive today as being good enough. Then tomorrow, try some more. Many people find the following approach to be helpful in learning to truly forgive.[26]

AN EXERCISE IN FORGIVING

Think of a person you harbor negative feelings toward. On a blank sheet of paper, list down the left-hand column the specific feelings you are harboring that make it difficult for you to forgive this person. Next, using a scale of 1 (not at all intense) to 10 (so intense I can hardly tolerate it), rate the level of intensity of each feeling. Put the sheet away someplace you'll remember.

Next, on a second sheet of paper, compose a list of what you most want for yourself in life; let's call them blessings. Then visualize the person you want to forgive receiving each blessing on the list. Do this once or twice a day for two weeks. At the end of that time, return to your original list. Notice how your intensity ratings of the various resentful feelings may have lessened.

Forgive Yourself

Scratch the surface of an unforgiving person, and you will find someone who feels ashamed of themselves and convinced that they don't deserve to be forgiven. We all harbor pains suffered from the lousy things we have done. Work to forgive yourself. The closest we come to perfection is when we recognize how we have erred, and adjust our behaviors to repair the wrong. Remind yourself that, more often than not, you've done the best you could, given what you knew about life and about yourself at the time. And take note of how you have applied lessons learned from your mistakes. Practice treating yourself with the same kind regard and nurturing encouragement you would show to a child who was truly sorry for a mistake.

Always Give a Little *Lagniappe*

There's a wonderful South Louisiana tradition of "always giving a little *lagniappe*" (a little something extra). A crucial piece of advice about letting go of what's holding you back in love and work evokes the spirit of lagniappe: As you move through your life, take every opportunity to be extra generous and gracious to others.

If you allow yourself to let go of what holds you back, you'll hear and see signs and opportunities for lagniappe all around you…

"His job was to be my doctor. But the way he treated me made him my friend."

"You went above and beyond your obligation to me in this contract. I'll never forget the extraordinarily great service you provided to my company."

"After all these years of being married, you still touch my heart with how kind you are to me."

"She always leaves the outside light on for me, if I'm coming home after dark. She makes me feel welcomed home."

"My boss is a busy and important man. He didn't have to come to my father's memorial service to show his respects. But I'll tell you this: I'll never forget that he did."

CLOSING THOUGHTS

Heroes create safe spaces for other people. They do this by surrounding others with caring interactions, one dot at a time. The process creates resilience for the giver and the receiver. We close with a single question: What's holding you back from being a hero to the people you love and work with? Whatever it is, let go of it!

CHAPTER 5

Changing from the Inside Out

"What made you successful won't keep you successful."

Lew Platt, former CEO, Hewlett-Packard

It's a rare person who enjoys it. Most of us fear it, grapple with it, and tire of it. Many even dread it. But once it hits, we usually find our way through it, then start again. And no one goes very long without having to face it. No matter what our stage or station in life, if we are to thrive, we all will have to deal with change—and few of us know how to recognize and manage the psychological aspects of change.

One of our patients put it best: "I've been to more coping-with-change seminars than I can count. I've learned what happens when work teams have to change, what stages organizations go through when changing, and how to solicit 'buy-in' from coworkers who are resisting change. But no course my company has offered has taught anything about what's most important to me: How do I cope with my most personal change battles?"

In this chapter, we address the internal, psychological processes that affect your ability to change. We will outline six keys to changing from the inside out:

1. Make peace with the need to change.
2. Beware of the false hope syndrome.
3. Understand your awkwardness when changing.
4. Beware of your dysfunctional psychological legacies.
5. Recognize your coping patterns and pitfalls.
6. Work through the stages of change.

Learn to recognize and manage these psychological factors and you can let go of whatever might be holding you back.

Make Peace with the Need to Change

Thriving is not an endpoint. It's not a static outcome we achieve or a destination we finally arrive at. Instead, it's a dynamic process. Thriving in our personal relationships and at work requires adapting, coping, and moving forward, all the while accumulating new layers of strength, skill, and confidence.

In today's fast-paced world, fearing change is a big handicap. Learning to get comfortable with changing is one of the most important 21st-century survival skills. To put it simply, thrivers make peace with the fact that they will need to reinvent themselves on a regular basis.

Many people rebel against this fact, believing instead that there must be someplace that is immune to this drama. This is especially evident in the workplace, where change-avoiders dream of another company, another division within their company, or perhaps another industry where the job descriptions, production goals, and required skill sets remain stable. They're chasing ghosts of days gone by.

We could fill this chapter with anecdotes and research studies that make our point, but instead we'll offer a few examples from recent conversations with professional consultation clients. The industries differ but the content remains the same: change.

Insurance sales professionals faced a crisis in early 2000. Having already built successful businesses selling homeowners' and auto insurance, they were asked by their mother company to move their emphasis from selling "tire and shingle" insurance (auto and homeowners) to selling financial services instead. And so they did. In 2004, just as these professionals successfully adapted to this change, their corporate leaders implored them to rebolster their efforts to sell homeowners' and auto insurance, reminding them that "these products are the bread and butter of our industry."

Airline reservationists already stressed to their production limits were given even more stringent performance goals, including a monitored "two-minute limit" on each telephone transaction. At the same time, they were informed that their pay and retirement benefits were being cut because of financial difficulties at the corporate level.

Distinguished educators in Louisiana in the early 2000s were handpicked from experienced teachers and charged with the task of revamping faculty and curricula in under-performing public schools. Many were "rewarded" at midyear with reassignments to new schools in need of similar re-engineering. These high-performing change agents were given no time to enjoy the fruits of their labors—always moving from one newly functioning school to another school in distress.

Information technology experts deemed to be the "cream of the crop" survived massive personnel cutbacks and were then required to absorb into their already overflowing workloads the projects of their newly departed colleagues.

Cardiovascular surgeons faced income cuts of 50 to 75 percent over a period of five years as a result of new technology that allows cardiologists (nonsurgeons) to insert drug-coated stents into arteries, thus drastically reducing the need for heart surgery.

Fire chiefs throughout the world gathered to discuss unprecedented staffing challenges stemming from a new commitment to work/family balance being demanded by young firefighters.

Directors of pharmacies gathered to discuss management challenges stemming from unpredictable drug recalls, mandates to counsel patients and not just "count pills and stick labels" when filling prescriptions, and difficulty motivating today's workforce to assume leadership positions.

Of course, the workplace is not the only place that's constantly changing. Our families and friendships never stop evolving. There is no roadmap for the contemporary relationship or family. We are making it up as we go and no matter what you did to be successful at one stage, the latest stage will bring new challenges that pull you in new directions. Never before has the conversation between men and women been so complex. Never before have families come in so many forms. Never before have so many families been impacted by such an ever-changing global environment.

Add to this our fervent desire to achieve ever-greater personal enrichment. We're constantly striving to get into better shape, have a more comfortable work/life balance, recapture the spark that seems to have dimmed in our romance, be more spiritually aligned, and enjoy ourselves more along the way.

Whether we're talking about work, relationships, or self, successfully adapting to change requires more than a set of simple coping strategies. You must learn to identify and manage your deepest psychological doubt about your ability to handle the way things are different from what you had expected or hoped for. This "new normal" that change creates must be embraced if you are to thrive.

Beware of the False Hope Syndrome

We've got good news and bad news. First, the good news: Whether your goal is to rejuvenate your marriage, lose weight, or boost your teamwork and productivity at work, the easy part is getting started. As Mark Twain observed, "Stopping smoking is easy. I've done it hundreds of times."

Consider your own experiences with changing. In the spaces below, list three things you'd like to change. Focus on behaviors or emotional habits that you have struggled with repeatedly, those that you've tried to change, over and over again. [Hint: You've probably included these on your New Year's list of resolutions, year after year after year . . .]

_____

_____

_____

If you are like most people, you included in your list things like exercising more, spending more quality time with loved ones, and/or doing something productive about a work or career dilemma.

Isn't it interesting that a person with your collection of skills, talents, and abilities has such a hard time changing something that seems so basic to your happiness? The truth is that if making these changes were simple, you would have done so long ago.

And this takes us to the bad news. In fact, this is the most unpopular news we have to deliver: If you're looking for a quick fix, you'll be disappointed. Changing for good is hard work, and the hardest part is sticking with it. Changing for good takes considerable effort exerted over long periods of time.

This necessity for hard work over time to achieve a difference is one of the foundation concepts of our counseling and consulting. Most of our clients can relate because they've already been disappointed by quick-fix promises. Once we've been through enough disappointment after trying quick-fix cures, we get ready for the real deal: we take responsibility for doing the hard work involved in letting go of what's holding us back, we dig our way out of the psychological pitfalls that have sabotaged our thriving, and we learn to recognize and avoid those pitfalls as we continue our journey.

When it comes to changing for good, you must avoid two costly mistakes. First, don't *under*-estimate how hard it will be to change, and second, don't *over*-estimate the benefits that will come with making the change. This combination of errors is what psychologists call the *false hope syndrome*. Let's examine this more closely.[1]

As soon as you decide to make a change, like going on a diet, your mood lifts. Bear in mind that you haven't actually *done* anything different yet. You still weigh the same as you did the minute before you decided to try this new diet. You might even be munching on a handful of potato chips as you read the magazine article that shows the fit and smiling models who supposedly got that way going on the easy-to-follow diet that you are about to embrace. And, sure enough, you start to *feel better* as soon as you decide to give the new diet a try. What boosts your mood are all those fine notions about the rosy future in store for the slimmer, healthier version of yourself that the advertisers promise will evolve—*by just going on this magic diet!* In fact, research suggests that measures of self-confidence and positive self-concept spike in the days immediately following the decision to make *any* positive change—like when you first join a health club, go on a budget, or decide to seek professional help for a problem.

Then the hard work of actually making that change begins. *Way too soon* after a burst of progress, you're confronted with the sobering fact that no matter how motivated you were at the start, you won't be the first person in the history of the human race who makes this change effortlessly and perfectly. Instead of feeling and looking like a magazine model, you feel bored and possibly frustrated with the hard work involved in making this change, and the person you see in the mirror looks like the same old you. Soon, frustration about your slow progress festers into downright grouchiness.

As you reach plateaus or even backslide, those inflated expectations about how easy this was going to be come tumbling down. Even if you have succeeded in making great progress toward the targeted change, around the same time that staying the course gets hard, you realize the sobering truth that the "new you" still has the same day-to-day life that the "old you" had. The cherished change hasn't made *that much of a difference in your overall life.*

Counting on a quick-fix strategy will leave you on shaky ground. Disillusionment and change fatigue will soon put you at risk of giving up and backsliding into your old habits. Far better to plant your feet solidly on level ground by being realistic about the work ahead of you, the likely consequences of making the change, and the psychological factors you'll have to overcome if you are to be successful.

When we are coaching a new client about changing, once we've gotten an overview of what the client wants help in accomplishing, we ask two seemingly simple questions: Do you feel that you deserve to change, to grow out of your ruts, to thrive? Do you give yourself permission to clarify who you really want to be and to make this version of you come true?

Most everyone responds initially with answers like "Of course!" or "You're darned right! I'm ready to feel better." But your true answers to these questions may be more complicated than you know. Evaluate whether you are really ready to change with the "I Know I'm Changing for the Good" test that follows.

Which of the following statements most accurately describes the feelings of someone who is making healthy, lasting psychological change?
   a. When I behave in this new way, I feel elated yet peaceful.
   b. When I behave in this new way, I am bored to death.
   c. When I behave in this new way, I feel a vague sense of discomfort, like I'm faking it.
   d. When I behave in this new way, I feel the approval of others.

Although it doesn't seem obvious, answer "c" may be the best indicator that you are moving toward real change. That's because, no matter how badly we may want to thrive, changing for good does not feel natural.

Understand Your Awkwardness when Changing

Of all the factors that can sabotage your attempts to change, the most common is that feeling of awkwardness you get when you're trying to replace an old habit with a new one. True and lasting change seldom feels natural; rather the opposite is true. If you've ever tried to change your golf swing, learn a new dance step, or improve your posture, you know that creating a new behavior pattern doesn't feel natural right away. This is doubly true for creating new emotional habits.

As we will discuss shortly, this awkwardness is sometimes due to deep feelings that get stirred when you change in a way counter to an old psychological pattern or habit. At minimum, unfamiliarity with the new skill you are trying to develop will leave you feeling awkward. Even if you're 100 percent committed to changing, repeating a new behavior enough for it to become second nature and emotionally comfortable takes time.

To truly let go of what's holding you back, you must live with the awkwardness that comes with changing. Sometimes, the vague feeling of "faking it" lasts long after the new behavior has become a habit.

Here, three of our clients talk about their experiences with the awkwardness of changing. Each of them faced a different change challenge.

Gordon, a 55-year-old successful auto and homeowners' insurance agent, was trying to adjust to his company's mandated new goal of pushing more life insurance and financial services business; Molly, 63, was trying to get more exercise; and Jake, 37, was trying to become less work obsessed and better at spending relaxed time with his family. Yet they all shared the same response: Each of them felt like a fake.

"I've built my business by being authentic with my clients," Gordon said. "That starts with believing I've got something to sell that they need, that will help them. I'm not so sure about these new products. I can see how life insurance and smart invest- ments can help my clients, but I feel like a fraud when I bridge our conversations from auto or homeowners' into discussions about long-term financial security."

"Who am I kidding?" Molly said. "I've never been athletic. What am I doing, acting like exercising is the most important part of my day? Every other person in the gym seems to have a glint of glee in their eyes, like they were born for this. I'm just trudging through the exercise session, feeling like an imposter."

Jake's feelings echo the others': "I'm frankly confused about this whole work/life balance stuff. I love my job, and I love the feeling of relief I get when I've gotten important work done. But my wife keeps warning me that it's time to 'stop and smell the roses,' that our kids are growing up without me. So I limit my after-hours work so I can join in the family life. I sit there playing with the kids or having a dinnertime conversation, looking perfectly contented and involved. But I'm not. Half the time I'm thinking about what work I have left undone. As much as I love my fam- ily and enjoy being with them, I feel like a phony, like I'm faking it."

Gordon, Molly, and Jake were not faking anything. All three were following through with commitments to change they made to themselves, and they were trying to grow accustomed to what this "new normal" felt like. Each was experiencing the most fundamental psychological aspect of changing. This is a process that takes getting used to. New behaviors seldom feel authentic; that's all part of creating a new normal.

Practice a new behavior for six to twelve months, and much of the awkwardness will wear off; but not all of it, all of the time. Twelve months of practice will very likely calm Gordon's sales anxieties and Molly's awkwardness about exercising. But the unrest that Jake feels when he fights his tendency to work compulsively is likely to last years, despite his best efforts. What determines the length of the struggle to reprogram your emotions is the depth of the programming that drove you into the old behaviors and patterns in the first place.

Beware of Your Dysfunctional Psychological Legacies

The most important task in changing for good is learning to recognize and manage the effects of your dysfunctional psychological legacies. We are referring here to those over-learned and self-limiting world views, judgments, fears, or behavior patterns that stem from past experiences and relationships, those that play in your subconscious like automatic messages that promote self-fulfilling prophecies and sabotage you. These psychological legacies and our responses to them show up in many guises. If misunderstood, they can lead you to change only superficially as you trade one problem for another. Here are a few examples of what we mean.

Counter-Script Change

Here, you do the opposite of what hurt you, but you're still not choosing for yourself because your behavior is still scripted by the old hurt. This is a brittle form of changing. It is fueled by outrage, hurt, or other unresolved feelings. It's the sort of temporary changing that follows this predictable pattern:

"Because I still harbor _____ (feelings) from the fact that _____ (something or someone hurt you), I commit to _____ (being different than the person or situation that hurt you)."

Example: Cary came for help with headaches, insomnia, and mood swings. The root of his problems was a counter-script change that went like this: "Because I still harbor unresolved hurt and outrage from the fact that my last boss was verbally abusive, I committed to never allowing myself to get angry when dealing with anyone I supervise."

As well intended as these counter-script changes may be, they are based on self-limiting and unhealthy psychological bargains. In Cary's case, constantly squelching the normal feelings of irritation and aggravation that surface periodically in any relationship kept him from learning how to effectively deal with negative feelings and healthily resolve conflict with employees. He didn't learn new emotional management skills that would truly move him beyond his abusive boss's way of mismanaging anger. Instead, he simply committed himself to not acting like his abusive boss. Being a man of his word, Cary never verbally abused others. But his stuffed-inside emotions were taking their toll on his sleep, his body, and his ability to manage his moods.

Here's another example of counter-script change.

Claire's world was shattered when her parents divorced without warning when she was 12 years old. She reacted by committing herself to staying loyal in relationships, no matter what the costs. Her counter-script contract read like this: "Because I still harbor unresolved grief and anger from the fact that my parents divorced for what seemed to me to be no good reasons, I committed to never giving up on relationships."

"And following through with this commitment," she explained, "has caused me

to struggle in these ways: I stay stuck in relationships with friends and lovers who are not very nurturing of me. I give far more than I get in relationships, and I feel mistreated, misunderstood, taken advantage of, and abused."

Consider whether you are trying to change in some counter-script way. Honestly fill in the blanks below:

Because I still harbor _____ (feelings) from the fact that _____ (something or someone that hurt you), I have committed to _____ (being different than the person or situation that hurt you).

And following through with this commitment has caused me to struggle in these ways:

_____

_____

_____

Confusion About "Rising Above Your Upbringing"

The case of Sara and Bill highlights the complex feelings that can get stirred when you make changes that discontinue your dysfunctional psychological legacies.

Sara's frustration about Bill's lack of warmth and nurturing brought them into marriage counseling. After seven years of struggling with these issues, Sara had become pessimistic that things would change. She openly discussed her fear that Bill's upbringing in a family where love and warmth were seldom expressed openly had scripted him to be emotionally unexpressive for life.

Bill did love Sara and very much wanted his marriage to survive. He was ready to change. Sara, happy about Bill's desire to be more warm and loving, began to share with him ways that he could demonstrate his love for her. Immediately and dramatically, their marriage improved.

But after several weeks Bill and Sara came to a session very distressed. It seems that all their progress had disappeared and things were back to square one. Both said there had been no major conflict or stress in their relationship, and they were both at a loss as to why their positive changes had disappeared.

An individual session with Bill provided the answer. He admitted that the improvement in his relationship with Sara had been a blessing and that he had been feeling proud of the changes he was making, when, "as if out of nowhere," he began to feel like a phony, like someone "pretending" to be good with emotional closeness, someone very different from the person he was brought up to be.

What Bill did not realize is that changing in some positive way might stir self-defeating feelings and thoughts. Often, self-limiting thoughts and feelings that hold you back were mentally or emotionally "recorded" during your experiences with only a handful of very significant people in your life, but these experiences shaped and wounded you at crucial moments in your development. *You may actually feel a sense of shame when you are abandoning a dysfunctional script from childhood.* It's as though you are violating some ancient taboo against "rising above your upbringing." The healthier you get, the more you will challenge the psychological messages that held you back in the first place. And it probably won't feel comfortable, at least at first.

It may seem to you that the most successful people are immune to the sorts of self-doubts and insecurities that plague the rest of us. Nothing could be further from the truth. In fact, we have never known anyone who did not harbor at least some hauntingly painful effects from living in a world that was not constantly nurturing and safe.

Here are a few examples from our clinical practice.

We once counseled a beautiful, extremely bright, and talented young woman we'll call Crystal who was failing to thrive in her college career. Despite her wonderful and supportive family life, her off-the-chart IQ, her good study habits, and the fact that she entered college with a stellar high school education, her college grades were disappointing. Test-taking anxiety seemed to be her problem, and nothing she had tried previously had helped her to perform better.

In a case like this, it's tempting to get overly clinical and search for all sorts of psychological ghosts that might be sabotaging a client. We try to resist this temptation because these psychological witch-hunts may promote shame and blame, and they can become a way of denying responsibility for what is required to solve your problems. It is important, however, to accurately identify the psychological factors that are holding you back. Only then can you do something about them.

Crystal's description of how she felt leading up to taking a test was revealing of what she needed to better manage before she could change. "When I'm walking to class to take an exam, I feel the same sort of shaky feeling inside that I used to feel just before basketball practice in high school. It's like I can't forget how nervous and awkward I felt all those times when Coach Felling criticized me in front of the team."

Even our most high-performing, successful clients have some version of this type of psychological wounding. As author John Lee observed, the heart of a child is so tender that even a sideways glance can pierce it and make a scar that lasts a lifetime.

Here's another example.

A heart surgeon who struggled with anger control once told us, "I'm just a knucklehead from West Virginia who rose above his upbringing. I'm lucky that I even got into college, much less into medical school and a heart surgery residency program. I get tense about the constantly changing technology I have to master to keep up in my field, and when I'm tense, I act mean. I've read every anger management book I can find, but nothing's taught me to deal with the source of my tension. I feel like a knucklehead in disguise."

Now that we've mentioned it, you'll likely start to notice that we're all battling negative ideas about our less-than-perfect lives. We all sometimes feel like "knuckleheads in disguise."

The late Ray Pelletier, a fabulously successful speaker, consultant, and author, spoke of how, despite the solid emotional foundation given to him by his loving family, a cruel third-grade teacher's constant criticism and humiliation left him floundering in self-doubt and underachievement for most of his life.[2] Similarly, television personality Dr. Phil McGraw speaks of the wounds to his self-esteem that came from an overly critical grade school teacher and his lifetime skepticism about trusting authority figures that stems from another teacher's disloyalty and criticism of him during a crucial time in his development.[3]

Closer to Home: In-Script Changing

Our first family (the family we grew up in) is our original learning laboratory. For most of us, no experience more powerfully shapes our expectations about what the world has to offer us and what our place will be in that world. These expectations get indelibly recorded in our brains and function like tapes playing in our heads, reminding us of what is important. If you were lucky, the tapes in your head tell you that you are worthy, valued, supported, and loved.

But even the best of families may pass on certain self-limiting legacies. Psychological patterns that sabotage thriving can get handed down from generation to generation. And these family patterns that hold you back can be difficult to pinpoint or painful to admit to. That's because the emotions that come with these patterns are so familiar to us that they feel "normal." These patterns are particularly hard to recognize when the content of your struggles differs from that of your parents or other close relatives. Look closely and you may see that you are living out a *process* that is very similar to theirs even though the *content* is very different and even though you swore you would never be like that.

For example, it might be that you come from a long line of family who wrecked their lives with alcoholic behavior. Perhaps you responded by swearing off alcohol completely. Even if no alcohol ever passed your lips, being sober wouldn't immunize you from being affected by the psychology that drives compulsive drinking. Though you are not sabotaging your life with alcoholism, you would be well advised to be on the lookout for variations of the family theme of failing to take responsibility for good health habits that may be showing up in your life. Do you abuse your body in ways other than alcoholism? Do you work compulsively, then numb yourself and distance yourself from your family with compulsive television watching? Are you addicted to quick stimulation fixes that come from gambling, pornography, or compulsive spending? If so, the net effect of your compulsions may be very similar to the effects of your Uncle Bill's drinking binges: damaged self-esteem, blunted health and productivity, and strained family relationships.

And it will be just as difficult for you to change your problem behaviors as it was for Uncle Bill to not take a drink. Underestimate this fact, and your script to live unhealthily will sabotage any move on your part to thrive, and the old family pattern will continue to hold you back.

Here's another example of what we're talking about.

John came for help to stop his chronic philandering. Throughout the course of his ten-year marriage, he had carried on a constant string of extramarital affairs. He was tired of living with the guilt of lying to his wife and the anxiety that he might get caught. He seemed ready to change. But he admitted that he had been "ready to change" many, many times before. Despite his repeated vows to himself to end his lying ways, his fidelity never lasted very long.

We asked John to describe what he typically felt when he was beginning an affair. Here's what he said: "If I'm honest with myself—and I'm not always—I can tell when one of these dangerous relationships is set into motion. And that's the best way to describe what I feel: I feel like these relationships sorta happen to me; that I get caught up in the momentum of the relationship. It seems that things happen whether I want them to happen or not, the relationship grows into something more than it should be, and then I feel that I'm stuck in it. Sure, I always have a choice about whether to return a phone call or make the phone call myself that sets up a dinner or a drink after work. But it seems that some momentum takes over and short-circuits that voice yelling inside my head, 'Don't do this! Don't go there! Just say no!'"

Most people cringe when they hear a confession like John's. It's easy to criticize someone who makes destructive choices, and then claims to be a victim. Maybe it's painful because it hits close to home. Your content may differ (and we hope it does!), but how different is John's sense of helplessness from your own futility and refusal to take responsibility for changing what's holding you back?

Using John as an example, let's walk through how you can uncover the psychological factors that you need to manage if you're to change for good. To begin, refer back to your list of changes you'd like to make. Pick one. In the spaces below, describe how you have typically felt in the past when you have tried to make this change.

_____

_____

_____

Now notice the words you chose to describe what it feels like when you try to make this particular change. Your descriptions provide clues to your psychological tapes that make changing this difficult for you.

Look at the words John used to describe how he goes about having an affair. He describes feelings of helplessness, passivity (he reacts, rather than takes charge), being victimized, agonizing, and having guilt, fear, and anxiety about what is happening or is about to happen.

Now look at the words you used to describe the feelings you experience when you try to change in this way, and think about where else in your life you have experienced these sorts of feelings. We're searching here for another problem in your life that you wish you could change. The emotions that come with a self-defeating script will be stirred whenever you try to change in a healthy way; they don't just rear their ugly heads when you try to change in one area.

For example, in one of our counseling sessions John realized that each time he vowed to exercise more, eat more healthily, or stop smoking, he struggled with emotions very similar to those he encountered when he tried to end his extramarital ways. In his words:

"I give myself a pep talk and convince myself that I'm going to do it this time. But then I actually start getting anxious and scared about being in certain circumstances where I know it will be hard to resist the 'pull' into my old ways: to overeat, talk myself into skipping an exercise session, or to bum a cigarette from a buddy. I get that old-time feeling of dread, agony, and weakness—and I know that I'm going to give in to the temptation."

John traced the origins of his change-squelching tapes to his first family experiences. He was raised in a family driven by his self-focused father's irresponsible behaviors. Whether drinking too much, precipitously quitting yet another job, or gambling away his family's rent money, John's father lived his life in a way that created emotional chaos for his family. This is the emotional memory John encounters when he tries to make his life a more orderly, healthy psychological territory. If he fails to acknowledge the pain of this material, he has no chance of managing it. But once he identifies what gets stirred psychologically when he tries to change, he can gather his resources and use them to help scale these hurdles in the path of ultimate change.

Use the following exercise to identify dysfunctional psychological legacies that might be holding you back.

Identify Your Psychological Legacies

Think of a family member who struggled with a life problem that negatively affected your well-being. Don't limit yourself to thinking of your parents.

Include siblings, grandparents, your spouse, or any significant loved one whose struggle caused you distress. In concise terms, describe that person's struggle and how it affected you. Write your responses in a journal or notebook that is for your eyes only.

What emotional patterns did you identify that you will need to acknowledge and manage if you are to achieve lasting change?

A final lesson from the case of John: Beware of in-script changing. We sometimes think we're changing for good when, in truth, we're merely trading one problem for another. This is what happens when we stay in-script and trade problem content, but keep the same self-defeating process. For example, John might decide to swear off having affairs but remain "helpless" about his many bad health habits. We call this type of "different content, same old process" change in-script changing.

You might wonder what's wrong with this kind of change. After all, isn't it true that staying stuck in fewer ruts is better than staying stuck across the board? And who would argue with the fact that, even if John keeps floundering in his bad health habits, stopping his lying and his affairs does improve his life?

No doubt about it. We agree. But here's the problem with in-script changing: The emotional distress that comes if we mismanage any one area of our life tends to "contaminate" our best efforts in other areas. In John's case, if he continues to take such poor care of himself physically, the odds will increase that his pattern of denying responsibility will set the stage for him to backslide in his primary area of desired change—remaining faithful to his wife.

While we don't expect you to be perfect, it is a fact nonetheless that the odds that you will stick with a change in one major area increase in proportion to how integrated you are in taking care of yourself across the board. We'll say more about this in Chapter 8, when we discuss the concept of fencing in your life's territory.

Letting go of what's holding you back from ending a dysfunctional psychological legacy is a true act of courage. In fact, we believe that people who do it are the true everyday heroes. When you end a dysfunctional legacy—refusing to continue treating yourself and others in limiting ways—you justify your lifetime, even if you do nothing else.

Let's recap the keys for changing for good that we have discussed thus far:

- Make peace with the need to change.
- Beware of the false hope syndrome.
- Understand your awkwardness when changing.
- Beware of your dysfunctional psychological legacies

We trust that by now, one of our major points is clear: In order to change for good, you must not only change your behavior, but also recognize and dislodge any deeply rooted ideas about yourself that might otherwise hold you back. As you do this you are likely to feel a surprising sense of doing something wrong, something inauthentic. Change feels uncomfortable because it is unfamiliar and goes against the theme of age-old role models and scripts that have contributed to your thinking, feeling, and acting in the very ways that you are now trying to change. Your discomfort doesn't mean the new, healthier way of being is not really you; it means that you are letting go of what has been holding you back, and you haven't yet grown accustomed to the new normal you are creating.

Managing the psychology of changing requires you to dig beneath any superficial understanding of yourself and identify the origins and pitfalls of your coping patterns. This takes us to our fifth key for changing.

Recognize Your Coping Patterns and Pitfalls

How you cope with life, including the special challenge of coping with change, is a result of your unique personality and what has happened in your life. Personality development is a complex process and there is no universally accepted theory about how it happens. As food for thought, we present key concepts and pearls of wisdom from three perspectives that we have found to be useful. The three theories are: the psychodynamic perspective; the integrative, coping perspective; and the transactional analysis perspective. Each of these perspectives can help you to identify some of the hurdles you will likely encounter as you orchestrate lifetime changes.

The Psychodynamic Perspective

Psychodynamic theory proposes that coping behavior is shaped by underlying emotions like anxiety, shame, guilt, sadness, anger, and sexual arousal. Fears develop in response to these repressed feelings, and these fears fester into exaggerated needs, which in turn cause self-defeating behaviors to arise.[4]

For example, if you fear conflict or rejection, you may develop an exaggerated *need for affection and approval*, which may drive you to overly conform to the wishes of others, even when doing so holds you back from getting your own needs met.

If you fear abandonment or being alone, you may develop an exaggerated *need for a partner to adore and be admired by*, which may drive you to prove yourself lovable by taking on the role of self-denying rescuer.

If you fear the consequences of expressing yourself or making demands of others, you may develop an exaggerated *need to restrict your life within narrow borders*. This may lead to a lifetime of holding yourself back by squashing your ambition, remaining in second place, and believing that excessive modesty and self-denial are of supreme value.

If you fear what will happen if you make a mistake or share control, you may develop an exaggerated *need for power* that will lead you to become overly dominant in relationships and intolerant of "weakness" of any kind (in yourself and others)—leading to relationship styles that will make it difficult for you to keep harmony in long-term relationships.

If you fear being exploited, shamed, or humiliated, you may develop an exaggerated *need to manipulate others or to appear perfect to others.* The result will be that you treat others like objects to be used for your own gain or to drive yourself to always be "the best" by defeating others.

Finally, if you fear what will happen if you love or need others, you may develop a distorted *need for self-sufficiency and independence* that compels you to stay detached from others. If you begin to attach to another person, a team, or a group, on the other hand, your primitive insecurities will get stirred and lead you to behave in ways that sabotage your relationships.

Splitting

One of the most useful concepts from this psychodynamic perspective calls attention to what's "lurking in the shadows" of our personality. The notion here is that early in life we develop "good self"/"bad self" psychological splits that are based on what pleases or distresses people who are important to us— and not necessarily on what is actually good or bad in any moral sense of the terms. Our "good self" contains the characteristics that please those around us, based on their needs, not ours. We learn that expressing these "good self" behaviors, thoughts, or feelings allows us to either gain pleasure and acceptance or avoid pain and rejection.

On the other hand, any thoughts, feelings, needs, or desires that meet with disapproval, discomfort, or shaming from significant others (largely based on their needs and comfort zones, not ours) get repressed and stored in the unexpressed or "bad" aspect of self.

For most of us, as life unfolds, we accumulate much more practice expressing our "good" traits and relatively little practice expressing the psychological traits that we've learned to identify as "bad." This is why changes that involve becoming a more integrated, healthy person by expressing the thoughts, feelings, and needs that have resided in your "unexpressed" self may stir those vague anxieties about doing something fraudulent or "wrong" that we mentioned earlier.

If you remain unaware of the "split-off" parts of your personality, they can cause you problems. You may develop unhealthy coping patterns that are fueled by your fear that openly expressing what resides in your "bad self" will result in pain, punishment, or humiliation, rather than in nurturance. Staying psychologically split will leave you out of touch with your "authentic self." We'll have more to say about identifying and clarifying your authentic self in Chapter 6.

The good news: You can let go of the "hold" these deep conflicts have on you by recognizing the fact that you are still a work in progress and you get to *choose* what happens next.

An Integrative, Coping Perspective[5]

No one has to remain stuck with splits and scars from childhood. Psychological development continues throughout life. Early life experience is only one of several factors that shape personality. Your current environment and the people in it, the status of your contemporary relationships, and the choices you make all converge to shape your present coping style. The idea here is that your coping style distinguishes you, and that style is ever changing.

The true challenge is learning to be equally adept at the two kinds of coping: *problem-focused coping* and *emotion-focused coping*. Problem-focused coping uses logic to solve the problem at hand. When you are dealing with a stressor that can be changed, controlled, or managed, problem-focused coping leads to an increased sense of control.

But problem-focused coping has negative consequences when it is *misapplied*. For example, if you use problem-focused coping strategies when you are facing an *uncontrollable* stressor, not only will your efforts fail, but the very act of trying to take charge of something that cannot be controlled will simply compound your stress. It will also hurt your body, as research has shown that misapplying problem-focused coping increases blood pressure and general cardiovascular stress responses.[6]

A different kind of coping is called for when the stressor is uncontrollable. This type of stress is most uncomfortable for high performers who are accustomed to taking charge and solving the problems they face. When the stress is not controllable, emotion-focused coping is more productive. Emotion-focused coping relies on your ability to manage your responses to uncontrollable circumstances. Here, you must learn to reinterpret the situation in some way that soothes you. You must learn to distract yourself from obsessive thinking about how you might change the situation, to soothe yourself in appropriate ways, and to seek and receive support from others. This sort of coping, in contrast to problem-focused coping, has been shown to lower symptoms of stress when facing situations like the death of a loved one, a disappointing set-back like losing your job, or the need for surgery—situations that are uncontrollable.[7] Emotion-focused coping can also help to ease the frustration that comes when another person fails to conform to your expectations.

Remember that each mode of coping has its advantages. Emotion-focused strategies are more effective in calming upset nerves in the short term. Problem-focused strategies are more effective over the long run. Choose how you cope respecting both your need to solve problems and your need to feel reasonably good, even when problems cannot be readily solved.

Transactional Analysis Perspective: Coping Patterns and Pitfalls

A commonsense way of understanding the coping patterns and anxieties that hold you back from thriving is a theory called transactional analysis.[8] This theory holds that we each develop some combination of six coping themes that tend to drive our ways of thinking, behaving, feeling, and dealing with others. These "drivers" can become problematic when they are overused.

- **Being Strong.** If you were taught that your role in life is to be stoic, never complaining about your pains and fears, you probably are driven by a Being Strong personality theme.

- **Being Perfect.** If you drive yourself with a Being Perfect personality theme, you are probably accustomed to feeling anxious, irritable, and guilty.

- **Trying Hard.** Some of us learn to equate self-worth with fatigue. When caught in Trying Hard, you cope by narrowly focusing on the tasks at hand, pursuing your goals relentlessly, and resting only when your fatigue builds to exhaustion.

- **Pleasing Others.** If you have difficulty being appropriately self-focused and self-nurturing without feeling guilty, then you are probably driven by a Pleasing Others personality.

- **Being Careful.** If your personality driver is Being Careful, it is highly likely that you often feel anxious, even when there is no objective reason to be bothered. You are probably a real pro at anticipating what might go wrong even when all is going well.

- **Hurrying.** If you are driven by a Hurrying personality, you probably live with an internal sense of urgency, and, when forced to slow down (by health problems, the "slowness" of others, or your own limitations), you probably feel anxious, frustrated, and irritable.

Each of these ways of coping can be helpful; each works sometimes in some situations. But coping problems develop when we overuse our most familiar drivers. They essentially create a script for our role in life that is limiting and often destructive if we follow it. As can be seen in the table opposite, overusing any of these coping drivers can lead to stress symptoms that stem directly from your coping style.

Coping Patterns and Pitfalls

If you cope rigidly in this way:	Your underlying hope probably is:	Your stress symptoms will likely be:
Being Strong	*To be nurtured*	*Loneliness and numbness*
Being Perfect	*To feel good enough*	*Guilt, irritability, and obsessing*
Trying Hard	*To feel deserving of rest and enjoyment*	*Exhaustion and joylessness*
Pleasing Others	*To feel understood and appreciated*	*Guilt, anxiety, and withdrawal*
Being Careful	*To feel safe*	*Fear and difficulty making decisions*
Hurrying	*To feel finished*	*Anxiety and urgency*

Which of these coping patterns best describes you? Changing for good will necessitate your practicing coping flexibility and accurately identifying and appropriately satisfying the needs underlying your coping drivers.

Use the information in this section to help you flag and control your coping-based stress symptoms. When you notice yourself experiencing any of the stress symptoms listed in the preceding table, try asking others for something that might soothe the actual underlying hope that corresponds with your driver. For example, if you find yourself feeling lonely and numb, it may be that you are hurting yourself by staying stuck in a Being Strong driver. The information in the table suggests that these stress symptoms might indicate that you're having difficulty giving yourself permission to nurture yourself or to ask others for support and encouragement. To rejuvenate your energies, take the risk of sharing your concerns and worries with a trusted loved one.

Similarly, if you notice a loved one acting in ways described in the "stress symptoms" column of the table, you can use this information to help them get some of what they're having trouble giving themselves. First, assume that your loved one's stress symptom comes at least in part from not having his or her underlying hope satisfied. Next, offer a nurturing "gift" that might soothe that underlying hope. For example, if your partner is acting joyless and exhausted, you might offer encouragement that he or she has worked hard enough for now, and deserves a little recess.

Work Through the Stages of Change

Whichever of these theories resonates with you, use it to understand what you need to change and what might get stirred psychologically as you begin to take better care of yourself. Most important is that you realize that, regardless of what your psychological legacies have been, you can let go of what's been holding you back. Take charge of writing the remaining chapters in your life script. Make peace with the need to change and accept that making lasting change takes work.

You won't change until you're ready, no matter how much other people beg you to. And, if you're like most of us, even once you're ready, you won't change all at once. Most people pass through a series of distinct stages on their way to making lasting changes. Acquaint yourself with these stages and pay attention to your passage through the five phases of change identified by psychologist James O. Prochaska and colleagues.[10] For our purposes, we've renamed the stages to show how most of our clients respond when we ask them how ready they are to change:

Stage I: I don't need to change.

Stage II: Sure, I'll change, but not right now.

Stage III: I'm going to change soon. I want to get ready.

Stage IV: Let's do it!

Stage V: I've had a slip-up. What now?

We will describe the work of each stage using examples drawn from one of our clients who had anger management problems. His temper outbursts were creating problems in both his career and his family life. While some examples will be specific to changing anger behaviors, the principles they demonstrate can be used to help you change any pattern.

Stage I: I don't need to change.

"Everyone harps on how I speak to them. Maybe *they're* the ones who need to change! I'm just pushing for excellence, and they can't keep up." If this sounds like you, you're not likely to change any time soon.

To move forward: Ask yourself why the people who care about you are encouraging you to curb your anger. Then, examine your reasons for saying you don't need to. Look at what you're likely to gain by communicating more calmly when you are upset versus what you're likely to lose by continuing on as you are. If you're honest, you'll see the wisdom in others' encouragement that you change.

Stage II: Sure, I'll change, but not right now.

"I know I should learn to manage my anger differently, but now is not the time." If this sounds like you, then you're making progress. When you openly acknowledge that you need to change, you're taking a big step toward changing for good.

To move forward: Start the habit of self-observation. Notice the circumstances and sorts of interactions that stir your anger. When is it easiest and hardest to control your temper?

List the high-risk circumstances and relationships in which it is hardest for you to control your anger. For example: "It's hardest for me to control my temper (1) during my Monday and Wednesday sales team meetings; and (2) during dinnertime at home, when everyone is squabbling and talking at once."

Begin learning about anger management strategies. Even though you're not yet ready to put these into practice, learn what others do to manage anger. Information makes the unknown more familiar and increases the odds that you will give it a try. Here are some things you can do:

Take note of how someone you admire handles tense interactions. What kinds of words do they use? What's their tone of voice? If your relationship with that person is trusting enough, ask how they manage to do that.

Tell your loved ones or friends that you're thinking about learning new ways to deal with anger and conflict, and ask for their suggestions on how to start.

Browse the self-help section of your favorite bookstore, and thumb through the contents of books on anger management, being sure to note the topics covered and the steps involved in a successful program.

Stage III: I'm going to change soon. I want to get ready.

Committing yourself to changing is not enough. You've also got to plan your strategy. In this stage, you prepare and motivate yourself for the hard work ahead.

To move forward: Immerse yourself in everything possible regarding what you plan to do. It's now time to actually read some of those anger management books you've only scanned, and take notes! Buy an anger management tape or CD and listen to it when you are driving.

List the reasons why you want to change, emphasizing the benefits you will gain by changing. Make multiple copies of the list, and post them where you'll see the list frequently, both at home and at work. For example, I want to manage my anger because doing so will:

- make my relationships better
- improve my quality of life
- enhance my career
- make it easier for the people I care about to feel comfortable when they're around me
- protect my health
- make me a more effective leader
- generate more respect in regard to my opinions
- allow me to feel more in control of my emotions

Prepare to start by writing down exactly what you plan to do during the first week of your change program, noting specifically what you will do in those high-risk situations and relationships you've already identified. What will you do that's different from your typical pattern? For example:

What I'll do:

1. I'll start by consciously relaxing for at least five minutes before the start of the two high-risk times I've identified: team meetings at work on Monday and Wednesday and family dinnertime.

2. During work meetings and family dinnertime, I'll practice being a better listener and less of a director.

3. Because I know it's hard for me to stay quiet when I disagree with someone, I'll take written notes during work meetings and mental notes at home about things I think I might otherwise challenge out loud. I'll save these for review, and keep quiet about the topic for at least two days. If I remain convinced that I need to speak up, I'll revisit the topic.

How long I'll do it: I will try this strategy for two weeks and then review my plan.

Before starting, look over your plan. What are the odds that you will follow through? On a scale of 1 to 100, with 1 being "no confidence" and 100 being "absolutely confident," how confident are you that you will follow through with this plan? Research shows that people follow through with an action only when they are at least 70 percent confident they can do it. In other words, if you have less than a 70 percent confidence rating that you'll stick to your plan, chances are you won't. When this is the case, either modify your goal to make it more attainable, or determine what would help you surmount the obstacles in your path.

Finally, prepare by promising yourself a reward for completing your plan. When making any change, if you celebrate the small steps, you're more likely to stay motivated throughout your journey.

Stage IV: Let's do it!

Stack the deck in favor of success. Focus on small, manageable steps you can easily take. Remember, it takes time and many, many experiences to get comfortable with a new behavior.

To move forward: Commit to your "new normal" by signing a change contract with yourself. We know that this might feel too formal, but we urge you to do it anyway. Research shows that we take things more seriously and follow through with action when we "formally" contract to do so. Here's a sample contract you may want to use.

Change Contract

I, _____, during the week of _____, will do the following:

_____.

I will do this on the dates and at the times noted below:

Dates: _____.

Times: _____,

at the location(s) I have listed:

_____.

My support person(s) will be _____.

I will reward myself for doing this by:

_____.

From 0 to 100 percent, I rate my confidence in my ability to complete this activity at:

0   10   20   30   40   50   60   70   80   90   100

(Adjust your contract until you are within the 70–100 percent high-confidence zone.)

Stage V: I've had a slip-up. What now?

"I'm listening more and arguing less, but I'm still a long way away from being Mr. Mellow. How do I make sure I don't fall back into my old ways?"

Developing new habits takes time, and no one does it perfectly. Slip-ups and setbacks are not the same as full-blown relapses into old ways; they're part of the change process, not signs of failure.

To move forward: Handle setbacks by seeing each one for what it is—a misstep, not a sign of weakness.[11] Resist the urge to criticize and shame yourself for experiencing a setback. Just get back on track. Ask yourself, What can this setback teach me that I can make use of as I continue to change?

Make your environment conducive to change. If you were trying to stop drinking, you wouldn't take a job bartending. By the same token, if you're trying to manage your anger, don't spend time in conversations that stir your irritation or watching newscasts that get you riled up.

Use common sense when making change. Describe your desired change in concrete and specific terms, for example, "I will exercise for 30 minutes four times a week" rather than "I will get more exercise."

Remember that team support is important. Let your family and colleagues know that you need and appreciate their help and support. Beware of circumstances that commonly trigger setbacks. No matter what you are trying to change, negative emotions put you at risk of slipping back into undesirable habits. Anxiety, boredom, depression, irritation, and stress increase the odds that you may react in unhealthy ways.

CLOSING THOUGHTS

We hope that our frank discussion about changing from the inside will guide you to think clearly about the hard work that changing requires and to stay the course as you change. Millions of people make life-affirming changes every day. You can be one of these success stories.

By using the tools outlined in this chapter, you can write the remaining chapters of your life's script with your own hand. Most of us would start to squirm if we were given a blank page and told to write a new script for our lives. How exactly would you like your life to be? What do you want? Who do you want to be with? And where do you want to be? It's time to choose for yourself. It's time to specify how you want to fill the limited time you have left on this earth.

Now that you know the truth about creating permanent change, you will have the opportunity to make such choices. Compared to the way you are living, how would you like to live? Compared to how you typically feel, what would you like to feel more or less of more of the time? Compared to the ways you manage your health, your relationships, and your career choices, how would you like to be? In answering these and other key questions, you will start to clarify your chosen self.

CHAPTER 6

☼ Clarify Your Chosen Self ☼

☼

"Your playing small doesn't serve the world. There is
nothing enlightened about shrinking so that other
people won't feel insecure around you."

Marianne Williamson, A Return to Love[1]

☼

"Each human being is born as something new, something that never existed before. Each is born with the capacity to win at life. Each person has a unique way of seeing, hearing, touching, tasting, and thinking. Each has his or her own unique potentials—capabilities and limitations. Each can be a significant, thinking, aware, and creative being—a productive person, a winner."[2]

So begins one of the books that launched our modern-day self-help craze. *Born to Win*, published in 1971, has sold more than four million copies worldwide. Fast-forward to 2007, and we find millions of people *each day* watching television and listening to radio programs that promise to make us better. We seem to be searching for something we have lost: some state of excellence; some sense of greater peace and harmony. We are hungry for authenticity in ourselves and in our relationships. But finding that authentic center is harder than it seems. Because we have learned to hold back, we have lost contact with the core of who we are.

For reasons that we have talked about in earlier chapters, including the negative ways we were interacted with as children, the defensive behaviors we developed in reaction, and the superachiever culture we live in, we become adults with a wall between how we live and who we really are. Other people's judgments, expectations, and slights added some of the bricks to this wall, while other bricks we placed ourselves. These are the internal factors: your own conclusions, decisions, and perceptions about what you need to do to survive. These self-limiting beliefs are the result of your very own flawed views of yourself. They hold you back and straitjacket your potential, and only you can change them.

You were not born with flawed views of yourself. Just look at small children before the reactions of others change them. They are passionate, ever curious, energetic, and resilient. They are affectionate, congruent (what you see is what you get), and clear about what they think, feel, need, and want. You, too, were that way and, if you were lucky, you still are that way.

If you were not so lucky, you can still rediscover your authentic self and, thusly empowered, change your life.

It Doesn't Have to Be This Way!

We invite you to work from the assumption that you are free to choose how you live your life. You are not merely a product of your past or someone else's expectations. You have a chance to have it all, and you have the right to get it. But you're probably selling yourself short because of some combination of three factors:

1. Your own fear of changing
2. The fact that you've grown accustomed to defining yourself and your life options in very limited ways
3. The probability that some of the important people in your life will be uncomfortable if you do change

For now, let's focus on you. You've got to determine whether you're selling yourself short by accepting some pre-scripted notion of what is possible for you. Are you living out someone else's plan for your life or a limited version of your own dream? Have you grown so accustomed to meeting everyone else's expectations that you've lost sight of what it would mean for you to truly thrive? Are you caught in a rut or a predetermined momentum—like water finding its path, then sticking there, confined by the walls of the rut and predetermined to go in the direction the rut takes it?

To answer these questions, you must dare to break with old ways of thinking and let go of any notions that base your worth on comparisons with others or approval from others. You've got to find your own voice and become a creative force in your own life. To discover your voice, you have to clarify your true nature and your deepest values, and then set goals that involve using your talents and passions to create a life of your choosing.

Think Big, Think New, Think Ahead

We encourage you to dream. No one else is looking. No one's listening. No one will laugh or make fun of your dream. This is your most private, unbridled wish list.

Coming up with such a list is uncomfortable because we've learned to be afraid of stepping outside the box created by all the "shoulds" we were taught and all the messages to "grow up" and "be realistic" we have internalized. Along the way of trying to figure out how to follow all these rules, most of us stop using our most powerful tool for making healthy changes: our belief in our own vision.

Daring to dream is not only permissible, it's crucial to thriving. Researchers find that a common characteristic of great and successful people from all walks of life is that they have the courage to continually sharpen their vision about what is possible for them. They spend much of their time thinking about what they want and how to get it. They think about their future, pinpoint the hurdles in their path, and develop the skills they need to make their dreams a reality. And, despite their inner fears and insecurities— the same types of fears and insecurities we all have—they do the work required to make these dreams come true.

Are You Aligned?

A hidden stressor in the lives of many people is that they spend so much of their life's energy responding to the needs of others that they have drifted into what we call "unalignment." Unalignment happens when you go too long behaving in ways that do not express your truest self. Rather than expressing your special talents, deepest values, and most honest emotions, you behave otherwise: acting cold when you feel affectionate; saying yes when you want to say no; working in a job that you don't believe in. Each of these is an example of unalignment. Living out of harmony with your values is like trying to drive a car by jamming one foot on the accelerator and the other foot on the brake. A tremendous amount of energy is wasted going nowhere, and you burn out.

Psychological Boundaries

An important aspect of discovering your authentic self is to understand your psychological boundaries and how they function in your life. Your psychological boundaries have to do with two things: first, whether you can accurately identify and *accept* what you truly think, need, and want; and, second, how you manage closeness and distance with other people.

Our life experiences lead us to formulate convictions about ourselves and others that are likely to stay with us for a lifetime. We may change these convictions based on new experiences, but most of us return to these ways of perceiving and coping with the world when we're stressed. These convictions drive the behaviors that determine our psychological boundaries. Simply put, how you treat yourself and others is determined by whether you believe you are basically good, trustworthy, and to be valued, and whether other people are basically good, trustworthy, and to be valued.

Clarifying boundaries is a key to thriving. Without clear boundaries, you won't feel comfortable in relationships. You'll fail to adequately protect yourself, your family, or your work team from outside influences or, alternatively, fail to let in the kinds of human connection or new information of the sorts we all need. Healthy, flexible boundaries provide safety, connection, and the opportunity to grow. Our psychological boundaries can be too porous, too rigid, or healthily semi-porous.[3]

Your Boundaries Are Too Loose!

If we discount ourselves, we develop boundaries that are overly porous. We are plagued by doubt or being downright unclear about our own opinions, feelings, needs, and wants. Driven to please others and be perfect (in the eyes of others), we pay more credence to what others think or want than to ourselves.

For example, a new manager has been called in to revamp your rather unproductive department. The lowest performers on your work team start complaining and spreading gossip about the manager.

A too-porous boundary response: You keep quiet about the fact that you actually agree with many of the manager's decisions, and, in an effort to fit in, you participate in the office gossip.

Constantly driving yourself to please others and live up to their expectations is an exhausting way to manage relationships. And it backfires! Do this for too long and you'll begin to resent the very people you're working so hard to please. Because of your lack of boundaries, other people will begin feeling invasive to you and you'll either start to avoid them or resort to indirect ways of setting limits. For example, "I'm too depressed" or "I'm feeling too sick" can be ways of saying the "I don't want to" that we dare not utter for fear of displeasing someone.

Your Boundaries Are Too Tight!

Some people develop overly rigid boundaries. They have rigid opinions and often are intolerant and judgmental toward others. But their sense of self is brittle and masks underlying insecurities and fears stemming from unresolved hurts that have left them distrustful of the intentions of other people. Basically, someone with rigid boundaries learned that staying within the confines of their own ideas and opinions is safer than venturing out of or letting other people into their psychological space. Painful life experiences have taught them that living unto themselves is safer than being open and vulnerable to others.

If your boundaries are too tight, you are probably an expert at getting rid of others or keeping them at a distance. Driven to be careful about trusting or becoming involved with others, you're likely to selectively perceive flaws in people, find ways to disagree with them, or act in ways that alienate people or intimidate them into leaving you alone. Or, you might simply keep your physical distance. Isolating yourself becomes a lifestyle. You justify your stance by remaining angry or suspicious. Others cooperate by avoiding you and your barbs.

For example, you and your wife are leaving her partner's office holiday party, where you were introduced to the two new associates she has been raving about for months.

A too-rigid boundary response: "Well those two seem like jerks to me. He's obviously a fool, and she's a hypocrite. Did you notice that she contradicted herself about what she did at her last job? I don't see what you like about those people. In fact, your office seems to attract people who are caught up in one form of bull or another."

The Worst of Both: Too Loose Sometimes and Too Tight Sometimes

If you discount yourself and distrust others' good intentions, beware of the tendency to give others the contradictory and confusing combination of messages to "come close" and "go away," all at the same time! Your complaining or suffering may invite other people to try to help you by offering suggestions or other input. But if you don't really trust that others care about you or that they are competent enough to be offering advice that would really help, nothing they offer seems good enough to you. At its worst, this pattern results in a chronic case of the "yes-buts." Whatever others suggest or try to do to help you is shot down by one of your "yes-buts." Your low opinion of yourself leads you to discount your right to be happy, so between these two dynamics you get nowhere with regard to solving your problem or having positive connections with other people. Eventually others tire of trying to help and they go away, confirming your suspicion: "I knew I couldn't trust others to understand or love me."

For example, you complain to your spouse, "We just don't make love often enough. It's not like it used to be." Later, your spouse approaches you romantically.

A too-porous-and-too-rigid boundary response: You passively participate but clearly do not enjoy the encounter. Or, even more blatantly, you say something like: "You know that I always want to make love, but now it's too late. Why did you have to wait until now to approach me? This just makes it worse."

Your Boundaries Are Just Right!

Fortunately, a healthy alternative does exist: semi-permeable boundaries. This means that your sense of self is firm enough to protect your psychological space yet "porous" or flexible enough to let information, people, and ideas in.

If you operate from the decision that both you and others are trustworthy and valuable, you are able to take care of yourself and participate in healthy relationships with others. You can negotiate a comfortable balance between closeness and distance in relationships without resorting to negative emotional dramas. By being reasonably clear about what you think, feel, need, or want, and trusting others enough to be interested in the same about them, you can negotiate an "in-between-the-two-of-you" understanding that is at once self-respecting and respectful of others. You know how to say, "Yes, come in and let's get to know each other." But you also know how to say, "No thanks; I'm not available for that."

Returning to the case scenarios we used earlier, here are examples of good-enough boundaries.

The low performers in your work team spread gossip about your new manager.

Appropriate boundary response #1: "I know you guys don't like the new manager or some of the decisions he's making, but let's at least give him a chance. I actually like a few of his ideas. Maybe some of these changes will help."

Appropriate boundary response #2: Just don't participate in the gossip.

You and your partner leave your partner's office party.

Appropriate boundary response: "Well, you've got an interesting bunch of colleagues. Some seemed to be very nice. I wasn't crazy about those two new associates, but I don't know them like you do. Help me understand more about what they are like."

Your partner approaches you after you have complained about your sex life.

Appropriate boundary response: "That's a nice invitation. I appreciate that we can always talk about things, even the difficult stuff. I love making love to you. But I'm really tired right now. How about if we make a date for tomorrow morning?"

SO HOW ARE YOUR BOUNDARIES?

Which boundary pattern do you naturally drift to?

__Boundaries too rigid

__Boundaries too loose

__Both rigid and loose boundaries

__Boundaries just right

Do you take different positions depending on the circumstances?

_____

Which circumstances lead you to take one of the unhealthy

boundary positions?

_____

Are you more likely to assume certain boundary positions with certain people?

_____

What do you typically do and say and how do you typically feel when you are in each boundary position?

_____

_____

It takes work to keep your boundaries healthy. Commit yourself to honing these skills: assertion, conflict resolution, comfort with intimacy, ability to tolerate the discomfort of saying no, open-mindedness, and the capacity for being comfortable with your own thoughts and opinions. Healthy boundaries make healthy relationships—which, in turn, make healthy individuals.

Rediscover Your Authentic Self

It's time to get clear and take charge. Using the exercises that fill this chapter, we invite you to clarify your most important values, honestly assess whether or not you are "aligned," and specify your desired version of the future.

What are your goals? How do you want to live? Take a few minutes to complete the exercises that follow. Each can help you to develop a clearer understanding of your authentic self. As you complete these exercises, ask yourself the following questions:

- What are my priorities?
- Am I living my life in ways that are consistent with these priorities?
- If not, what are the barriers?
- What strategies can help me to accomplish these priorities?

What Are Your Highest Values?

Start by specifying your highest values. These are the things that you stand for, the things that make your life worthwhile, elements that hold meaning for you. Here's one way of figuring out your most prized values.

PICTURE THE END OF YOUR LIFE

Imagine that, from the position of an after-life, you are viewing your own funeral. Seven speakers comment on your life:

- One of your children (if you have any)
- Your spouse or life partner (if you have one)
- One of your extended family members
- One of your friends
- A colleague from work
- One of your clients or customers
- A member of your church or one of your community organizations
- A stranger with whom you crossed paths casually in some public place—like when waiting in a line; riding on a bus, plane, or train; or when seated in a theater or restaurant

What would you like them to say about you? What would you hope would be said about the impact you had on them? What personal and professional characteristics, contributions, and services would you hope to have mentioned? How would you like to be described? By writing these various aspects of your eulogy, you can clarify the values that you hold most dear.

Answer the Hard Questions

Another effective way to clarify your values is by answering the questions that follow. These value-clarifying questions from a number of self-help experts[4] are divided into groups related to self, health, work, and family life.

Self

What makes you feel important?

What raises your self-esteem?

What increases your sense of self-respect and personal pride?

What have you accomplished in your past that has given you the greatest sense of pride and satisfaction?

What would you like to be known for?

Which of your many life roles is most important to you?

What vision do you have for your life?

What would you most like to learn more about?

What have you always wanted to do but been afraid to attempt?

What do you love to do? If you could do any job or full-time activity all day, without needing to be paid, what would it be?

What kind of service would you like to give your community, your church, your neighborhood, and others in need?

Health

How important is your health?

What do you do to maintain and enhance your health?

When you visit your physician, what do you worry you'll be told you need to do more or less of to care for your health?

How important is it to you to devote time each day to taking care of your physical health?

Work

Why did you enter your profession?

Does this motivation still apply?

Does your current position allow you to live out this value?

Do you believe in the brand or service or product you represent?

What are your true talents?

Where does your passion lie?[5] (Hint: It is something you love to do and when you are doing it, time stands still.)

What would be your perfect job?[6]

What would you be doing?

Where would you be doing it?

Who would you be working with?

What level of responsibility would you have?

What skills and abilities would you have?

What goals would you be accomplishing?

What status would you have in your field?

Family and Other Important Relationships

Think of your family and closest friends, focusing not on your list of wishes about how others might change but on your most personal wish list instead.

Who would you like to see more of? Less of?

Which feelings would you like to express more, and to whom?

Which relationship struggles would you like to stop getting trapped in?

How would you like to spend time with your loved ones—doing more and less of which things?

CHECK YOUR ALIGNMENT

Another way to clarify your values is to read a list of attributes and pick the ones that seem most important to you. We've included below some frequently mentioned choices, but obviously the possibilities are extensive. By identifying how you would like to be seen by others, you clarify what it is that you truly value.

honesty   compassion   kindness   sincerity   beauty   intelligence   friendliness loyalty   patience   generosity   strength   sense of humor   spirituality thoughtfulness   playfulness   financial success   modesty   family ties physical fitness   team player   good parent   hard-working   easygoing

Next, rank the items you circled in order of your top five values. On average, of the 168 hours that comprise each of your weeks, how much time do you spend behaving in ways that actually express these values?

It might be sobering to do a real-time analysis of your lifestyle. Suppose your weeks are filled as follows:

Work (including commute time)..........................50 hrs.

Sleep..49 hrs.

Meals (purchasing, preparing, or eating)................14 hrs.

Chores.. 10 hrs.

Showering, dressing, grooming............................7 hrs.

TOTAL: 130 hrs.

This would mean that a total of 38 hours remain open each week (168 hours minus 130 hours = 38 hours) to choose activities that express your values; to show that you value anything other than working and attending to your most basic physical needs for food, sleep, and cleanliness.

Now this: According to *USA Today*, in the year 2004, the typical American watched 1,669 hours of television. That's 32 hours per week! Unless you ranked "being entertained" as your highest value, if you're watching television for 32 of the available 38 hours each week you have to align your behaviors with your truest values, you're in trouble!

Live Like You Were Dying

There's a reason the song "Live Like You Were Dying" by Tim McGraw became such a mega-hit. It tapped into a collective angst so many of us feel—the fear that we are living out of harmony with our truest selves; that life is taking us in directions we never intended and don't want to go.

Just like the song says, once the shock of receiving a diagnosis of a terminal illness wears off, people often use their awareness of impending death to make changes that heal their lives. And these changes typically involve letting go of what's been holding them back from loving more deeply, forgiving more sweetly, appreciating more frequently, and dancing more joyfully.

IF I KNEW THE END WAS NEAR…

Imagine that you just learned that you have only two or three more years to live:

How do you imagine you would react to this news?

What would you take time to begin doing more or less of?

With whom would you choose to spend your precious, remaining time, and what would you be sure to do and say during this time?

Which aspects of your life would you look back on with pride?

What would you need to forgive yourself and others for?

Which new experiences would you finally take the time to orchestrate?

Which simple pleasures would you allow yourself to mindfully enjoy on a daily basis?

Taking Charge

It's time now to specify what, exactly, you plan to change. Our final exercise in this chapter helps you to see how you are now living, compared to how you want to live in each of these areas: your family life and relationships; your work; your health; and your sense of self.

THE PERSON I'VE FINALLY BECOME . . .[7]

Imagine that it is exactly one year from now. As you rummage through your bookshelves, you notice this copy of *Letting Go of What's Holding You Back*. You pause and realize, "I have made a number of good changes in my life during the year since I read this book. Compared to the way I used to be, I have finally become a person who..." You are visualizing what you would like to have accomplished in a year's time. Use the space below to complete the thoughts cued by the accompanying sentence-starters. Remember, this is your *imagined*, changed self.

The person I've finally become:[7]

I treat others in these ways:_____

_____

_____

I care for myself in these ways:_____

_____

_____

I tend to think about the world and other people in these ways:

_____

_____

_____

I approach my work and career with this attitude:

_____

_____

_____

I regularly make time for_____ in my life.

I've finally been able to let go of these struggles:

_____

_____

_____

_____

In this exercise you have specified what kind of person you would like to become—how you would like to treat others, care for yourself, think, manage your time, and cope. Now, move to the column below and list how you are living here-and-now in each of these areas, noting any contrasts between how you are living now and how you would like to live.

These days, I live like this:

I treat others in these ways: _____

_____

_____

_____

I care about myself like this: _____

_____

_____

_____

Here's how I tend to think about the world and other people:

_____

_____

_____

_____

I approach my work and career with this attitude:

_____

_____

_____

The time of my life is filled with these activities and roles:

_____

_____

_____

I struggle with these issues or people:

_____

_____

_____

Finally, write at least one small step—like committing to an exercise plan, scheduling regular feedback sessions with your boss, or making a list at the end of each day of things you are grateful for—that can move you from the description in the second list to being the person you described in the first list. These are the sorts of little changes that bring your behaviors into alignment with your values.

Renew and Remind Yourself

Value-based living requires the courage to make choices that dismantle the brick wall that blocks full expression of your authentic self. Some people break through the wall dramatically. A life-changing experience leaves them yelling, "Enough! It's time to stop holding back who I really am."

Far more frequently, people dismantle their walls without much drama. They make small changes that are the equivalent of chiseling out and discarding one brick from the wall at a time. Forgive this. Rethink that. Start behaving in this way instead of some other way. This is the course of letting go that most people take. Even if you dealt with a three-story wall by removing one brick a day, you would eventually dismantle the entire structure. The key is to remain steadfast and committed to living in harmony with your values.

We recommend that you review your goals and your priorities at the start of each month. Are you making choices day-to-day that align your behavior with these goals and priorities? If not, what do you need to do more or less of in order to achieve alignment?

As you complete these life reviews, remember to remain flexible. Keep sight of the larger issues that are important to you, and accept that living in harmony with your values can come in many forms. For example, if you value having quality relationships with your family, recognize that you can keep these relationships alive in many ways that may not correspond with what you learned in your upbringing. The home-cooked-meal scenario you may have been taught to believe is the major sign of healthy family life might not match your busy lifestyle. This doesn't mean you can't live in harmony with your value; it means you have to find a creative way to show that you value your family, even though you aren't going to be spending a lot of time cooking over a hot stove. It might mean a regular night out with your family at a local restaurant. Or if your teenage daughter seems to dread those "parent-child" talks, but you have a need to offer advice, encouragement, and feedback, writing letters, notes, or emails may have to do instead of the proverbial family chat. The key is to behave in harmony with your underlying value and to resist the temptation to compare your lifestyle with some script that was written in another day for another family (even if that family was the one you grew up in).

Most people find that, at minimum, these periodic self-reviews clarify one glaring point: "I need to learn to say no more often than I do." Another fundamental bit of advice we always incorporate into our life coaching is this: *Consider carefully where you choose to spend your precious 168 hours each week.* If you want to get to the next level in your career, now may not be the time to train for a marathon. Or if you want to overcome a lifetime of low self-esteem about your physical self, maybe now is exactly the right time to make exercising a time priority. Remember that value-based living comes with costs, and saying no makes most of us uncomfortable. But only by learning to say no to what's holding us back can we truly and congruently begin saying yes to what helps us to let go.

CLOSING THOUGHTS

Finally, let us caution that clarifying your values and comparing your current lifestyle to your chosen self can stir discomfort. Feelings like anger, sadness, and resentment are not unusual if you realize that you've been living someone else's life, not your own. The best balm for this irritation is a day spent living true to your chosen self. And then another and then another and another . . .

CHAPTER 7

Learn the Truth About Resilience

"The world breaks everyone. And afterward some are
strong in the broken places."

Ernest Hemingway, A Farewell to Arms

Being psychotherapists and consultants brings us bittersweet experiences. We spend most of our days in the presence of real-life heroes—spouses, mothers, fathers, friends, lovers, or colleagues who are trying their best to create safe spaces for others and for themselves. And it certainly is gratifying when we're able to help good people who have gone astray find their way back into the light of a healthy life.

Alternatively, we get very private, painful glimpses into the inner workings of tragic lives. Abusive families; abandoned and rejected lovers; hard workers who've been double-crossed by career setbacks or sabotaging coworkers; happy people who become devastated by unwanted medical diagnoses—we've seen them all.

Both types of experience have renewed our belief in the potential inherent in each of us to be resilient. We believe strongly that each of us is born with an innate self-righting ability that can be hurt or helped by the circumstances and people we encounter, but most people move ahead through difficult times and grow stronger because of them. That's what resilience is all about.

For the past half-century, researchers have investigated the keys to resilience.[1] We now know that resilience is shaped by a combination of internal and external factors. Some (like intelligence and temperament) are givens. Others (like family dynamics, beliefs, participation in spirit-lifting practices, coping skills, and positive interactions with others) can be taught or learned.

In this chapter we will outline the basics of resilience and ask you to consider making them a part of your life. These basics include developing the right way of thinking about your life, finding meaning in something greater than yourself, looking for what is right rather than what is wrong in yourself and others, keeping your expectations challenging but realistic, remaining flexible, learning patience, and creating positive, affirming relationships with others.

Develop a Resilience Attitude

How you think affects how you feel, which affects how you deal. The fuel for great achievement is real passion. And you cannot achieve great passion unless you believe. Resilient people, families, and work teams believe in themselves and they believe in each other. They also keep sight of the higher purpose they serve. This resilience attitude comes in many forms.

A survivor of Hurricane Katrina who lost both his home and his business in the flood that devastated New Orleans in 2005 put it this way: *"I have what it takes to get through this. I've been through a lot of hard times, things that would have caused most people to fold their tents and give up. I don't give up. I'm a good man, and I work hard to do good in my life. I deserve to get through this, and I will."*

A real estate executive who was facing a depressed market had this to say: *"We've been through tough times before, and we will survive this, too. If you're successful in this business, you've learned to ride out the peaks and the valleys. I'm just thankful for the people and the organization I work with. We provide a quality service that our community will always need and value, and we know how to weather market storms."*

This is from a woman who had recently discovered that her husband of 27 years was having an affair: *"This hard time right now is just a bad chapter in our very long, very good marriage. We'll survive this. We've got more good chapters to come."*

This is from a recently diagnosed heart disease patient: *"Being a heart patient was nowhere on my wish list. The diagnosis shocked me. But I'm learning what I need to know about how to live a full life as a heart patient. I put this in the 'stuff happens' category. Being a heart patient isn't my whole life; it's just a part of what I hope will be a long, satisfying journey."*

This is from a physician going through the disillusionment and headache of a medical malpractice suit: *"After all the sacrifices my family and I have made for my career, this is hard to take. But I try to focus on the fact that the vast majority of my patients do appreciate what I do for them. I've dreaded the thought that this might happen during my career. But now that it's here, I refuse to let this turn me against a profession that I love."*

Each of these people was facing his or her own unique challenges. But their comments show that they are thinking about their challenges in ways that researchers have found distinguish resilient people:[2]

- They truly understand and acknowledge the problems that confront them.

- They define their problems as challenges that must be coped with, and they commit to doing just that.

- They develop or access the resources they need to proactively address these problems and maintain a reasonable sense of control over themselves.

- They keep sight of the big picture rather than narrowing their focus to a single problem.

What you think about the world and your ability to cope with it strongly affects how you deal with life and whether you will remain resilient. Neither "pie-in-the-sky" nor "the-sky-is-falling" attitudes are helpful. Resilience isn't about cheerleading or pretending. The resilience attitude is never about denying or lying. Looking the other way won't make a problem go away, and calling your problem something different won't make it something different. At the same time, resilient people keep things in reasonable perspective. They don't think in catastrophic terms. Notice from our examples that no one was thinking like this: "My life was going along just fine, then 'X' happened to me. And now my life is a wreck." Instead, they were thinking like this: "My life is just fine, it goes along. And now I'm dealing with 'X.' I didn't particularly plan on 'X' happening, but now it's a part of my life and I'll deal with it."

To stay resilient, acknowledge any threats to your happiness, health, or productivity, and then accept the challenge of doing something about them.

Think, "What can I do to adapt, to cope with this?" You must regularly and honestly evaluate yourself with positive intentions. Look at each important area of your life with the goal of noticing what's good and fixing what's not.

Personally: Take time at least once a month to review your life's goals and how you are spending your time. Are you living in harmony with how you want to be? The guidelines for alignment we outlined in Chapter 6 can help here.

In Relationships: Regularly seek feedback from your loved ones. Find out how they feel about their relationship with you. If you never ask, you will never learn anything new from the people most important to you about how you can be a better part of their lives.

At Work: Learn to solicit, offer, and receive constructive criticism about what it's like to work together. And evaluate regularly how your team is doing relative to realistic performance benchmarks and market or company challenges. Don't make the management mistake of believing that your team or company is invulnerable. Do this, and your complacency will cause your performance to slip.

Once you assess each of these important areas and identify the problems you face, see whether you have the resources you need to solve them. No amount of positive thinking will overcome skill deficits. What do you need to learn in order to more competently deal with some part of your life? How can you hone these skills? Be proactive: Don't wait for a life or career or relationship crash to start doing what it takes to correct your course. Do it now!

How do you know what you need to work on? How can you identify where you lack competence and where your skills are strong? At minimum, we recommend that you assess yourself with regard to the following competencies that are crucial to thriving. And don't limit yourself to the competencies we list below. These are just a few examples.

Key Competencies for Thriving

On a scale of 1 to 10, rate yourself on your abilities in the following areas:

1-----2-----3-----4-----5-----6-----7-----8-----9-----10

Extremely poor   Extraordinarily competent

Key Competencies for Personal Change	*Score*
Motivation to make this specific change	_____
Humility about my need to change this	_____
Realistic about how difficult changing this will be	_____
Stamina (in sticking to my commitment to change)	_____
Ability to delay gratification	_____
Willingness to celebrate small victories	_____
Comfort soliciting support for my efforts to change	_____
Confidence that I can make this change	_____

Key Competencies for a Healthy Family Life	
Loyalty	_____
Dependability	_____
Ability to show affection	_____
Ability to show love	_____
Cooperation	_____
Ability to forgive	_____
Playfulness	_____
Communication	_____
Other-orientedness (opposite of self-centered)	_____
Ability to resolve conflicts without damaging one another	_____

Key Competencies for Career Success	
Skilled in areas specific to the job	_____

Ability to prioritize and produce   _____

Acts proactively   _____

Dependable   _____

Team player   _____

Communicative   _____

Customer/service oriented   _____

Key Competencies for Managers[3]

Planning   _____

Organizing   _____

Staffing   _____

Delegating   _____

Supervising   _____

Measuring   _____

Reporting   _____

Next, circle your strongest and weakest competencies in each area. Note that no matter how strong your strong suits are, *your overall effectiveness in a given role will be determined by your weakest competency.* For example, no matter how much you love a family member and show your affection, if you periodically are violent or otherwise act in ways that damage the other person's trust and comfort with you, your incompetent behaviors will place a very low ceiling on the relationship's ability to grow. The good things you do will count, but many of the benefits you'll derive from these positives will be erased by the damage caused by your weakest competency.

How you think also matters. Acknowledging your problems, strengths, and weaknesses is about *what* you think. But *how* you think is the final common pathway that determines how you feel. Your ways of thinking create "lenses" that color your perceptions of and reactions to the outside world.

⚔

Your thinking style is key to your resilience for a variety of reasons. First, thoughts stir at least momentary emotional states like joy, confidence, anxiety, or anger. These emotions affect your body and your behavior. For example, we now know that we literally take emotions "to heart." Here's what we mean. Studies that used heart imaging found that when patients with hardened arteries simply recalled an event that had made them angry in the past, the hardened segments of their arteries constricted severely.[4]

Fortunately, researchers have documented that we take positive thoughts "to heart" as well. For example, try this: Think of someone you care deeply about, someone you love so unconditionally that you simply "melt" inside whenever you see or hear from them. Vividly picture a pleasant image of that person, and hold that thought or image in your mind.

Did you notice a warm glow in your chest when you thought of your cherished loved one? Know why? Because loving thoughts relax heart functions, which causes arteries to dilate and allow blood to flow more smoothly.[5]

So pay attention to how you are thinking. Your body certainly does. And what your body registers when reacting to your thinking can either boost or drain your resilience. If you habitually think negatively, the negative emotions your thoughts create also become habitual. So by thinking negatively on a regular basis, you move from being someone who is angry or anxious right now to someone who is an angry or anxious person in general. Your negative emotional states become traits of your personality.[6] And the behaviors that come with these traits affect resilience.

Resilience at work is certainly affected by how you think. Consider these findings from research on employees with high trait anger or trait anxiety, meaning that, as a rule, they would be described as angry or anxious or potentially angry or anxious people. Anger or anxiety are traits of their personality. This study compared their behavior in the workplace to the behavior of colleagues who had low trait anger or anxiety.

Workers with high trait anger . . .[7]

- argue with coworkers more

- sabotage coworkers more

- engage in more acts against the organization

- are more disruptive of teamwork

- cause undue turnover

- use more organizational resources, like time spent managing
  personnel issues caused by their anger

Workers with high trait anxiety . . . [8]

- have more frequent absences from work

- show higher levels of frustration

- complain of more health symptoms and poor well-being

- have higher levels of job dissatisfaction

- report more work-related anxiety

- have higher levels of perceived interpersonal conflict

- are less clear about their work roles

- report more role conflict

- show low levels of autonomy

Optimism and Pessimism

No discussion of resilience and attitude would be complete without mention of the mother lode of all resilient attitudes, optimism. Decades of research have documented the power that our thinking style has in shaping our health, happiness, and productivity. Studies have shown that unchecked pessimistic thinking is dangerous. In fact, pessimists are eight times more likely to become depressed when bad events happen; and they do worse at school, sports, and in most jobs. Compared to optimists, pessimists are less happy and have poorer health, slower recovery from surgery, and shorter life spans.[9]

Maybe these differences come from the fact that optimists take better care of themselves than their negative-thinking brethren. Believing that their efforts can have an effect, optimists are far more likely to go to the doctor, eat healthier foods, and exercise than are pessimistic people who see themselves as doomed to suffer the whims of fate and their genes.

The good news is that optimistic thinking habits can be learned. Start by assessing where you fall on a continuum of optimistic versus pessimistic thinking on the test below, developed by psychologists Michael Scheier and Charles Carver.[10]

LIFE ORIENTATION TEST

Indicate how much you agree with each of the items below, using the following scale:

4-------------3-------------2-------------1-------------0

Strongly Agree   Neutral   Strongly Disagree

__1. In uncertain times, I usually expect the best.

__2. If something can go wrong for me, it will.

__3. I always look on the bright side of things.

__4. I'm always optimistic about my future.

__5. I hardly ever expect things to go my way.

__6. Things never work out the way I want them to.

__7. I'm a believer in the idea that "every cloud has a silver lining."

__8. I rarely count on good things happening to me.

Reverse scores for items 2, 5, 6, and 8 (for example: If you answered "3," score it "1." If you answered "0" score it "4" and, of course "2" remains "2").

Now, total your score: _____

Interpretations

A score of 20 or above indicates that you are optimistic.

A score of 19 or below indicates that you are pessimistic.

When something goes wrong, a pessimist explains it in the following way: "Things will never be the same, I can't do anything about this, and this is all my fault." In other words, they see their problems as being permanent, pervasive, and due to their personal shortcomings. When something good happens, on the other hand, a pessimist discounts the event: "The good times won't last, this won't make much difference in my life, I just had a moment of luck."

Optimists do just the opposite of pessimists. When something goes wrong, the optimist writes off the bad event as something temporary: "Things will get better. I can learn from this experience. I just ran into a little bit of bad luck." They see setbacks as surmountable, particular to a single problem, and resulting from temporary circumstances or other people. When something goes right, the optimist embraces the good fortune: "That really turned out well and life should just keep getting better. My hard work paid off!"

Even if you avoid locking into full-blown pessimism, your thinking will have much to do with how you manage stress.

ARE YOU A STRESS THINKER?

Check any that apply to you:

___*All-or-nothing thinking:* I tend to see things in terms of black or white.

___*Personalizing blame:* When things go wrong, I assume it's because of something I have or have not done.

___*Catastrophizing:* I tend to imagine worst-case scenarios, and then I feel as though they have come true.

___*Selective perception:* I scan for negatives and tend to ignore the positives in any given situation.

___*Mind reading:* I tend to assume the worst about others' intentions.

___*Blaming:* When things go wrong, I blame someone else.

___*Shaming:* When I'm stressed, I strike out at others and try to make them feel guilty.

Whether you need to break a pessimism habit or simply disrupt the thinking-suffering loop—thinking about your problems so negatively and globally that the thinking itself generates more suffering in the form of self-doubt and lowered self-esteem—here are a few suggestions to help you.[11] Are you using words like "all," "nothing," "totally," "completely," and "forever"? Are you thinking of this as a situation you are stuck with, using words like "always," "never," and "from now on"?

Are you assuming the worst possible outcome for the situation? Ask yourself, "What are the odds that things will really go as badly as I am speculating they will? Even if this does happen, what would I do? Would this truly be a catastrophe? How could I turn it into an opportunity?"

Are you overlooking your strengths? Ask: "What positive attributes do I possess that I am ignoring? What situations like this have I handled before and how did that turn out?"

Are you blaming yourself for something that was beyond your control? Ask: "Even though I might have chosen differently (in hindsight), did I exert at least a reasonable effort to keep this from happening?"

Are you expecting perfection from yourself or others? Ask: "Where did I ever get the notion that I or anyone else should be perfect?" Work to develop more humble expectations of yourself and more gracious responses to other people's imperfections.

How could you have handled this situation differently? Other than the stress-thinking perspectives you may be engaging in, what are three alternative ways you could explain this event to yourself?

Finally, consider what difference this will make in a week, a year, or ten years? Ask: "Will anyone really care or judge me in the future, simply and solely based on this situation or mistake?"

Examine the phrases and images that flow in your mind during stressful times, and you will be better able to control your emotions and behavior.

Believe in Something Bigger Than Yourself

"Meaning is the antidote to burnout." These sage words by physician Rachael Naomi Remen capture the essence of yet another characteristic of resilient people: they keep their sights on the higher ideals and meanings that help them to rise above the stress of the moment. Some do this by committing to a set of religious beliefs. Others find meaning in their political convictions, their commitment to raise a healthy family, or their participation in a personal recovery program. Still others believe so strongly in the good that comes to people because of their company's products or services that the meaning of their work helps them transcend the struggles of the moment.

Do what you love or find a way to love what you do. Learning to love what you have to do is a key to happiness and high-level performance. A physically fit person doesn't whine about the difficulty of a workout. She sees the workout as part of her higher commitment to stay physically fit. Loving parents don't whine about having to take extra care of a sick child. They just do what needs to be done to live up to their commitment to being great parents.

High-performing work teams don't waste their time and energy grousing about yet another set of new corporate goals. They accept that industry and company changes are inevitable and that coping with change quickly and efficiently is what distinguishes a dynamic team from a less effective team.

Remind yourself that doing the work required in the roles you choose is the definition of a good time or a good day. And make time regularly to direct your gaze upward and outward, past your personal struggles. Believe in something and do it!

A Word About Spirituality and Religion

Resilience has to do with more than managing mind, body, and relationships. Let's not ignore the fact that we are also spiritual beings. Facts suggesting that we are a spiritual-seeking culture abound. Consider the phenomenal book sales of Christian authors like Rick Warren and Joel Osteen, and gurus of nonsecular spirituality like Deepak Chopra, Wayne Dyer, and Marianne Williamson. In different ways, they all propose that we should consider viewing ourselves as spiritual beings, not as physical beings that have occasional spiritual experiences.

Consider also the fact that 67 percent of Americans rate religious and spiritual beliefs as very important in their lives; and 82 percent want greater spiritual growth.[12] And when the going gets tough, even people who have never set foot in a place of organized worship tend to pray for protection. For example, 97 percent of surgery patients claim that they found prayer to be very helpful to their recovery.[13]

Many studies have noted the relationships between spirituality, religious participation, health, and happiness. For example, people who state that they believe in God, pray regularly, and actively participate in a faith community are healthier and happier than those who do not. They also take better care of themselves and live longer. Compared to the nondevout, the more religiously devout drink less alcohol, smoke less, and have safer sex. They also report lower levels of anxiety, depression, and anger compared to those who rely less on faith. It seems that religion can also help some marriages. Couples who integrate religion into their marriage have been found to have less marital conflict, more verbal collaboration, greater marital adjustment, and more perceived benefits from marriage.[14]

There is evidence that the type of higher power you believe in can affect health and happiness. A nurturing and forgiving higher power helps to short-circuit nonproductive worries and doubts and increase a sense of inner control. In contrast, believing in a punitive higher power has negative health consequences. This may be due to the fact that living in constant fear of punishment leads to chronically elevated levels of anxiety and depression.

In nearly 30 years of counseling people who have faced all sorts of life challenges, *every person we have known who was able to get through their hard times and come out stronger drew strength from their belief in something bigger than themselves.* Some dropped to their knees and prayed. Others committed themselves to being better providers, spouses, community members, or employees if given the chance to recover from the setback they faced. Each grew noticeably more wise and mature in the wake of their setback.

However you do it, develop rituals that remind you of the purpose of your journey. Take time to clarify your higher purpose.

CHECK YOUR SPIRIT

The questions that follow are taken from various inventories.[15] We present this not as a list of "shoulds" but as food for thought about what soothes you, brings you peace, and connects you to a higher meaning.

- Do the challenges you are now facing have a special meaning to you with regard to your beliefs?
- What is your source of strength or hope during times of great difficulty or sorrow?
- Do you find strength in your religion or spirituality?
- Do you feel spiritually at peace, or are you spiritually searching?
- Do you have some sort of ritual that helps you to feel joy and lifts you out of your daily concerns?
- How have your coping challenges affected your faith or spiritual beliefs?
- Which activities in your daily life give you the most peace and a sense of connection with a larger whole?
- Which experiences help you to feel deep inner peace or harmony?
- What do you do to renew yourself spiritually?
- What gives you a sense of stillness?
- What is your favorite quiet place, where you go to reflect and renew?

Think about ways to enrich and renew yourself spiritually. Whether it's going to church, praying, driving through the mountains, writing in your journal, meditating, or having a quiet conversation with your favorite person about the meaning of your life—do something! Whatever it takes, develop and use rituals that connect you with your higher meaning. At minimum, try a combination of these strategies:

Develop philosophies that will help you deal with disappointment. Understand that everyone is disappointed at times; that disappointment is not a sign of personal or family failure; that setbacks are part of a full life.

Practice the serenity prayer.

Think about which people, places, and events make you feel better about yourself and your life after you have contact with them. Never let a week go by without doing some of these things, communicating with these people, or visiting these places.

Focus on Your Strengths

Psychology often focuses on *what is wrong* with people rather than *what is right*. The tragedy in this is that it keeps us from seeing some of the wonderful strengths we have—and using them. For most of us, this means breaking the lifelong habit of focusing on weaknesses, deficits, and disappointments.

What do you notice about yourself and others most often—your strengths or your weaknesses? When you look in the mirror, do you spend more time noticing the part of you that you like the looks of, or do you immediately focus on your blemishes? When you think of loved ones or friends, do you habitually celebrate what's good about them or focus on how they worry or disappoint you? Notice how often you participate in negative gossip at work, complaining about some company policy or a coworker, compared to how often you comment to a friend or coworker about what you appreciate about your job and your company.

As always, the purpose of identifying where you aren't living like you want to is so you can change. Develop the habit of noticing in detail what is good, hopeful, and to be appreciated—about you, your relationships, and your work—and talk about it! We're not encouraging you here to brag about yourself in superficial ways or to give others meaningless compliments. We're talking about regularly assuring yourself and others that what is right in your life is more powerful than anything that is wrong. The challenge is to stay aware of the problems you face while drawing on your strengths and those of your loved ones and colleagues to solve your problems. Communicate the belief that the current problem can be successfully overcome.

Identify your strengths through any process that appeals to you. The important thing is to learn where you are strong and accentuate those positives so that you can use those strengths when you face a coping challenge.

Set High But Realistic Expectations for Success

Many times and in many ways throughout this book we have asked you to evaluate the match between your reality and your ideals. We hope that when you do this you will bear in mind two guidelines from resilient people.

First, give up any quest for perfection. There are no perfect people, relationships, or workplaces—and neither you, nor your loved ones, nor your workplace will prove to be exceptions to this fact. When evaluating your very real life, don't fall prey to the fictitious standards of perfection. At the same time, don't sell yourself short and don't settle for mediocrity. Strive for full expression of your authentic self, your best teamwork, and your deepest passions.

Neither foolishly chasing perfection nor settling for mediocrity will make you resilient. The energy that fuels high performance stems from regularly stretching our abilities. *Goals that are set too high simply demoralize, while those set too low fail to motivate or energize.* The highest performers regularly push themselves beyond their normal limits.

Develop Coping Flexibility

High performance and coping flexibility go hand in hand. In Chapter 5 we talked about alternating taking action (problem-focused coping) with self-soothing (emotion-focused coping). High performers develop wisdom about when to use each coping style.

Taking action is most effective when you are facing something that is within your power to control. For example, if you're stressed by the clutter of your office and by the shaky market in your industry, you can immediately do something to change one of these stresses (the messy office), but not the other (the overall condition of your marketplace). Or if you're anxious about developing a health problem, you can take action by improving your diet, stopping smoking (if you do), controlling use of alcohol, and exercising regularly, but you can't totally control whether or not you get a disease.

People, in general, are most stressed by those aspects of life that are highly demanding or important to them but out of their control. High-demand/low-control stress might come in the form of worrying about the choices your children make as they go about finding a life partner; worrying about the overall economy and its effects on sales within your industry; or fearing for the health consequences of a loved one's poor lifestyle.

There is no action you can take to eliminate these sources of stress. Problem-focused coping won't work. Trying a problem-focused strategy in a situation that is not controllable will only make you more stressed and frustrated. Instead, learn to put your energy into soothing your reactions to the stress rather than struggling to change what you cannot control. Here, it helps to focus on your emotions (not on the problem) and use self-soothing strategies:

- Distract yourself from your worries by enjoying healthy pleasures.
- Remind yourself that you're doing all you can to deal with the manageable aspects of the problem.
- Ask for support from friends and relatives.
- Use prayer, meditation, or relaxation techniques to calm your nerves and slow your mind.
- Reframe the problem in a way that calms your anxieties. For example, instead of thinking of your current problems as signs that you will be miserable forever, think of them as temporary setbacks that are teaching you and your loved ones valuable life lessons.

Commit and Give It Time

We hope that by now you've gotten one of our main points: Truly letting go of what's been holding you back will take a while. Lasting change takes time, patience, commitment, and maturity as you work through the awkwardness that comes with embracing a new way of coping.

Build Positive Relationships

The most powerful factor affecting your resilience is your ability to establish and maintain positive relationships, both at work and at home. High performers work hard to maintain friendship, communication, and intimate connections at home and equally hard to foster collaboration and collegiality at work. But stress and struggling make narcissists of us all. It is easy to become self-focused and lose sight of our connection with others. Tough times constitute a call to character in this respect, and, in their response to this call, high performers distinguish themselves.

When the going gets tough at work or at home,

high performers . . .	low performers who burn out . . .
respond with inquisitiveness about what new things they need to learn in order to make things better	respond by getting more rigid, narrow-minded, and closed off to outside input
respond with humility	react with self-righteous indignation about how things have changed
grow more other-oriented	get more self-centered
forgive	get vindictive

When times get tough it's okay to put your nose to the grindstone and keep going. But don't forget to regularly look up at your fellow travelers, noticing the effects you are having on them. Staying open and positively connected to others in times of stress is truly a characteristic of those who thrive.

CLOSING THOUGHTS

In the most fundamental ways, resilient people take responsibility for themselves. They do not justify self-defeating or team-sabotaging behaviors by leaving open "escape hatches" that allow them to run away from responsibility. They don't store up negative feelings, and then "cash in" with bouts of self-abuse, other-abuse, or violation of loyalty to their relationships or company. In a nutshell, the biggest truth about resilient individuals, families, and work teams is that they have integrity: They integrate their behaviors with their truest value of commitment to excellence in both self-care and service to others.

CHAPTER 8

Fence Your Life Territory

"One man cannot do right in one department of life whilst
he is occupied in doing wrong in any other department.
Life is one indivisible whole."

Mahatma Gandhi [1]

"I really hate living here. I swore I'd never live in a city this big. But what can I do? This is where my career took me. But that's not my problem. My problem is my marriage."
—Terry, banker

"My affair has nothing to do with my depression. In fact, that relationship is the only happy part of my life. I just want to learn how to feel better, in general."
—Susan, homemaker

"I'm a mess. I need to drink less, exercise more, and spend more time with my family. And I'm sorta bored with my job. Maybe if I got a new job, it would jump-start me to take charge of myself. A new job would be the new begining I need."
—Carlisa, pharmaceutical sales representative

Each of these people presents a basic dilemma that we see frequently. Each is ignoring a glaring problem in their life while focusing on something else. Terry wants to ignore the poor fit between where he truly wants to grow roots and where he is now living, and, instead, try to make his marriage good enough to soothe his chronic dissatisfaction about living in an environment he finds toxic. Susan wants to overcome depression without fixing the most depressing aspect of her lifestyle, her chronic dishonesty in her marriage. And Carlisa thinks that quitting her job—and thereby dismantling the one part of her life that is not broken—will be a step toward taking charge of what she truly does need to change in order to thrive.

How's Your Life Territory?

It's impossible to thrive unless the situations, relationships, and processes that structure your days create a nurturing, supporting "fence" around the territory of your life. Your *situations* are your life's *where* factor. This can include your job, your community, your church, your clubs or organizations, and so on. By *relationships* we mean the *who* factor—who you spend your time with. This includes not only your most intimate partnerships, but also the other people in your life: family, friends, colleagues, and acquaintances. Your *processes* are the ways that you treat yourself. This is your *how* factor—how you define yourself, how you treat your body and spirit, how you manage your coping patterns, and the way that you generally live your life.

In simple terms, Terry, Susan, and Carlisa have "holes" in their life's fencing. Terry's got a *where* problem; his life *situation* does not fit him well. Susan's got a *who* problem; her dishonest relationship will put a ceiling on how much she thrives, no matter how well she does in other areas of her life. And Carlisa's got a *how* problem; her life *process* is filled with unhealthy behaviors.

A crucial step in letting go of what's holding you back is to ask a profoundly simple question: Is the who, where, and how of my life territory toxic or nurturing?

Toxic is anything that makes you feel frightened, anxious, miserable, uncomfortable, or stuck in a painfully familiar emotional struggle. Nurturing, on the other hand, is anything that makes you feel reasonably safe, appreciated, acknowledged, secure, and energized.

Take a look at the fencing around your life territory. Is it in good shape or does it contain holes? Any unmended "hole" will hold you back from thriving. Letting go starts with being honest about what needs to be mended in order to create a safer life territory. Resist the temptation to avoid dealing with the real problems that compromise your happiness, "fixing" something else, instead. Adding layers to a well-maintained side of the fence—that is, doing more of something you're already doing well—or distracting yourself from your real pain by stirring up problems in another area are pseudo-solutions that may satisfy your need to do *something*, but do nothing to fix the real problem. And your weakest stretch of fencing will define how safe or unsafe your life territory is. Your life territory will only be safer if you fix the part that's broken.

Many people live high-stress lives that involve a good deal of toxicity. Yet they soldier on with courage and strength, all the while becoming more and more symptomatic. These same courageous people often run in fear from the idea of changing anything about their territory to make it safer. When our clients get stuck like this, we tell them the tale of the traffic dodger.

"Traffic dodgers" are people who live unprotected in the middle of a busy intersection. They spend every day dodging traffic. Of course, periodically a traffic dodger is going to get hit—it comes with the territory. When they're bleeding badly enough, they go for help. But here's the tricky part. They don't walk in the door saying they suffer from massive vehicle trauma; they say their marriage is bad, or that their kids are disrespectful, or that they can't seem to lose weight. Traffic dodgers essentially ignore the major cause of their pain: *Their lifestyle is keeping them in the middle of a busy intersection and, as a result, they keep getting hit!*

If these characteristics describe you, our first bit of advice is to encourage you to get out of harm's way. Dodging traffic all day is not a very good way to live. It is only when you find the courage to change what is truly toxic in your life—to repair the pieces of your life territory's fencing that leave you vulnerable to harm—that you will be able to get an accurate picture of your other problems.

We remind you of the words of Mahatma Gandhi that opened this chapter: "One man cannot do right in one department of life whilst he is occupied in doing wrong in any other department. Life is one indivisible whole." Is there a situation, relationship, or process in your life that is toxic? If there is, you can be sure it is holding you back.

It May Not Be Simple

Sometimes it's easy to see the way different areas in our life affect each other. Ever notice that you're much more likely to stick with a healthy eating plan if you also exercise regularly? On the negative side, how many times has a disappointment in a relationship given you permission to start smoking again, eat a quart of ice cream, or otherwise stop taking care of yourself physically? It's clear and obvious what we're doing, and yet we do it anyway. At other times, the ways different areas of our lives impact each other, good and bad, are not so obvious.

Painful, But Not Confusing

Bob, a young investment banker, was coerced into seeking our help when his firm threatened to fire him because of his harsh way of dealing with colleagues, clients, and staff. Faced with the threat that he might lose his dream job, Bob crumbled. In our first session with him he poured out a flood of emotions that had been boiling inside him and fueling both his ambition and his rage.

"Okay. You're right. I do tend to go numb and store up anger. Let me explain it to you; let me make it perfectly clear. I'm 39 years old, and I cannot remember not working. I've been striving to be the best since grade school. And working harder than the next guy is how I got successful. Now, I'm told I'm 'too intense.' My managing partners at work say I deal with clients 'too intensely.' My secretary and support staff—they all claim to fear me because of my 'intensity.' Even my wife tells me I look 'too intense,' even when we're supposedly having a nice time.

"My problem is that I don't know any other way to be. I didn't make the grades that earned my MBA by being 'laid back.' And half-stepping it isn't how I earned partnership in this firm. So you tell me: How do I lighten up my intensity and stay successful? What's going to fan my flames and keep me going?"

As you work to change, you might notice your own version of Bob's despair and sense of betrayal. When we honestly evaluate our feelings and attitudes, it's not uncommon to notice outrage at what has been holding us back from thriving—those holes in our fencing. Beyond the outrage, you may be surprised to find sadness and a longing for what you have never gotten, and still do not get, enough of. Here, the comments of Bob's wife, Ellen, are enlightening:

"I don't know what to do to help Bob. And I'm so sad and angry most of the time I don't know what to do to help myself either. I am the loneliest 40-year-old woman I know.

"My husband has been basically absent since he became a partner in his firm. I keep from being furious with him by staying furious with his firm. I blame the senior partners in Bob's company for the pain in my heart; they're the ones who constantly push him to bring in more business, and that's the reason he's gone all the time.

"I used to blame my husband, but now I just see him as a victim. No matter how much money we make, we live above our means. And no matter how successful he gets, he can't seem to satisfy this drive he has to be the best.

"Sometimes when I look at him I feel like crying. I miss his energy and enthusiasm. He's got that numb look that we used to joke about seeing on the faces of all the miserable 'old people.' I don't know how to stop this. Our life is on a skid."

At least Bob and Ellen know where their pain is coming from: Bob's excessive working and the emotional and physical toll it's taking on his mood and his home life. This situation is painful, but not confusing. Even more distressing is the situation in which dissatisfaction fills your days for reasons that are not apparent to you. Paul was a case in point.

A Loss of Passion

Paul seemed to be living a charmed life. The father of three healthy children and husband to beautiful Suzanne, he became a top producer in his law firm within the first five years of practice. Then his productivity leveled off. When the accolades stopped coming, Paul began questioning whether he was burned out. He sought our counsel with the following question: *"Maybe I need a career move. I'm trying to decide whether to switch to a new firm or leave practicing law altogether."*

As we explored this further, Paul's description of his work didn't match his plan to change jobs or careers.

"I've always loved practicing law. One of my private quests has been to help return our profession to 'most respected' in the public's eye. My firm is one of the finest, most dynamic groups I've ever seen, and we do make a positive difference in our community. Plus, I really do enjoy working with most of my clients."

As we got to know Paul better, it became apparent to us that he spent more time observing than participating in his life.

"You're right about that. In fact, even when I'm with Suzanne or the kids, I find myself drifting into that one-step-removed position. I can't stop fantasizing—about another job, another house, even another lifestyle. I constantly daydream about how it would be to start over.

"One thing that bothers me is that Suzanne never questions this rut we're in. She seems to be satisfied seeing our same friends, doing the same stuff with the same routine, over and over again.

"Now, don't get me wrong: I love my wife, and I like my friends—and the things that we do, they're things I usually enjoy. But something's wrong.

"I've lost that edge that I used to feel when I was learning and creating. That's what I've always loved to do: learn and create new things. I used to resent having to sleep because it took away time I could be exploring some new idea or project—and not just at work. Whether it was golfing or fly fishing, remodeling our wonderful house or coaching my kids' sports teams, I used to get involved passionately, and passion in one project seemed to fuel my passion about others.

"I know it's my fault. I just don't follow through anymore when I'm interested in something. Somewhere along the way, I started chastising myself about 'wasting

time.' If I've heard that phrase once, I've heard it a million times in my life. But now I'm the one saying it!

"'Stop wasting time on those hobbies!' 'It would be a waste of time to get to know the new guy at our club. He probably doesn't need a new friend, anyway.' 'Why waste time doing something that won't help pay the bills?'

"I've learned a thousand different ways to talk myself out of doing something that interests me. So these days, I just work, come home to a few gin and tonics, and veg out until Suzanne says we've got to go to another get-together with our same old friends."

We repeat: The most fundamental way to examine the stress of your life is to ask a simple question. Is the territory of my life more toxic or nurturing to me?

Think about the who, where, and how of Paul's life territory. His life *situations* are reasonable: good job, good house, and good community. In general, however, his life situations don't challenge him or satisfy his need for variety.

His *relationships* are sound, but not intimate. He loves his wife and his children. He basically likes his friends, but his social routine has become a rut to him. He is not growing in any of these relationships. Instead, he's observing himself playing various roles and he's not open and involved with the people around him. He doesn't act on his natural curiosity or explore his interest in new people.

Most obviously, the *processes* of Paul's lifestyle are causing him pain. He spends his energy observing himself becoming stagnant. He is plagued with doubt and self-criticism. His actions are not aligned with his inner thoughts, feelings, needs, or wants. He fantasizes about a different life, but does nothing to initiate change. Most painful is Paul's growing habit of discounting his own accomplishments. He constantly notices all that he is not and all that he has not done, and he only halfheartedly notes the positives in his life.

Our practice is filled with people who can relate to Paul's story. There's nothing major wrong with their lives, but they are unfulfilled; they're not thriving. They've lost enthusiasm for what used to give their lives meaning: getting educated, finding a partner to love, establishing a good life, getting promoted, or creating a family. They've lost their passion.

Much of Paul's discontent came from staying stuck in the same lifestyle, even though he regularly felt pangs of motivation to do something different and change his life.

Your longings for a different way of life may show up as relatively small stirrings—curiosity about a new movie or acquaintance or work routine. Don't make the same mistake Paul made when he discounted his stirrings. Your inner unrest and your daydreams tell you something about yourself that's worth paying attention to; they are worthwhile. The exact content may be an exaggerated version of what you need. But the theme of the daydreams is usually worth taking seriously. Let yourself explore their content and see how you feel. Do a values check to see if the inner unrest is from living out of sync with what is important to you. Then do a reality check, looking at the actual situations of your life and the resources you have available to you, and decide if, when, and how to begin to change things.

What Are You Waiting For?!

A special variant of holding back is the "wait-until" syndrome: We talk ourselves out of doing what we know would help us feel better, rationalizing that we'll get to it once we finish some huge task or accomplish some enormous goal or once we get to the next stage of life. In the process, we grow accustomed to living a life of waiting. This psychology of postponement comes in many flavors:

"Once I complete this project, then I'll start spending some quality time with my family."

"Once I learn my way around this new organization, then we'll be able to enjoy our life together."

"Once we get out of debt, then we'll start feeling successful."

"Once our kids prove that they've got sense enough to make good life choices, then I'll relax and enjoy parenting them."

"Once we raise the kids, then we'll get back to being romantic."

Postponement can become a very dangerous habit. As the years progress, we suffer the cumulative effects of neglecting whatever we're postponing. Remember that both positive health and distress or illness result from small choices that seem unimportant in the moment.

Couples who "wait-until" they have time to attend to their relationship risk losing each other. As their children's needs and their own work demands take precedence over their relationship, keeping energy in their marriage moves lower and lower on their list of priorities. They become disconnected from each other and lose their intimacy—and sometimes even their friendship. Managers who wait too long to let colleagues and staff know they are appreciated lose team unity. And if you wait too long to create reasonable balance between your emotional, spiritual, and physical needs, you will suffer burnout, illness, or worse.

So, how's your life territory? The checklist that follows will help you answer this question by evaluating the situations, processes, and relationships that define your life.

Evaluating Your Life Territory [2]

Using the following scale, rate how nurturing versus toxic you find each aspect of your life listed.

1---------------2---------------3-------------4--------------5

Very Nurturing   Benign   Very Toxic

Situations:

My work____

My club activities____

My church activities____

My community activities____

My neighborhood____

My city or town____

Processes:

My health behaviors____

My spirituality____

My modes of relaxing____

My hobbies____

How I spend my time away from work____

Relationships:

With my life partner____

With my extended family____

With my children____

With my grandchildren____

With my colleagues at work____

With my friends____

CLOSING THOUGHTS

Make it part of your life to regularly reevaluate and adjust the situations, relationships, or processes that structure your days. Even for those who can't or won't change the circumstances of their lives, there is hope. Stress-hardy people manage their lives by managing themselves. They deal with stress from the inside out. By controlling your own attitudes, coping tendencies, and relationship dynamics, you too can disrupt coping patterns that would otherwise hurt you and your relationships.

CHAPTER 9

Stress Matters

"It's easy to forget that stress is the body's warning signal
that something is out of whack and delude
yourself into thinking that it's normal."[1]

Doc Childre and Deborah Rozman

The right amount of stress for a reasonable period of time is actually good for you; it can keep you healthy, stimulated, interested, and interesting. But let it continue unchecked and your health, happiness, and productivity will suffer.

Stress is what happens when we are faced with the need to adapt or adjust. Both internal events (thoughts) and external events (noise, barking dogs, or barking bosses) can trigger stress reactions. So, too, can both desired and unwanted changes.

Too often, we oversimplify the topic of stress. The first and most frequent mistake is assuming that absence of symptoms means you're not overstressed. In fact, camouflaging symptoms with medication or simply going numb may mask signals that might otherwise warn you that you are drifting into dangerous territory.

Pay attention to even minor symptoms of stress, such as chronic muscle tightness or gastric upset. Your body may be months or years ahead of your mind in detecting a stress problem.

It's also a mistake to assume that all stress is bad or that a busy lifestyle and health and happiness are mutually exclusive. There is, in fact, *healthy* stress. When your challenges are interesting and meaningful to you and your abilities and resources make you feel competent to meet those challenges, stress can be energizing and renewing, both physically and emotionally.

This chapter will provide you with the right information to help you differentiate between good stress and bad stress, and will help put both in the proper perspective.

When Stress Is a Good Thing

We know you didn't buy this book hoping to get lessons in physiology and anatomy. But any intelligent discussion of stress requires familiarity with a few facts about how the body works. So bear with us through this short course on stress, from the inside out.

Let's start with the basics. *Stress is not dangerous; strain is.* In the normal stress reaction, arousal is followed by calming, and no harm is done. Here's how a healthy stress reaction works. When something demands our attention, the sympathetic branch of the autonomic ("automatically acting") nervous system turns on, preparing us to cope. If what's causing the stress is specific and if it can be resolved in a short period of time, the stress response is brief and is followed by calming. (In technical terms, sympathetic arousal ends when the parasympathetic branch of the autonomic nervous system kicks in and relaxes the stress response.) If you were to chart the turn-on, turn-off pattern of a normal stress reaction, the graph would look sort of like a healthy heartbeat pattern: rise, fall; rise, fall; rise, fall; and so on.

It's also important to know that healthy stress is not only not dangerous, it can be good for you. When you are dealing with situations that require you to focus and that stretch your skills, but that still leave you feeling in reasonable control, blood pressure and heart rate lower, and your body's autoimmune system balances itself.

Stress vs. Strain

Our bodies weren't built to deal with the stress assault that comes with our BIG LIFE. A constant barrage of rushing, emails, traffic jams, media coverage of more bad news than good, role juggling, and rude sales clerks (they're overstressed too!) overload our stress system. *The basic problem is not our initial reactions to stress; it's our failure to recover quickly enough once we first feel stressed.* Most of us do not relax frequently enough or long enough between bouts of stress. Eventually, our "turn-on; turn-off" system stops functioning properly, and then the damage occurs. When you constantly rush or worry, your body reacts as though it were dealing with a specific stressor, over and over again, and it can't make it go away. The result: an upwardly moving, jagged graph of stress reactions that never fully calm down.

As mismanaged stress turns into *strain*, we enter the danger zone. Strain can cause or complicate any of the Big Bad 5 psychological conditions that are health threats: unchecked worry and anxiety; chronic struggles with depression; anger and hostility; isolation from others; and chronic marriage or family conflict. And it's when we are strained that we are in jeopardy of suffering negative physical changes.

In the book *The End of Stress As We Know It*, the preeminent stress researcher Bruce S. McEwen, Ph.D., of Rockefeller University in New York City offers a detailed explanation of exactly what happens inside the body when mismanaged stress turns to strain.[2] Dr. McEwen explains that while the "fight-or-flight" response, which requires us to respond to a threatening situation by either fighting or fleeing, is the stress reaction that most of us are familiar with, there are a variety of others. And some of these physical reactions prove that stress is not all about psychology and what you are thinking. Here's a reader-friendly description of just how ugly or damaging things can get when stress reactions go unchecked.

The new brain, or cortex, is the largest and most highly developed part of the brain, the part that's in charge of abstract thinking, reading, writing, and reasoning. If we could put the cortex in charge of all of our reactions, we would have fewer fears, worries, and concerns; we'd keep our problems in perspective, separate thoughts from feelings, and move on.

But it's not that simple. Because of the actions of the old brain and a couple of special structures—the hippocampus and amygdala—and special chemical messengers throughout our body, we sometimes have stress reactions that bypass all rational thinking found in the cortex. When this happens, we experience pure emotion without any understanding. Let's look at the players involved in old-brain responses.

The old brain is the oldest part of the nervous system. Having developed in prehistoric man, it is the part that takes care of most of the body functions we need to survive, like heartbeat, breathing, blood pressure, and muscular reflexes. It contains the spinal cord and brain stem and the areas that surround them, including the limbic system. Our basic needs are registered here, and some translate into actions in response to emotions—mating, fighting, and bonding, for example.

Two special structures in the limbic system are the hippocampus and the amygdala. The hippocampus is a banana-shaped structure located deep in the brain that stores memories and monitors reality, comparing the outside world with the brain's representations of it. It develops sometime around the age of two.

The almond-shaped amygdala sits adjacent to the hippocampus. It is the brain's emotional alarm center, a repository of emotional memories that lack any information about context. In other words, the amygdala stores emotions without information about who, when, where, and how. Sometimes, it acts as a cauldron of sloppy generalizations. Frightening experiences activate the amygdala without having to travel to the higher tower of thinking and reasoning—the cortex. *Because the amygdala's action is not controlled by the cortex, mere thoughts can't stop its physical and psychological responses.*

Once it is stimulated, the amygdala scans for two basic pieces of information: Is this dangerous? And will this hurt me? If the answer to the first question is yes, your level of fear increases. If the answer to the second question is yes, your level of anger increases.

One way to think about the amygdala is that it stirs "low road" stress reactions: those that prompt us to escape first and ask questions later. And as stress hormones increase, the amygdala kicks into overdrive, making us emotionally hyperactive without any thoughts about why. Dr. McEwen points out that a memory manufactured completely in the amydgdala will be a nameless nonspecific sense of fear or dislike, an anxiety not attached to any specific reason or worry.

Next come the neurotransmitters and neurohormones. These chemical messengers relay signals throughout the nervous system. We've got a bunch of these. They pass the alarm throughout your body.

Once you're alarmed, adrenaline (or epinephrine) begins to fuel the fight-or-flight reaction and directs blood clotting to speed up, so you won't bleed too much when you fight or flee. Too much adrenaline leaves you feeling jittery, unfocused, irritable, and unable to concentrate. Adrenaline also affects the heart directly. It steps up sympathetic arousal, increasing your heart rate and blood pressure to drive more oxygen to the large muscles of your arms and legs.

And sudden surges of adrenaline activated too often can cause damage to the blood vessels in the coronary arteries. The damaged places can then become clogged with a sticky buildup that sets the stage for hardening of the arteries. Repeatedly turning on the fight-or-flight without quickly turning it off can also lead to excess fats and glucose not getting metabolized. These remain in the bloodstream, contributing to plaque formation inside the blood vessels and increasing the odds of developing diabetes.

Stress can interfere with clear thinking. Ever notice that, once you calm down, solutions become apparent that seemed impossible to find when you were stressed? That's because during the fight-or-flight reaction, less blood flows to the prefrontal cortex, making it hard to think and reason clearly. Rather, stress activates the danger-based limbic system, making it more difficult, for example, to see another's point of view in an argument. A flood of stress hormones also causes the hippocampus to function improperly. Remember, it's the hippocampus that monitors reality. If it functions improperly, we can't think straight! Without help from the hippocampus during a stress reaction we literally can't differentiate friend from foe.

What Happens When You Are Stressed [3]

- *Your heart rate speeds up.*

- *Your heart pumps blood to your muscles.*

- *Your arteries narrow and your heart beats faster, raising your blood pressure.*

- *Your breathing becomes shallow and fast, moving oxygen to your blood more quickly.*

- *Your muscles tense to get ready for fight-or-flight.*

- *Your fibrogen (a blood-clotting agent) levels increase.*

- *Less blood flows to the higher reasoning brain centers (the cortex) as more blood flows to the primitive (limbic) part of the brain.*

- *Digestion stops.*

- *You sweat more—to help cool your body.*

- *Your pupils get bigger and your senses heighten. For example, your senses of smell and hearing become stronger to help you perform your best.*

- *Arteries around your heart become inflamed and strained.*

- *Your immune system is diminished.*

Endorphins, the body's natural painkillers, are released to keep us functioning during the crisis of fight-or-flight. Contrary to the popular notion that endorphins are feel-good hormones, many scientists today believe that these painkillers contribute to the "going numb" syndrome we discussed earlier. If stress goes on and on, your body reacts as though it's in danger (because it is!), and endorphins are secreted to allow us to continue the fight. This may serve us well in the short term, but it makes us vulnerable to long-term damage.

Excessive stress causes an imbalance in the give-and-take action of two other important players in our internal checks-and-balances system. Gamma amino butyric acid inhibits neurons, telling them when to slow down and become less active. Its counterpart, the excitatory neurotransmitter glutamate, tells neurons when to speed up. Excessive stress overactivates glutamate, which causes damage to nerve cell neurons involved in memory. Excessive glutamate may also lead to too many free radicals, unstable compounds that can damage cells, proteins, and DNA.

Finally, there's the all-important cortisol. This is a steroid hormone made from cholesterol. By regulating the metabolism of carbohydrates, cortisol replenishes energy depleted by the rush of adrenaline. It also fuels coping action and hunger. When left to function normally, cortisol assures that our immune response is balanced—activated enough to protect us, but controlled enough to calm over-reactions that can cause ailments like allergies or asthma. But the wrong amount of cortisol can lead to all sorts of negative physical effects. A chronically high level of cortisol can hurt you in several ways: It can damage the hippocampus permanently, leading to poor memory and other cognitive or "thinking" problems. It can dampen the effects of insulin and has been linked to the development of insulin resistance, a risk factor for type II or non-insulin-dependent diabetes. It can lead to bone mineral loss.

It can even make you fat! Ever notice that when you go through a long period of stress you get fat and stay hungry? That's because strain results in fat being deposited at the abdomen rather than the hips or the buttocks. Once again, excess cortisol is the culprit here. During times of stress, cortisol releases glucose into the blood. But when the stress doesn't cease, cortisol levels remain elevated and it sends fat into storage at the waist.

To make matters worse, constant stress affects your body the same way that constant exercise or physical working does: Assuming that your energy supplies are being drained, your liver converts energy into glycogen and fat (forms of long-term energy), and stress hormones stimulate the brain to trigger food-seeking behavior. So we get caught in a vicious stress cycle that goes like this: When we're stressed, we get hungry, assuring that we'll eat to replenish our energy supplies. And what we eat when we're stressed turns quickly into body fat that is deposited in our abdominal area—for quick retrieval, should we need more energy.

While increased cortisol levels can be detrimental, so can an *under-production* of cortisol, causing yet another wear-and-tear effect. Cortisol acts as its own thermostat: It slows production of other stress hormones and reins in the immune system and reduces inflammation and swelling from tissue damage.

Lack of sufficient cortisol leaves your immune system to run wild and react to things that do not really pose a threat to the body. This can lead to a whole list of health problems, including allergies, asthma, arthritis, fibromyalgia, chronic fatigue syndrome, and skin rash.

The Potential Effects of Prolonged or Severe Stress

Prolonged or severe stress can:

- *weaken your immune system*

- *strain your heart*

- *damage memory cells in your brain*

- *deposit fat at your waist rather than the hips and buttocks (a risk factor for heart disease, cancer, and other illnesses)*

- *interfere with digestion*

- *hasten aging*

- *erode bone minerals*

- *fuel depression*

- *increase the odds of developing rheumatoid arthritis and diabetes, among other illnesses*

- *interfere with sleep, which increases stress, which leads to an increase in all of the above*

CLOSING THOUGHTS

It occurs to us that this discussion of the dangers of unchecked stress has perhaps stressed you out. But remember a foundation concept in our work: You don't have to be afraid of stress. You simply have to learn how to avoid strain. In our next chapter, we outline eight ways you can do just that.

CHAPTER 10

Do Not Fear Stress

"Stress is inevitable.
Struggling is optional."

Wayne and Mary Sotile

Every approach to stress management has its own emphasis and validity. Some tout the benefits of learning relaxation or meditation skills. Others focus on time management, thought control, or exercise to soothe upset nerves. Still others emphasize the importance of mindfulness and countering the multitasking habit. Many believe that loving interactions with other people is the best medicine for soothing stress ailments.

Each of these approaches works. And the reasons why have to do with a few facts about the physical side of stress.[1] Positive thoughts, caring interactions with others, and commonsense health practices like exercising have something in common: Each stirs calming or soothing physical reactions and boosts our mood. Consider:

- Oxytocin is a hormone that lowers blood pressure, heart rate, and cortisol levels for up to several weeks (when injected). It is triggered by pleasant stimuli such as touch and warm temperatures. It's also the neuropeptide that is produced during social interaction and bonding; it bathes the brains of a mother and child during breastfeeding. The effects of oxytocin may help explain how social support improves health.

- Prolactin is another hormone that has a calming effect on the brain. It, too, is released during breastfeeding and other forms of loving interaction. One effect of prolactin is that it serves as an inherent remedy against anxiety for both males and females.

- Exercising regularly increases brain-derived neurotrophic factor (BDNE) and nerve-growth factor, which play roles in learning and memory.

- Finally, virtually anything you do that's good for you—from positive thinking to positive health behaviors—helps to boost the presence of neurotransmitters like dopamine and serotonin, which improve mood.

In this chapter, we will highlight eight ways you can boost the flow of these soothing body chemicals. These are the same eight strategies we teach our clients who are interested in better managing stress. Our focus here will be on ways to counter the physical stress reaction.

Eight Steps to Better Stress Management

1. Fight the Right Fight

Stress is inevitable; strain is optional. For decades, we have taken the stance that any single stress management strategy is best practiced within an overall program that promotes effective emotional management. In this sense, a stress management strategy may be necessary, but no single strategy is sufficient for thriving. It's a lot easier to manage stress when you're not angry, anxious, sad, lonely, worried, or otherwise distressed; and mismanaged stress increases the odds that you'll settle into one of these deeper emotional pits.

To truly manage stress, you must manage your emotional and physical energies to hasten your recovery time when you do get stressed. You must do what it takes to increase your actual or perceived sense of control over the situation. This means changing some aspect of the actual stressful situation or changing how you perceive or think about the situation. For most of us, this means developing new behaviors or thinking patterns.

Be realistic about your goal. Stress is inevitable. It's not possible to get through any day without getting stressed. The key here is responding to the call to character that stressful times issue. It's easy to take appropriate care of yourself when things are going smoothly. It takes character, self-discipline, and a commitment to excellence to take care of yourself on your worst days. The goal is to avoid compounding stress with choices that create strain.

2. Disrupt Stress Pile-ups

The sad truth is that most of us create stress pile-ups by making poor choices when we are stressed. Beware of stress pile-ups like these:

Stage 1. Something goes wrong at work or home and you react by speeding up your multitasking, hoping to catch up or get beyond the stress wave that's pushing you.

Stage 2. In your rush, you skip over opportunities for stress recovery. Rather than pausing to admire a job well done, you rush to the next thing on your ever-growing to-do list. You avoid a moment of chitchat that might make you laugh and allow you to switch off the worry and intensity channel that you're locked into. Instead, you rush to get more done.

Stage 3. As the day unfolds, you reach repeatedly for artificial energy boosters like caffeine, simple sugars, and simple carbohydrates. Each gives you a momentary energy boost, but each has a bad stress management downside: once the "buzz" wears off, you crash to lower and lower levels of quality energy. The result? As the day unfolds, your unsoothed stress reactions accumulate like an upwardly moving stock market graph, and your available high-quality coping energy reserves diminish.[2]

Stage 4. Day's end finds you exhausted, frazzled, and feeling emotionally deprived. So you give yourself permission to skip exercising or otherwise taking healthy care of yourself. Instead, you rationalize that you "deserve" to self-soothe with some yummy (and unhealthy) carbo-loaded meal or dessert while you vegetate in front of the television and wash away your stress with additional mind-numbing drink or drugs.

Stage 5. The strain of the day, combined with your poor choice about how to spend your evening, leaves you restless at best and your sleep is disturbed, if it comes at all. You awaken the next morning feeling more exhausted than refreshed, and the pattern starts all over again.

Time and energy management researchers claim that most people spend anywhere from two to four hours each working day participating in energy- and time-sapping habits.[3] Moving mindlessly from task to task without completing any, allowing multiple interruptions while working on a task or failing to be periodically mindful of your own breathing pattern are examples of energy- and time-sapping habits. Replace these with energy builders! Disrupt stress pile-ups by setting limits on stress time and curbing your use of energy "boosters" like caffeine that increase stress responses in the short run and drain you in the long run.

Allow yourself to recover more fully between bouts of stress. Pause. Take a moment to notice what you've just gotten done and feel good about it before moving on to your next task.

Rather than reaching for another cup of coffee or sugar-filled snack, develop the habit of drinking water throughout the day. Recognize that your constant reaching for another energy boost is what takes you into strain. Too much salt, sugar, fat, cholesterol, and caffeine will lower your performance levels. Caffeine acts as a diuretic; it drains your body of the water you need for optimal functioning and with that water go significant chemicals that are necessary for your brain to function most effectively.

Take energy-boosting breaks. Taking several brief breaks during each half of your day can work wonders to counteract the cumulative effects of hassles. Especially in the midst of a busy day when you think you have no time to spare, take a few moments periodically to create a quiet environment, close your eyes, and think of a pleasant thought or practice deep breathing or some other form of relaxation. We know you're busy. But you can afford to take several two- to five-minute breaks to interrupt your stress build-up. The results will be worth the effort.

3. Learn a Relaxation Technique and Use It!

The most obvious way to counter a stress reaction is to turn on the relaxation response. Relaxation is good for you: It lowers your heart rate and blood pressure, eases muscle tension, enhances concentration, and soothes anxiety and fear. Relaxation even helps you cope with pain or anything else that bothers you. And it boosts the functioning of your immune system, thereby lowering your risk of developing certain diseases.

How to Take a Break[4]

When

- *Take two short breaks each morning and each afternoon.*

- *Sandwich unpleasant tasks between breaks.*

- *Take a break after dealing with an energy-sapping person.*

- *Take a break when you're in any of these six common conditions: lack of motivation, tension, high-concentration work, procrastination, complex work, and mental blocks.*

What to Do

- *Choose an activity or location that is different from your current task or site. (If you've been sitting, stand up and stretch. If you've been staring at a computer screen, look out the window at the sky.)*

- *If you've been doing something that requires concentration and accuracy, switch to doing something physical.*

- *If you've been doing something that requires creativity and complex thinking, switch to doing a routine task like filing or unpacking your briefcase.*

- *If you've been working alone, go interact with someone else.*

- *Eat lunch. Take a 20- to 60-minute energy-building lunch break. And make it a true break. If you dine with a friend or colleague, steer the conversation to topics other than work and worries. Avoid rich, high-fat, sugary, or salty foods. These will drain your energy for the two hours following lunch.*

What's the best way to relax? It depends on what your particular strain symptoms are. If you carry tension in your body, then you'll probably respond best to relaxation techniques that calm you physically. Try taking warm baths, yoga, massage therapy, breathing exercises, progressive muscle relaxation, and physical exercise. If your strain shows up mentally in the forms of worry,

---

Why Relaxation Matters

The relaxation response

- *decreases heart rate*
- *slows breathing*
- *lowers blood pressure*
- *relaxes muscles*
- *decreases anxiety and fear*
- *increases concentration*

- *eases sleep*
- *lowers awareness of pain*
- *lowers risk of heart disease*
- *eases anger*
- *boosts immune system functioning*

---

fatigue, and loss of zest, try mind relaxers like meditation, visualization, positive imagery, or distracting yourself from your worries with a good book or an interesting movie. A combination of body and mind relaxation strategies works best for most people. The bottom line is that it doesn't matter how you do it, just find a healthy way to relax that works for you, and do it often!

4. Make Time for Active Leisure

At the end of a stressful day, it may seem like cruel and unusual punishment to ask yourself to find the energy it'll take to change clothes and go hit a few golf balls, work in your garden, or invite a friend to join you at the tennis court. But these forms of active leisure have no downside and a great upside: They actually rejuvenate drained energy reserves, boost your mood, increase the flow of soothing endorphins, and quiet cravings for artificial "relaxers." Motivate yourself with this fact: Research has shown that passive sitting before television and channel surfing actually leads to increased tension and dips in your mood. According to the researchers, watching primetime or late-night television can leave you more rattled and less relaxed as you head for bed.[5]

Techniques for a Quick Relaxation Break

Belly Breathing

Change your breathing pattern, and you'll change your stress level. Place one hand on your chest and one on your belly, right above your belt-line. Inhale as much as you can, concentrating on breathing into your stomach. If you do this properly, your bottom hand will move outward while the hand placed on your chest will remain still. Next, exhale twice as much air as you inhaled. Again, your lower hand should move (inward this time) while your top hand remains relatively still. Breathe this way ten times and notice your body relaxing.

One Muscle at a Time

Sit or lie comfortably. Take between five and ten "belly breaths," then breathe normally as you clear your mind. Inhale and, starting with your hands, tense each muscle group, holding it tightly for five seconds, and then release. As you release, exhale and fill your mind with the word "relax." Move from your hands to your arms, shoulders, face, abdomen, buttocks, thighs, calves, and feet. Isolate each muscle group as best you can, tensing it, holding it, and exhaling when you release.

Imagine It/Recall It

One of the quickest ways to relax is to recall naturally relaxing experiences— those times when you have felt most relaxed, content, or at peace. Pause. Take a few cleansing breathes. Recall that special experience using all of your senses, especially what you hear, smell, and see when you do that relaxing thing.

5. Move It!

Regular aerobic exercise is a great elixir: It can help prevent or cure just about anything that ails you physically or emotionally. Want to relax your muscles, distract yourself from your worries, and give your brain a bath of chemicals that make you feel a deep sense of well-being? *Then get some exercise!*

For two simple reasons, exercising regularly can help anyone to manage stress better. First, exercising regularly lessens the amount of adrenaline that is pumped out during a stress response. And, second, once the fight-or-flight syndrome is turned on, regular exercisers turn it off more quickly than people who do not exercise regularly.

Research has proven that people who exercise regularly report reduced anxiety, decreased muscular tension and depression, increased overall stress management, and generally improved outlook, mood, and self-concept.[6] Exercising regularly also reduces food cravings and increases the odds that you will follow a healthy diet. In short, it's a sure way to help you feel better, especially when you are dealing with stress that is out of your control. The act of taking charge of your physical self gives you increased self-confidence that you will be able to cope, even with those things that are beyond your direct control.

The list of work-related benefits that come from regular exercise is astounding.[7] Research has shown that, compared to nonexercisers, those who work out regularly have

- fewer disability claims
- lower absenteeism rates
- sharper mental performance
- fewer errors
- better safety records
- improved ability to make complex decisions
- improved mood
- less fatigue during the workday
- higher levels of alertness
- better rapport with supervisors and coworkers
- higher levels of job satisfaction

How Much Exercise is Enough?

Have you ever known anyone who *didn't* say they felt better about themselves when they exercised regularly? We haven't. Given its benefits, you'd think we'd all be chomping at the bit to exercise our right to exercise! Wrong. About half of American adults admit to being totally inactive, and of those who claim to exercise, fewer than 15 percent do it often enough or hard enough to produce benefits.

How much you should exercise depends on your goal. For many people, even a 15-minute walk can be extremely effective in calming tensions. But a stroll won't necessarily protect your health or help you lose weight or keep it off. For these goals and for the most positive stress management effects, you have to exercise more vigorously. The best data on the question of how much exercise is enough came from the ongoing Nurses' Health Study. This study suggests that three hours of brisk walking each week or half that time spent in more vigorous exercises such as jogging or aerobic dance reduces the risk of heart disease by 35 to 40 percent.[8]

As for how much is enough, in their book *Take a Load Off Your Heart*, our friends and esteemed colleagues Joe Piscatella and Barry Franklin, Ph.D., emphasize that benefits like cardiovascular protection are apparent once you expend more than 500 calories a week in exercise. Optimal improvements come when you expend between 2,000 and 3,500 calories a week. When more than 3,500 calories a week are burned in exercise, there may be more risk of injury than benefit. Balance is best. Make sure your week includes some combination of these four components:

- daily physical activity
- aerobic exercise
- weight training
- flexibility exercises (stretching)

In general: Move more, sit less, and make sure you accumulate at least

30 minutes of moderate-intensity activity on most and preferably all days of the week. Ideally, the activities listed in each of these categories should reduce the amount of time you spend in passive leisure activities like watching TV and playing computer games.

6. Think "Energy Management"

How you manage your energy affects how you cope with stress.[9] We recommend that you develop the habit of asking yourself repeatedly throughout the day, "What will this behavior do to my energy level?" This can be a helpful way to cue yourself to skip a high-sugar midday snack or yet another cup of coffee; to pause and rest a bit before continuing your next task; to resist the temptation to check your email while in the midst of doing something that requires you to focus; or any number of other ways we waste rather than preserve our precious coping energies.

Try Something Different

Think of your coping energy as being divided into "fuel tanks." Each of these tanks serves a specific purpose, and whenever you need to adapt or cope, you draw energy from the appropriate tank. Perhaps your fuel tanks would be labeled fuel for office work, fuel for dealing with the kids, fuel for housework, fuel for fun, and so on. You burn energy from these coping fuel tanks in two ways: 1) when you *engage in coping behaviors* and 2) when you *think about what you have to do* to cope with particular stressors.

We get into trouble when we draw energy from a given channel for too long. For example, while you are dealing with housework, if you are also worrying about office work, you are draining energy from your office work fuel tank even though you aren't there, and it has no chance to replenish. When this happens, the stress response progresses from alarm to adaptation to exhaustion.[11] Bad things may begin to happen physically, emotionally, and

Exercise Tips*

- *Get an O.K. from your physician.*

- *Start slowly and have a reasonable goal.*

- *Make it fun.*

- *Join a group.*

- *Make an exercise contract with yourself and stick to it.*

- *Keep an exercise journal.*

- *Make exercising a family affair.*

- *Increase the amount you move in your normal activities.*

- *Park your car at the far end of the parking lot and walk.*

- *Use the stairs.*

- *Get up! Forgo conveniences such as television remote controls and drive-through windows.*

- *Make more trips. Unload grocery bags from the car one bag at a time.*

- *Clean up! Vacuum. Dust. Mop the floor. Garden. Each increases your activity level.*

- *Take time to stretch.*

- *Mix it up. Try various types of exercise to keep it interesting.*

from Take a Load Off Your Heart [10]

cognitively. First, the bath of stress hormones that comes with exhaustion complicates your overall physical health, causing premature wear and tear on your various body systems. A growing sense of emotional restlessness or aggravation leaves you psychologically rigid and struggling to cope. Eventually, neurochemical changes that correspond with exhaustion interfere with attention, memory, and creative problem solving.

The good news is that all you have to do to prevent or correct this problem is regularly "switch channels." Congruently switching your focus to new activities (like enjoying healthy pleasures) replenishes your coping energies. When you move to a different energy tank, the depleted tank begins to refill its supply of coping energy.

So, diversify! Research has shown that men and women who have a more "complex and diverse" lifestyle show fewer signs of stress, less depression, and fewer incidents of foul moods, colds, stomach pains, headaches, and muscle aches.[12]

Even taking brief pauses in your day can help you remain efficient and avoid exhaustion. Consider the alternative: Working too long at a task results in up to a 500 percent increase in the time it takes you to solve a problem.[13] Taking regular two-minute work breaks throughout the day, on the other hand, has been shown to boost productivity and mood.[14]

Get Help When You Can

If you enjoy tasks like grocery shopping, cleaning house, doing yard work, or gift-wrapping, by all means go ahead and engage in these activities. If not, use your resources to buy yourself time and energy.

Doing these sorts of life chores yourself is sometimes relaxing and centering; they can reconnect you with roles that you value. But we encourage you to be mindful here. If it seems like a hassle not worth your energies, if the cost/benefits analysis tips the scales in the "paying too much of my energy to do this" direction, *then don't do it!* Deciding to delegate or hire out some of these tasks today doesn't mean you'll never shop or clean for yourself. It just means that you're making an energy management decision that makes sense for right now.

Twelve Ways to Boost Your Energy:[15]

1. *Get proper rest.*

2. *Eat for high performance and peak energy: Avoid too much salt, sugar, fat, cholesterol, and caffeine; eat fruits, vegetables, whole-grain breads, and other foods high in fiber.*

3. *Drink six to eight glasses of water daily.*

4. *Get aerobic exercise daily.*

5. *Spend a little time alone every day.*

6. *Grow spiritually.*

7. *Have loving, intimate interactions with family and friends.*

8. *Have some fun.*

9. *Learn something new.*

10. *Make time for hobbies.*

11. *Take your fair share of vacations.*

12. *Remind yourself of the meaning and purpose of your life and work.*

---

7. Get Some Sleep!

Sleep is naturally healing and restores your ability to cope. When we do not get enough sleep, whatever is bothering us seems so much worse. Studies increasingly point to how important it is to get enough sleep. Sleep deprivation can interfere with concentration, mood, and body functions. In fact, sleep deprivation elevates blood glucose and cortisol for at least 24 hours. Habitual sleep loss can interfere with your body's ability to momentarily quiet the stress response, and this makes you more vulnerable to blood pressure surges that can cause heart attacks.

In a nutshell, poor sleep wears you down, weakens your immune system, and makes you much more susceptible to physical and emotional illness. And being sleepy is a surefire way to underperform at work. A recent study of young physicians found that following one night of disturbed sleep there was a 25 percent drop in cognitive performance, and two nights of sub-par sleep resulted in an amazing 40 percent dip in cognitive performance![16]

The best indication that you're not getting enough of the right kind of sleep is if you wake most mornings feeling tired, and this fatigue lasts throughout the day. Add to that nagging body aches and pains and lapses in attention, and you can be sure that you're sleep deprived.

If you're really interested in assessing your sleep, evaluate yourself using the same test that most sleep clinics around the country use when evaluating new patients.

The Epworth Sleepiness Scale [17]

Use the following scale to choose the most appropriate number for each situation:

0 = would never doze or sleep

1 = slight chance of dozing or sleeping

2 = moderate chance of dozing or sleeping

3 = high chance of dozing or sleeping

Situation	**Chance of Dozing or Sleeping**
Sitting and reading	____
Watching TV	____
Sitting inactive in a public place	____
Being a passenger in a motor vehicle for an hour or more	____
Lying down in the afternoon	____
Sitting and talking to someone	____

Sitting quietly after lunch (no alcohol) ____

Stopped for a few minutes in traffic while driving ____

Total score *(your Epworth score)* ____

Key

1–6   *Congratulations, you are getting enough sleep!*

7–8   *Your score is average.*

9 and up   *Seek the advice of a sleep specialist without delay.*

The Epworth Sleepiness Scale is used to determine the level of daytime sleepiness. A score of 10 or more is considered sleepy. A score of 18 or more is very sleepy. If you score 9 or more on this test, you should consider whether you are obtaining adequate sleep, need to improve your sleep regimen, and/or need to see a sleep specialist. These issues should be discussed with your personal physician

8. Manage Information Overload and Constant Interruptions

The more our concentration is interrupted, the more irritated, stressed, and drained we get. And the more we think we need to know, the more likely we are to mismanage one of the most insidious stressors in the "new normal" of modern times.

It is variously referred to as information glut, information overload, information smut, and infobog. It's delivered from a seemingly endless menu of sources: email, pagers, cellular phones, video conferencing, handheld PDA devices, chat rooms, e-news servers, 24-hour news television and radio shows—not to mention those "old" standbys snail mail, telephones, answering machines, faxes, and voice mail.[18] Wherever we get it, our constant access to massive amounts of information has raised our baseline level of stress. In fact,

Sleep Tips

- *Be sure you are comfortable. Have a comfortable bed and a quiet, comfortable room and temperature.*

- *If you have difficulty breathing, try elevating the head of the bed on wooden blocks of four to six inches or use pillows that elevate your chest, shoulders, and head. You might also want to try using a vaporizer. Warm moist air can make breathing easier.*

- *Avoid alcohol and caffeine late in the day, or smoking near bedtime.*

- *Eat your last meal at least three hours before bedtime.*

- *Do not nap in the afternoon or after dinner.*

- *Stay awake until you are ready to go to bed.*

- *Develop a routine:*

  o *Go to bed at the same time every night.*

  o *Get up at the same time every morning.*

  o *Get used to doing the same things every night before going to bed.*

- *Finish exercising at least four hours before bedtime.*

- *Use your bed and your bedroom for sleeping. If you do not fall asleep within 30 minutes, get out of bed and go to another room and do something routine until you feel sleepy again.*

- *If you wake up earlier than normal, try distracting yourself with pleasant thoughts or relaxation strategies. If you do not fall back asleep, get out of bed and return when you are sleepy again.*

- *Try not to worry about not getting enough sleep. If you create the proper environment, your body will fall asleep when it needs it* most of us don't even notice the effects of this stressor, much less control it. Consider:

- A Reuters Business Information survey of 1,300 mangers reported that one in four managers admit to suffering ill health as a result of the amount of information they are having to handle, and two-thirds say that stress from information overload increases tension with colleagues and lowers job satisfaction.[19]

- Research by Management-Issues.com suggests that today's managers and knowledge workers receive between 60 and 1,000 emails per day. These same researchers caution that good decisions do not necessarily stem from gathering large quantities of information, but rather from taking time to absorb and process information, reflect and analyze, and discuss the issue at hand with others.

- Carl Honore, author of *In Praise of Slowness*, claims that the typical office worker gets interrupted every three minutes by a phone call, email, instant message, or other distraction. But it takes about eight uninterrupted minutes for the brain to get into a creative state.

- A study of 1,000 adults carried out by psychologists in King's College London found that heavy text messaging and emailing causes a reduction in mental capacity equivalent to the loss of 10 IQ points.[20]

- Researchers suggest that six out of ten adults admit that they are addicted to checking email and text messaging repeatedly throughout the day. And 80 percent of managers surveyed say they spend more than a fifth of their day (at least an hour and a half) dealing with emails, while the average American employee spends about a quarter of their working day (around one and three quarters hours) dealing with email. Three out of ten spend more than two hours and 8 percent spend four hours or more a day dealing with email.[21]

Our distractions aren't always imposed by others. Have you ever found yourself stuck before your computer screen for hours, trying to complete some project but constantly distracted by the fact that you keep going off on yet another interesting tangent? Soon you're sitting with seven open "windows," the day has passed, and you seem to have accomplished little.

One simple stress management strategy related to this version of information glut comes from Pamela Kristan, author of *The Spirit of Getting Organized*.[22] Pamela tells the amusing tale of how she learned her most important time management tip observing herself training her puppy. In managing the puppy's enthusiasm about gnawing on whatever his little mouth could hold or simply running about with endless energy, Pamela found herself alternately saying in a firm voice "Drop it!" or "Stay!" Now, when she finds herself straying too far afield from her targeted task, she gets back on track with the self-admonition to "Drop it!" And when she's tempted to sneak a peak at email for the umpteenth time instead of remaining focused on the project at hand, a stern "Stay!" reminder serves her well.

Interruptions and the sheer volume of information bombarding us are not the only problems we face here. Our notion of what's necessary versus what's sufficient to know has also become blurry. Not all information is important. Much is just "noise" that can accumulate and contribute to stress overload. We are bombarded on a daily basis with more information than any prior generation in history.[23]

Given that the quality of your life is influenced by the kinds of information you take in, you should dare to discriminate.[24] You've probably already learned to do this with junk mail. Most of us caught on long ago to the fact that every piece of junk mail we receive doesn't warrant reading. Don't spend any of your precious time or energy on it. In fact, many people develop the time management strategy of sorting through their mail over a trashcan, anticipating that most of what they receive by snail mail will be most appropriately filed in the "trash" file.

It pays to exercise similar discretion with other information sources as well. Don't read every email you receive, and limit how often you check your in-box. Use spam blockers to eliminate "trash" emails. Avoid overloading on news stories. Update your awareness of world events regularly, but not continuously.

Use the technique of "firewalling" to block off periods of time when you are unavailable for information input—by phone, fax, email, regular mail, or even face to face. Periodically taking recess from information glut will refuel you and make you more productive.[25]

CLOSING THOUGHTS

People seem to come in two varieties. First are those who trudge through their days. Dreading what their day will bring, they get started with a moan. They strain to get through each hour, never fully engage, and don't enjoy the unrecoverable moments of their lives.

On the other hand are those people who seem to zoom effortlessly through each day. They get more done than the moaners, they switch from task to task with ease and anticipation; they even seem to be interested in doing what needs to be done. These thrivers seem to be enjoying themselves as they approach the same tasks that strain the moaners.

If you look closely, you'll discover that people in this second category all share a common talent that researchers have pinpointed to be the single most powerful predictor of resilience. It's also the most surefire way to keep stress from becoming strain: They learn to counter daily hassles with daily uplifts. Most of what we call stress management could be filed in this single category. The next chapter is devoted to this crucial topic.

CHAPTER **11**

The Power of Daily Uplifts

"Plan your joy as thoughtfully and
as frequently as you plan your work."[1]

Ann McGee-Cooper et al.

There are no perfect people. None of us enjoys perfect health or contentment. There are no perfect relationships, friendships, marriages, or families. And there certainly are no perfect workplaces. We all face unavoidable hassles, at home and at work.

But the great news is that it is not the presence or absence of hassles that determines whether we thrive or just survive. Thriving married couples squabble just about as frequently as those who eventually divorce.[2] Healthy people don't get or stay that way by living hassle-free lives. And resilient organizations face the same aggravating, relentless challenges and crises that sink others.

What makes the difference between thriving and struggling is the presence of daily "uplifts." To remind you, we're talking here about the moment of caring connection, the pat on the back, the flowers or music or deep breath, the prayer or moment of mindfulness—little spurts of pleasure or contentment that are the "small stuff" we've been misled to believe isn't worth sweating. In truth, it's not the big stuff, but the small stuff that matters most. Consider the facts:

- Daily minor irritants actually have a greater harmful impact on our health than do major life events.[3]

- Enjoying frequent, small pleasures, on the other hand, has a greater effect on positive mood and overall psychological health than do intense periods of feeling good.[4]

- In fact, researchers have shown that happiness is more affected by how much time you spend feeling good on a daily basis than by occasional "peak" experiences.[5]

- Stress problems have less to do with the absolute amount of distress in your life and more to do with the *absence of uplifts.*[6]

- Frequent uplifts will boost your quality of life even during periods of high levels of negative stress.[7]

- For example, a study of college students who were tested in early 2001 and again in the weeks following the September 11 terrorist attacks showed that positive emotions experienced on a regular basis—emotions like gratitude, interest, and love—accounted for both pre-crisis and post-crisis resilience levels and helped buffer the resilient students against depression and fueled thriving in the wake of the attacks.[8]

- Good feelings are good for your health. Experiments have shown that the best way to calm cardiovascular reactions to a negative event is to initiate positive feelings. As we mentioned earlier, while coronary arteries constrict when you think an angry thought, these same arteries open and allow blood to flow when you think a loving thought.[9]

- Research has also shown that focusing on something that lifts your mood will help you to recover more quickly from the cardiovascular effects of negative emotions[10] and lower your levels of stress-related cortisol.[11]

- Compared to their more grouchy or blasé counterparts, people who report having frequent bursts of positive feelings have reduced inflammatory responses to stress, lessened physical pain, and greater resistance to viruses.[12]

- Positive moods that come with mindfulness meditation have even been shown to improve brain functions and immune system activity.[13]

- In fact, there is convincing evidence that how frequently people experience good feelings even predicts how long they will live.[14]

- Orchestrating uplifts for those around you can boost workplace morale and productivity and lower your own levels of work stress.

- Compared to those who work without being praised, employees who receive regular recognition and praise are more productive, more engaged with colleagues, and more likely to stay with their organization; receive higher loyalty and satisfaction scores from customers; and have better safety records and fewer accidents on the job.[15]

- Organizational leaders who share positive emotions have work groups with more positive mood, enhanced job satisfaction, greater engagement, and improved group performance.[16]

Can Uplifts Make You Smarter?

Barbara Fredrickson, Ph.D., of the University of Michigan is one of our most prolific contemporary researchers in the field of positive emotions. She theorizes that positive emotions evolved in our ancestors because they increased productivity and the odds of survival.[17] Unlike negative emotions, which urge people to a narrow range of specific actions (e.g., fight or flee), positive emotions widen our thoughts and actions. For example, when we feel good, we're more likely to play and explore. This broadening generates more coping flexibility because it results in the building of personal resources, like social connections, coping strategies, and knowledge about the world around us. By contrast, negative emotions promote avoidant behaviors, leading to missed opportunities to learn more and to correct false impressions.

Many other studies and experiments support this notion.[18] To put it simply, good feelings alter your mindset in positive ways. When you are in a positive mood, your scope of attention is widened,[19] your intuition and creativity flow, and you are more likely to try a range of creative solutions when solving problems.[20]

Uplifts Can Make for More Creative Thinkers[21]

Forty-four experienced physicians were randomly placed in one of three groups. Group 1 got a small package of sweets; Group 2 read aloud humanistic statements about medicine; and Group 3 was the control group.

All were presented a complex case study and asked to think aloud as they rendered their diagnoses. The group with the sweets did best.

Similar results have been seen in studies with subjects as young as four years old. When experimenters first induce a positive mood, subjects tend to show more flexible and creative problem solving and fixate less on the obvious or easy answers.

As you can see from this brief overview of research, it's not far-fetched to say that uplifts—those ways of thinking, behaving, and interacting with other people that lift your mood—can help soothe virtually anything that ails you and help keep you resilient.

Assess your hassles-to-uplifts ratio with the following exercise.

What Is Your Hassles Quotient?[22]

Indicate whether each statement that follows is mostly true about you most of the time.

1. I am concerned about my weight (I'm either too heavy or too light). Yes____ No____

2. I have a good relationship with a spouse or lover. Yes____ No____

3. The rising cost of living bothers me. Yes____ No____

4. I have a sense of accomplishment. Yes____ No____

5. I have a lot to do to maintain my home. Yes____ No____

6. I have good friends. Yes____ No____

7. Misplacing or losing things is a problem for me. Yes____ No____

8. I am in good health. Yes____ No____

9. I have too much to do and too little time to do it. Yes____ No____

10. I get enough sleep. Yes____ No____

11. I am not satisfied with my physical appearance. Yes____ No____

12. I spend a lot of time with the people who are important to me. Yes____ No____

13. Managing finances and keeping records take a lot of my time. Yes____ No____

14. My home is pleasant. Yes____ No____

15. Someone close to me is in poor health. Yes____ No____

16. I eat out often enough. Yes____ No____

17. I am concerned about crime and safety. Yes____ No____

18. I have a sense of satisfaction in meeting my responsibilities.
Yes_____ No_____

Scoring and Interpretation

Count the number of odd-numbered questions for which you have checked Yes. This is your hassle score: _____. Count the even-numbered statements for which you have checked Yes. This is your uplift score: _____. Your stress level is high if your hassle score is either greater than four or greater than your uplift score.

This test is clearly not exhaustive of all possible hassles and uplifts, and it's certainly true that the same thing could be an uplift or a hassle for different people. Our intention here is to stir your thinking about the range of ways you might be hassled or uplifted.

Boost Your Uplifts!

Sounds simple. In many ways it is simple and yet it is more complicated than just using common sense. In the rest of this chapter we want to tell you how the thrivers do it. We'll offer research-based guidelines that stem from the study of people who, as a group, tend to be happier, healthier, and more productive than others.[23]

It's not just common sense and it's not always logical. For example, logic would tell us that a lot of thrivers just got lucky—by birth or some other twist of fate. The most obvious case for this "some have it easier than the rest of us" argument is wealth. It is true that uplifts come easier when you're not worried about paying your bills. Studies show a positive, statistically significant relationship between income and overall life satisfaction.[24] And getting a windfall of money feels great. For example, research has shown that lottery winners and people receiving an inheritance report higher mental well-being the following year.[25]

The truth is, however, more complex. For example, the rich gain less from extra income than poorer people.[26] That's because of a syndrome called "hedonic adaptation." As our incomes rise, we adapt to our new circumstances, the novelty wears off, and our expectations change. Interestingly, the well-being that comes with a windfall of money diminishes substantially after the first year and the size of the positive effect of income, in general, is small compared to other factors such as marriage, divorce, and unemployment.

Many wealthy people are very happy and many are not. Many beautiful people are very happy and many are not. Many smart and talented people are very happy and many are not. The common denominator across populations of people who construct happy, productive lives is their commitment to incorporating an abundance of uplifts into their journeys at work and at home. And you can become one of them, even if you don't win the lottery. Here's how.

Uplift Strategy 1: Do What It Takes to Get Along with Others

It's not enough just to have friends, relatives, and coworkers; you also have to get along well with people. As we explained earlier, having friends, being married to a supportive mate, having supportive relatives, and having supportive work mates all correlate with high levels of satisfaction with life.[27] But the flip side is equally true: Conflict with loved ones is toxic to mental and physical health; and relationship tensions at work lead to increased burnout, lower productivity, and sky-rocketing rates of turnover. Good relationships are crucial to thriving.

Uplift Strategy 2: Get Active!

We've said it before. Participating in some form of active leisure boosts your mood more than doing something passive like watching television or going to the movies. A passive leisure activity might distract you from your worries, but it won't lift your mood for long, and, sometimes, you might actually feel worse afterward. That's why people who report that they regularly exercise, play, or do some activity like work in the garden are more satisfied than those who do not.

Uplift Strategy 3: Do What You Need to Do to Feel Better

What seems like a potential uplift can simply serve to guilt trip you. This fact became clear in a 2006 study of 540 families that evaluated the emotional experiences of working mothers and fathers.[28] Contrary to logic, taking time for themselves before going home after work did not improve either mothers' or fathers' moods. In fact, mothers who took time for themselves after work experienced lower levels of happiness at home. The authors hypothesized that when taking time for oneself is seen as a tradeoff that takes time away from work or family members, the emotional benefits diminish.

So be true to yourself. Do what you need to do to lift your mood. If relaxing over breakfast while reading the morning papers gets you centered and starts your day on a good note, then dare to do it. If, on the other hand, getting a jump on your day's work first thing in the morning lifts your mood, treat yourself to a spurt of guilt-free work before you eat breakfast. The point is to honestly evaluate what works best for you, and do that thing.

Uplift Strategy 4: Vacation Wisely

We get good at what we practice, and most of us don't "practice" having fun nearly enough. We tend to turn potential "play" situations into work. Rather than enjoy spending time with a friend hitting tennis balls or cruising around the golf course, we ruin the mood by turning the activity into a competition. As parents, we contaminate precious moments with our kids by filling them with "instructions" that oftentimes feel like criticism or shame. We even tend to turn leisurely walks around the neighborhood into workouts.

Life is stressful enough. Don't let your hard-work ethic spill over into your times of recess. The need to "practice" enjoying recess is underscored when we look at how most of us deal with vacations.

Most couples make at least some of the following mistakes when planning and taking vacation.

- Launch into a full-blown work binge at least two weeks in advance of your vacation. ("Got to catch up and get a little ahead before I leave; otherwise I'll drown in accumulated work when I return.")

- Set off for your vacation exhausted and irritable from the binge.

- Spend your first two days of vacation withdrawing from the adrenaline overload that the preceding two weeks brought. As though the tension, restlessness, and irritability that comes with this withdrawal weren't enough, add fuel to the fire with a flurry of activities, ski or golf lessons, or other high-stimulation family activities.

- One of you moves into the "We're on vacation. Let's have some romance!" mode before both of you are ready.

- Let your children's endless demands and sub-par performance on the ski slopes or golf course fuel your own Type-A frustration.

- Spend Day 3 bickering or pouting about what did not happen on Day 2 (i.e., no romance).

- Finally having accumulated enough time away from work, notice that Day 4 brings the dawning of rejuvenation. As you both begin to remember what you like about each other, you let the fun begin (i.e., romance!).

- Make Day 5 so enjoyable that you start to wonder out loud, "Maybe we ought to buy a time-share or a second home here. This place is great!"

- On Day 6, start to get distressed about the end of the vacation having come so soon.

- Spend the entire return trip dreading what awaits you in your Big Life back home.

It can be better than this. Enjoying vacations is a learned skill and it starts with realistic expectations. Before leaving home, you and your mate should clarify whether you are about to take a family trip or a romantic getaway. Any single trip is unlikely to be both. Clarify your hopes, fantasies, and plans for how the trip might go. This simple step can make a difference.

Next, discuss what level of activity, stimulation, learning, or playing you want on this vacation. Be clear about your goals. Will this be a time to relax and play with your family, or a time to hone your skill at a sport or hobby? Make sure everyone is on the same page. We only half-jokingly advise most of our clients: *Never get certified in anything on a vacation.* You spend enough of your life together rushing, performing, and producing. Really take a vacation from those pressures.

Plan a more gentle re-entry back into your everyday life. A postvacation work binge can ruin the best afterglow. Consider using one of your vacation days for the purpose of gradually getting back to your routines at home and work. Give yourself time to catch up on mail, phone calls, and paperwork before your full-tilt work/life shuffle resumes.

Uplift Strategy 5: Find Something to Enjoy in What You Are Doing

You can almost always find something to enjoy in a situation, if you look for it. Pay attention to the "sweet" aspects of bittersweet experiences. For example, even though you may not like having to be away from your family for business trips, find ways to take advantage of the perks that come with the trip. Don't add insult to injury by exhausting yourself with overwork or guilt about being away from home. If you allow yourself to enjoy some aspects of the trip, you are more likely to return home rejuvenated. Enjoy room service. Treat yourself to a massage at the hotel spa. Relax and watch a movie. Don't spend every minute on the trip working. If you do, your family will suffer the double-whammy of having tolerated your being away, then having to suffer the effects of your exhaustion and stress when you return home. Take care of yourself so that you can arrive home at least somewhat rejuvenated and everyone benefits from your trip.

Even more important is to find pleasure and meaning in your day-to-day routine. Make it a habit to remind yourself how what you are doing *now* is connected to a higher meaning that you value. Even mundane routines like washing dishes can take on a new meaning when you link them to one of your core values like caring for others or taking pride in a job well done.

Uplift Strategy 6: Make Your Environment Uplifting

The long lines, traffic jams, crowded elevators, and overheard cell phone conversations in noisy restaurants and commuter trains, and the constant clatter and chatter that bombards us from every angle are bad enough. Noise and crowding increase our heart rates, tense our muscles, and raise our aggravation levels. But many of us add to our environmental misery by allowing unpleasant noise and clutter to contaminate our private spaces— our homes, automobiles, and private workspaces.

Do the look, sound, feel, and smell of your surroundings matter to you?[29] Imagine that you are walking into your house or apartment after a stressful day. You open the door and are hit with the blast of a radio playing in one room and a television blaring in another room. The phone rings, and one of your family members begins a loud conversation, adding to the din.

As you enter your kitchen, you glance around and note that, once again, it's a total mess. Newspapers are lying beside the breakfast table. The morning dishes are still in the sink. Articles of clothing are draped over the chairs. Last week's mail is piled high on the countertop. The smell of dirty dishes and the overflowing trash fills your nostrils. Notice how you feel as you vividly imagine arriving home to such a mess.

Now change the scene. Take a deep breath. Relax. In your mind's eye, picture your house or apartment as it is after you have straightened and cleaned it. Starting with the area you first enter as you open the door, see each room. Everything is in its place. Your clean kitchen is invitingly neat. Dishes and clothes are put away. Trash has been picked up. Throughout your home, things are clean, inviting, and fresh.

Now imagine walking into this clean, orderly house after a stressful day. This time you are met with the pleasant sounds of softly playing music and the inviting aroma of a bouquet of fresh flowers. Notice how you feel this time as you imagine entering your neat and tidy kitchen.

Don't add insult to injury. If you're already stressed, do what you can to de-stress your environment. Turn off distracting sounds or visuals. If need be, commute with your personal headphones and tape player or iPod that allows you to listen to what you choose rather than the invasive conversations of people around you. Make time to keep your workspaces, car, and home uncluttered so that stressful activities become less stressful. Do what you can to make your surroundings look, sound, smell, and feel the way you want them to.

You might want to make your space appeal to your whole brain:[30] pleasant colors and shapes—anything that appeals to your sense of beauty and humor—will engage your right brain, as will memorabilia. Anything that increases your ability to stay organized will engage your left brain. This includes items like files and folders, to-do lists, and a clean and tidy environment.

Finally, do what you can to create or discover a pleasant, relaxing personal space, and visit it regularly. This doesn't mean you have to regularly go on vacation to an exotic resort to manage stress. Rather, you should make it a part of your daily routine to visit some favorite spot in your yard, patio, home, or community. Even a favorite chair can be a private relaxation base.

Uplift Strategy 7: Connect with Your Higher Power or Meaning

If you find soothing and hope through connecting with a nurturing higher power, then you are well advised to do so regularly. Religious people who actively pray and participate in their faith communities are happier and healthier than the average person.[31]

Uplift Strategy 8: Join Something, and Attend!

Even shy or introverted people tend to get uplifted by participating with others in some meaningful activity. Going to monthly club meetings, doing volunteer work, spending time with friends or loved ones, attending church services—each of these forms of connecting have been found to boost happiness as much as doubling your income.

Uplift Strategy 9: Have Hope!

Good things come from maintaining hope. Even in hard times, believing that things can get better will sustain you and strengthen your will to do what it takes to better your situation. Hope has even been found to be good for your health. A 2005 study showed that people with higher levels of hope had a significantly decreased likelihood of having or developing hypertension, diabetes, and respiratory tract infections over a two-year period of follow-up.[32]

Uplift Strategy 10: Start Your Day Smoothly

Your mind is very receptive upon waking, so before you get out of bed, fill your mind with thoughts that set a positive mood for the day. Read something inspirational or calming. Enjoy music that makes you feel good. Mentally rehearse your day going smoothly. And here's a recommendation we make to most of our clients concerned about stress or anxiety management: Start your day with exercise. We know—many of you can't imagine finding the time and energy to exercise first thing each morning. But this is really worth making happen, even if you have to get out of bed an hour earlier than normal. Early morning exercising is a sure way to calm your nerves, and start you off with a feeling of self-satisfaction and confidence.

Uplift Strategy 11: Turn Aggravation into Opportunity

Turn minor annoyances like waiting in a line or for an appointment into opportunities to relax, meditate, or catch up on busywork or return phone calls. Time management experts estimate that you can "gain" an extra two weeks of productive time a year by utilizing these "in-between" times. And doing so lessens your aggravation at being kept waiting.

This requires that you be realistic. You know that certain hassles are inevitable parts of your day. The crucial question is how you take care of yourself during these high-hassle times and whether you take advantage of the opportunities that some of these very times afford you to enrich your life. Remember that "in-between" times—like when you are carpooling your kids to school or commuting to work with your life partner—can be times for connecting. Every parent knows that children—especially teenagers who might otherwise be hard to reach—sometimes become open to connection while being carpooled. But you have to be open to seizing the moment.

Start by noticing how much time you spend each day focusing on things you cannot control (like traffic) or that you dread. Take charge of what you do and what you think about during hassle challenges, and you'll feel better and be more productive.

Uplift Strategy 12: "Sandwich" the Hassles

Combine an activity that hassles you with an activity or mental strategy that boosts your energy or mood. For example, while rushing to get ready for work, listen to calming music or hold a soothing mental image in your head.

Uplift Strategy 13: Allow Enough Time

Be realistic about how much time you will need to do anything, then allow a little extra. For nonfrazzled commuting, leave home early enough to arrive at work feeling ahead of, not behind, schedule.

Uplift Strategy 14: Replenish Your Pictures of Things Going Well

Periodically throughout the day, replenish the soothing images and thoughts of things going well that you started your day with. During your commute, mentally rehearse the day going smoothly and productively.

Uplift Strategy 15: Prepare for a Peaceful Return Home

Let your commute home rest and uplift you. You've worked hard and long; now you're returning to your home and (we hope) the people you love. Review and renew: Recall what you did right or well that day; make a mental note of what you appreciate about your work, your colleagues, and your accomplishments of the day. Next, prepare yourself for a good re-entry into your home. Spend a few minutes thinking about each of the family members you'll see when you arrive home, and note at least two things you appreciate about each of them and why you love them. If you live alone, prepare for this last chapter of your day by focusing on what you plan to enjoy once you get home.

Uplift Strategy 16: Re-enter Your Home Gracefully

When you arrive home, resist being pulled into another multitasking flurry. Sequence your evening activities. Do one thing at a time. Even if you live alone, make time to touch base with people or pets you care about. Unwind from your day slowly. If you have chores to do or homework that has to be completed, set a time limit on the working part of your evening and stick to it. Schedule some healthy pleasure into your day, and give yourself the treat you promised. Doing so will rejuvenate your energies and serve you well tomorrow.

Uplift Strategy 17: Break the Procrastination Habit

A major hassle for most people is unfinished business, especially the stuff that accumulates because we've procrastinated doing it. The longer we put it off, the more insurmountable it seems, and the more hassled we become over the accumulated tasks.

Here are some thoughts about how to work your way out of this trap. These strategies for breaking the procrastination habit and time management can be used to address any area that requires change.

Make it easier for yourself. Don't set such lofty expectations that you paralyze yourself with performance anxiety. Remember the time-tested "Swiss cheese" method described by author Alan Lakein in the 1970s: The way to get something done is to break it into smaller tasks and do just one of the smaller tasks or set a timer and work on the big task for just 15 minutes.[33] By doing a little at a time, eventually you'll reach a point where you want to finish. We call our variation of this method "Picking the Low-Hanging Fruit." We recommend that you read through the steps in this process and the examples that follow before completing this exercise.

PICKING THE LOW-HANGING FRUIT

Step 1: Identify something you are procrastinating about that is related to a goal that's important to you: _____

Step 2: Make a list of the people you would have to deal with or the specific things you would have to do in order to complete this task. Next, rate each of these people or tasks on a "misery scale" that assesses how much you dread dealing with this person or doing this task. Use 1 to represent "I don't dread this person or task at all" and 100 to represent "I totally dread dealing with this person or doing this task."

Person or task	Misery rating
1. _____	_____
2. _____	_____
3. _____	_____
4. _____	_____
5. _____	_____
6. _____	_____
7. _____	_____
8. _____	_____
9. _____	_____
10. _____	_____
11. _____	_____
12. _____	_____
13. _____	_____
14. _____	_____
15. _____	_____

Step 3: Use the following table to divide your list into three categories—easiest, moderate, and hardest for you to deal with—as indicated by your misery ratings.

Easiest (misery rating of 1–30)	**Moderate** (misery rating of 31–60)	**Hardest** (misery rating of 61+)
1.	1.	1.
2.	2.	2.
3.	3.	3.
4.	4.	4.
5.	5.	5.

Step 4: Focus on the people or tasks on your easiest list. Once these are done, move on to the people or tasks on your moderate list.

If you approach what you are procrastinating about in this way, you will find that you build a momentum that breaks through your procrastination trap, the trap that's created when, for the sake of avoiding doing the hardest stuff, we tend to avoid doing *anything* relevant to the task.

Here's an example of how this method works.

Rick, an insurance salesman who was a midlevel performer on his agency's team, came to us for help in overcoming his habit of procrastinating doing what he knew was necessary to achieve his goal of selling more life insurance. He explained his dilemma this way: "This is not rocket science. My company has proven that simply calling existing customers and setting up face-to-face appointments to review their insurance needs significantly boosts an agent's sales figures. But I just don't make the calls. Each day, I dread making those calls, then beat myself up for letting yet another day go by without doing anything productive about this."

First, we had Rick make a list of 30 customers he could potentially call. Next, we asked him to rate each customer using our "misery scale." Finally, we had him divide the customers into three categories of easiest, moderate, and hardest to deal with. When he did this, Rick realized that he actually *enjoyed* interacting with many of the people included on the easiest and moderate lists. But, for the sake of avoiding the people he found hardest to deal with, he was also avoiding some of his favorite customers. The simple advice to start by calling the customers in the easiest category—"pick the low-hanging fruit first"—broke Rick's all-or-nothing approach that was fueling his procrastination habit. Incidentally, he also significantly boosted his sales figures.

Uplift Strategy 18: Manage Your Thinking

Every sane person knows that we can't always control what happens to us. But people who focus on what is controllable, even during uncontrollable times, do have higher life satisfaction and better overall health.

One of the most manageable aspects of your coping is one that we tend to relinquish control of when stressed: our thinking. We spoke earlier about the dangers of stress thinking. Here are three recommendations for thinking your way into uplifts.

Practice the Three Cs

Salvatore R. Maddi, Ph.D., and colleagues at the University of Chicago studied the stress reactions of employees who were involved in one of the biggest corporate downsizing cases in American history to date.[34] In 1981 Illinois Bell Telephone cut 13,000 employees in one year. Dr. Maddi and his associates followed more than 400 supervisors, managers, and executives before the downsizing occurred and on a yearly follow-up basis for the next six years. While two-thirds of the employees in the study suffered significant performance and health declines as a result of the extreme stress from the downsizing, the remaining one-third actually thrived during the upheaval. These thriving employees maintained their health, happiness, and performance and felt renewed enthusiasm.

What made the two groups so different? In a nutshell, Dr. Maddi found that the difference was attitude. Those who thrived maintained three key "hardiness" beliefs. Take a lesson from these resilient people, no matter what you're facing:

- *Think Challenge:* Try to view your stress challenges as opportunities for new learning.

- *Think Commitment:* Strive to be involved in what's going on.

- *Think Control:* Take control of what you can to influence the outcomes that matter to you, rather than languishing in passivity and powerlessness.

Even under the most extreme circumstances, choosing to think in these ways can make a tremendous difference in promoting your hardiness.

Research with Army reserve personnel mobilized for the Persian Gulf War in the early 1990s proved this point. Soldiers who used coping strategies that corresponded with the Three Cs outlined above showed a greater ability to experience combat stress without negative health consequences, such as post-traumatic stress disorder, than those who did not.[35]

Balance Achievements and Expectations

A surefire way to uplift yourself is to feel good about what you have and what you've done. Too often, no matter what we achieve, we demoralize ourselves by expecting more or by lamenting that things are not different. Even if you haven't yet accomplished a major goal, remind yourself of the value and worth of what you have done thus far relative to your goal. Remind yourself of the deeper meaning of your current experience. People who feel most satisfied with life view what they do each day as being related to what matters most to them. So set goals, commit yourself to pursuing them, and appreciate your every step along the way. Researchers have proven that doing so will significantly boost your overall life satisfaction and well-being.[36]

Reminding yourself of all the good that you have already achieved is an especially important way to uplift yourself during difficult times. Following one of our presentations, a surgeon in the audience shared with us a most poignant example of this last point.

Somewhat shyly, this rather stern-looking man asked us to accompany him to his hospital office. Once there, he placed before us a large scrapbook, saying, "This is what's kept me from burning out and giving up over the past 28 years of working as a pediatric transplant surgeon." We thumbed through thank you notes from grateful parents of children whose lives he had saved; and graduation, wedding, and birth announcements sent by former patients, now grown-up and thriving—tokens of gratitude that spanned nearly three decades, all for having given so many children the gift of continued life.

The surgeon explained: "Your comments about balancing achievements and expectations got to the quick of what this scrapbook does for me. I have my wife to thank for this. She talked me into keeping these notes. And she convinced me many years ago to never leave this hospital after one of my patients has died without first coming here and thumbing through these reminders of the many patients I have helped." Through his tears (and ours) he then spoke of how this ritual has helped him to grieve for children he couldn't save, then celebrate the fact that he has given so many others continued life.

Focus on What's Good About Your Health

A prime example of the importance of finding what's right about what you've got, rather than simply focusing on your deficits, faults, or losses, comes from research on what's called self-rated health. A number of researchers have found that how you think about your health is a more powerful predictor of how long you will live than is your objective medical status.[37] A landmark study of 7,000 Californians showed that males who were pessimistic about their health had a 2.3 times greater death rate than optimistic males, and pessimistic women had 5 times the death rate of women with optimistic attitudes about their health.[38]

The reason? People who focus on what is good and right about their health are more likely to benefit from the soothing that comes with peace of mind and more likely to continue to have hope and to stay involved in *living*— all of which translates into taking better care of themselves.

Self-rated health is also a powerful predictor of overall life satisfaction. Nothing more quickly takes the air out of our sense of well-being than an unwanted medical diagnosis. But researchers have long noted that health problems like heart disease, paralysis, and cancer have only short-term negative effects on life satisfaction for thrivers. They tend to adapt to their new health status rather quickly and find new supports and new attitudes about what's important in life.[39]

So don't just focus on your aches and pains and what you have "lost" due to your medical condition or age. Learn to think like people who thrive: Focus on what remains, on "residual capacities."

Make a Habit of Feeling Good About Your Health

In many studies, self-rated health has been found to be an excellent predictor of future health.[40] In general, would you say your health is . . . (circle one number)

Excellent	*1*
Very good	*2*
Good	*3*
Fair	*4*
Poor	*5*

Interpretation

The average score given in a study involving 1,129 people with chronic disease was 3.29.[41] How do you compare?

Uplift Strategy 19: Regularly Enjoy Healthy Pleasures

The health benefits of indulging in healthy pleasures are well documented. We emphasize that we're talking here about *healthy* pleasures; those that soothe without costing us our well-being. These do not include quick-fix mood changers like alcohol, binge eating, or other forms of unhealthy escapism.

In *Healthy Pleasures*, psychologist Robert Orstein and physician David Sobel summarized the many health benefits of small acts of healthy self-nurturing.

The Benefits of Healthy Pleasures		
Activity	**Decreases**	**Enhances**
Touch someone	*Heart rate*	
Get a massage	*Anxiety*	
Sit in a sauna or hot bath	*Stress hormones* *Pain*	*Serotonin* *Beta-endorphins* *Relaxation* *Sleep* *Resistance to infection*
Enjoy the sunlight	*Seasonal mood changes*	
View nature	*Sadness*	*Alpha brain waves* *Wakeful relaxation*
Listen to pleasant sounds and music	*Anxiety* *Pain*	*Endorphins* *Relaxation* *Immune-system functioning*
Smell pleasant scents		*Positive emotions*
Have moderate physical exercise	*Depression* *Anxiety* *Stress hormones*	*Relaxation* *Parasympathetic arousal* *Sleep* *Immune-system functioning* *Neurochemical processes*

Busy people often lose sight of what they truly enjoy. They know what they dread, what they are anxious about, and what they wish they had relief from. But they have difficulty specifying what they truly enjoy.

We recommend that you conduct a pleasure experiment. For one month, take time to experiment with different healthy pleasures each day, even if for only a few moments. Try things that you might not typically do and relish doing those you already know you enjoy.

Remember to match relaxation techniques to your individual sensory preferences—using music, for example, if you are particularly auditory or looking at something beautiful if you are particularly visual. Don't fall into the trap of trying to enjoy someone else's version of pleasure. Just because your best friend loves long hot baths, it's not necessarily going to be the case that you do. In fact, research has shown that people vary widely in their physical reactions to different types and levels of stimulation. For some, the best way to get peaceful and calm is to simply be still in a quiet, comfortable place.

But others find quiet and stillness more agitating than soothing; they are more calmed by external stimulation that distracts or entertains. It doesn't matter how you do it, just do it: Make time each day to switch channels and focus on something that takes your mind off whatever fills most of your day.

Uplift Strategy 20: Don't Forget to Laugh

Laughter can help to soothe anything that ails you, and laughing is good for your health. A good guffaw boosts your immune system,[42] calms stress hormones,[43] and increases your pain thresholds.[44] Laughing also exercises lungs, relaxes the diaphragm, increases oxygen in the bloodstream, improves mood, and makes parasympathetic calming reactions more readily available for up to 30 minutes afterward—getting you ready to more quickly calm down after facing your next hassle.[45]

So take time to laugh. Associate with people who make you smile. Allow yourself time to read at least a few of those silly emails you tend to delete automatically. Remember that a little playfulness while at work can significantly boost morale, creativity, productivity, and stamina.

Uplift Strategy 21: Be Childlike

There's a big difference between being childish (as in immature) and childlike (as in passionately involved in whatever you're doing, and enjoying yourself). Apply lessons learned from observing the most resilient members of our species: children. Author Ann McGee-Cooper observed that high performers often intuitively do just that. Consider the connections. Children are constantly

- jumping from one interest to another
- giggling
- fooling around
- finding ways to make whatever they're doing at least a little bit fun
- avoiding boredom
- dreaming
- having pleasant fantasies
- learning
- moving
- expressing emotions

And the happiest, most resilient people refuel their energy supplies repeatedly throughout the day by employing childlike strategies.[46] They

- find ways to have fun at what they are doing
- jump from one interest to another
- are curious and usually eager to try anything once
- smile and laugh a lot
- experience and express emotions freely
- are creative and innovative
- are physically active
- are constantly growing mentally and physically
- aren't afraid to try something new, even if they aren't good at it initially
- learn enthusiastically
- dream and imagine possibilities
- believe in the impossible
- don't spend much time worrying or feeling guilty
- are passionate

Uplift Strategy 22: Get Out of Your Head and Into Your Senses

Notice what you like about your surroundings, right now! What do you hear that you like? What pleasant smells do you notice? What body sensations are most comforting to you right now? Look around and be mindful of what you see that pleases or entertains you.

Quick-Hit Uplifts

- *Give yourself a compliment.*

- *Write out a list of ten things you admire about yourself.*

- *Make a list of ten of your happiest memories—things that still bring you joy when you recall them.*

- *Keep a gratitude list handy: What are you most grateful for having in your life?*

- *Listen to music that lifts your mood.*

- *Plan to eat a healthy meal or snack that you really love, and look forward to it throughout the day.*

- *Make contact with people who leave you with positive feelings.*

- *Get organized so you know when you'll get done the stuff that needs to get done; then you can afford to take breaks for pleasure.*

- *Do something kind for someone else—you'll both be uplifted.*

- *Find or create a special place in your home or community that soothes you, and visit that place often.*

How Much Is Enough?

Just how many uplifts are enough for staying happy, healthy, and high-performing? Researchers have actually tried to answer this question. For those of you interested in numbers, normal mental functioning is characterized by a ratio of positive to negative emotions of around 2.5 positive to 1 negative. Optimal mental health, on the other hand, requires that you experience between 2.9 and 4.3 uplifts for every one negative emotion.[47] Researcher John Gottman summarized two decades of research on marriages to conclude that unless a couple is able to maintain a ratio of approximately 5 positive interactions for every negative one, it is highly likely that their marriage will end.[48]

Can You Fake It?

You might fool others by pretending to feel happy when you really feel neutral or hassled, but your body knows the difference. Studies have shown that when we show nonverbal behavior that is disconnected from our true feelings—like when we flash a fake smile—both our brain[49] and heart functions[50] respond as though we just experienced a negative emotion.

CLOSING THOUGHTS

We hope this chapter did as much to remind you of what you're doing right and should continue to do as it taught you new ways of taking care of yourself. We encourage you to summarize the wealth of information presented here by answering these three questions:

- *What should I continue doing because it's working well?*
- *What should I start doing more of?*
- *What should I stop doing because it hinders more than helps?*

CHAPTER 12

Letting Go

We hope that, regardless of what attracted you to this book, the concepts and information we have presented will help you to take a next step toward being who you choose to be. Letting go of what's holding you back means different things to different people.

My (Wayne's) dad has a saying that began as he and my mom went about creating their family, which eventually included my four siblings and me: "Just when you think it's full, another child comes along and you find a piece of your heart you never even knew you had."

We have learned from our clients that there are many avenues to the sort of self-discovery and actualization that my dad spoke of. Sometimes, the catalyst of letting go is not a joyful event, but an unwanted setback. It all depends on how you choose to react.

If, even in small ways, the information we have presented stirs you to begin to let go of what might otherwise hold you back from exploring those parts of your "heart" that have been waiting for the light of your attention, then we have accomplished our goal. Whether you need to let go of something that is hurting you or simply lift the ceiling of joy you feel about your already good life, just do it!

Pace Yourself

We have filled this book with a multitude of strategies for letting go. No one uses them all, and we suspect that neither will you.

We offer a wide menu of change strategies because experience has taught us that people who make lasting changes do so with the help of a variety of strategies applied across a lifetime. The key is to regularly and honestly evaluate your progress, celebrate what is working well, and, if you are stagnating in some area, try something new. Even if you practice only two or three of these strategies at first, you will likely begin to change in ways that lead to transformations in your work, your life, and your relationships that you will want to continue. No matter where you begin, to keep your momentum going, use the other strategies we have described. So start someplace! Remember that letting go in *any* way is better than staying stuck in old ways that are holding you back.

The Signs of Letting Go

How can you know if you're letting go? On the most obvious level, you will start taking better care of yourself in work, love, and life.

But the deeper message of this book reflects the deeper psychological work to be done if you are to truly thrive. This is the work of ending self-limiting psychological legacies and starting, instead, to live in ways based on a newfound generosity and graciousness when dealing with yourself and others. We believe that this is the ultimate accomplishment.

> ### End Self-Limiting Legacies
>
> *When you end a self-limiting psychological legacy, you justify your lifetime, no matter what else you might do.*

You know you are letting go when you find yourself moving out of the "shadows" created by self-limiting patterns that hold you back, and move, instead, into the "light" that comes from taking responsibility for yourself and the impact you have on others. We hope that our words will stir you to . . .

- Let go of denial, and move toward accepting your life's truths and your own worth.
- Let go of despair, and embrace hope.
- Let go of passivity, and take an active role in shaping your future by changing your present.
- Let go of secrecy, and begin to let others know what you really think, feel, need, and want.
- Let go of isolation, and begin to connect with others in deeper and more meaningful ways.
- Let go of guilt or shame, and find forgiveness.
- Let go of anxiety and fear, and learn to trust in your own courage.
- Let go of cynicism, and find meaning and goodness all around you.
- Let go of loss, and embrace your "new normal."
- Let go of trying to change other people and, instead, try accepting them as they are.
- Let go of waiting and struggling, and start enjoying each moment of your journey.

Let go!

NOTES

Chapter 1

[1] Jim Loher and Tony Schwartz, *The Power of Full Engagement* (New York: The Free Press, 2003).

[2] This scale is adapted from seminal research on happiness conducted by E. Diener, E. Suh, and S. Oishi, "Recent Findings on Subjective Well-Being," *Indian Journal of Clinical Psychology* (March 1997).

R. A. Easterlin, "Explaining Happiness," *Proceedings of the National Academy of Sciences* 100 (2003): 11176–83.

M.E.P. Seligman and M. Csikszentmihalyi, eds., Special Issue on Happiness, Excellence, and Optimal Human Functioning, *American Psychologist* 55 (2000): 5–183.

M.E.P. Seligman, *Authentic Happiness: Using the New Positive Psychology to Realize Your Potential for Lasting Fulfillment* (New York: The Free Press, 2002).

B. Staw, R. Sutton, and L. Pelled, "Employee Positive Favorable Outcomes at the Workplace," *Organization Science* 5 (1994): 51–71.

[3] M. Fordyce, "A Review of Research on the Happiness Measures: A Sixty-Second Index of Happiness and Mental Health," *Social Indicators Research* 20 (1988): 355–81.

[4] C. Hermann et al., "Effects of Anxiety and Depression on 5-Year Mortality in 5,057 Patients Referred for Exercise Testing," *Journal of Psychosomatic Research* 48 (April–May 2000): 455–62.

[5] D. E. Bush et al., "Even Minimal Symptoms of Depression Increase Mortality Risk After Acute Myocardial Infarction," *American Journal of Cardiology* 5 (2001): 337–41.

[6] Dean Ornish, *Love and Survival: The Scientific Basis for the Healing Power of Intimacy* (New York: Harper Collins, 1997).

[7] R. Niaura, J. F. Todaro, and L. Stroud, "Hostility, the Metabolic Syndrome, and Incident Coronary Heart Disease," *Health Psychology* 21 (2002): 588–93.

[8] L. C. Gallo et al., "Marital Status and Quality in Middle-Aged Women: Associations with Levels and Trajectories of Cardiovascular Risk Factors," *Health Psychology* 22 (2003): 453–63.

Linda J. Waite and Maggie Gallagher, *The Case for Marriage: Why Married People Are Happier, Healthier, and Better Off Financially* (New York: Doubleday, 2000).

[9] J. Denollet et al., "Usefulness of Type D Personality in Predicting Five-Year Cardiac Events Above and Beyond Concurrent Symptoms of Stress in Patients with Coronary Heart Disease," *American Journal of Cardiology* 97 (2006): 970–73.

[10] C. Maslach, S. E. Jackson, and M. P. Leiter, *Maslach Burnout Inventory Manual*, 3rd ed. (Palo Alto, CA: Consulting Psychologists Press, 1996).

W. B. Schaufeli and D. Enzmann, *The Burnout Companion to Study and Practice: A Critical Analysis* (London: Taylor & Francis, 1998).

[11] Wayne M. Sotile with Robin Cantor-Cooke, *Thriving with Heart Disease*, 2nd ed. (New York: The Free Press, 2004).

[12] U.S. Department of Health and Human Services, *Mental Health: A Report of the Surgeon General* (Rockville, MD: U.S. Department of Health and Human Services, 1999).

13 G. E. Simon and M. VonKorff, "Recognition, Management and Outcomes of Depression in Primary Care," *Family Medicine* 4 (1995): 99–105.

A. S. Young et al., "The Quality of Care for Depression and Anxiety in the United States," *Archives of General Psychiatry* 58 (2001): 55–61.

14 R. C. Kessler et al., "The Epidemiology of Major Depressive Disorder: Results from the National Comorbidity Survey Replication," *Journal of the American Medical Association* 289 (2003): 3095–105.

15 W. F. Stewart et al., "Cost of Lost Productive Work Time Among U.S. Workers with Depression," *Journal of the American Medical Association* 289 (2003): 3135–44.

16 C.J.L. Murray and A. D. Lopez, "Alternative Projections of Mortality and Disability by Cause, 1990–2020: Global Burden of Disease Study," *Lancet 349* (1997): 1498–504.

17 Sotile, *Thriving with Heart Disease.*

18 For an excellent discussion of the following symptoms of depression, see: J. Preston, "Depression and Anxiety Management" (audiotape) (Oakland, CA: New Harbinger Publications, 1992).

19 Adapted from the American Psychiatric Association, *Diagnostic and Statistic Manual of Mental Disorders*, 4th ed. (Washington, DC: American Psychiatric Association, 1994).

20 Redford Williams and Virginia Williams, *Anger Kills* (New York: Harper Paperbacks, 1993).

21 R. Niaura, J. F. Todaro, and L. Stroud, "Hostility, the Metabolic Syndrome, and Incident Coronary Heart Disease," *Health Psychology* 21 (2002): 588–93.

22 K. L. Zellars and B. J. Tepper, "Abusive Supervision and Subordinates' Organizational Citizenship Behavior," *Journal of Applied Psychology* 287 (2002): 1068–76.

23 Nic Paton, "Bad Bosses Cause the Most Workplace Misery," www.management-issues.com, 13 January 2006; accessed 16 January 2006.

24 J. Ferrie et al., "Injustice at Work and Incidence of Psychiatric Morbidity: The Whitehall II Study," *Occupational and Environmental Medicine*, 12 May 2006.

M. Kivimaki et al., "Justice at Work and Reduced Risk of Coronary Heart Disease among Employees: The Whitehall II Study," *Archives of Internal Medicine* 24 (October 2005): 2245–51.

25 M. Friedman and D. Ulmer, *Treating Type A Behavior—and Your Heart* (New York: Alfred A. Knopf, 1984).

26 Wayne M. Sotile and Mary O. Sotile, *The Resilient Physician: Effective Emotional Management for Doctors and Their Medical Organizations* (Chicago: American Medical Association Press, 2002).

27 Gallo et al., "Marital Status and Quality in Middle-Aged Women."

Waite and Gallagher, *The Case for Marriage.*

28 R. C. Brown, "What Sparks Threats on the Job?" *Forsyth Medicine/Business Coalition Meeting Report* (Winston-Salem, NC), 10 September 1999.

[29] Used by permission of Scott Stanley and Howard Markman. See Howard Markman et al., *12 Hours to a Great Marriage* (New York: Wiley and Sons, 2004).

Chapter 2

[1] Rebecca A. Clay, "Making Working Families Work," *Monitor on Psychology* (December 2005): 54.

[2] N. Chesley, "Cell Phone Technology Is Linked to Increased Psychological Distress and Lower Family Satisfaction in Working Men and Women," *Journal of Marriage and Family* 67 (December 2005): 1237–48.

News release, Blackwell Publishing.

[3] "Free Days," *The Strategic Coach*, www.strategiccoach.com/resources/articles/coach-article/article/free-days.html, posted 18 August 2005; accessed 16 July 2006.

[4] D. H. Olson and A. K. Olson, *Empowering Couples: Building on Your Strengths*, 2nd ed. (Minneapolis: Life Innovations, 2000).

[5] Kimberly Durnan, "Leaving the Job Behind," *The Charlotte Observer*, 5 December 2005, 3D.

[6] Tony Schwartz, "Going Postal," *New York Magazine*, 19 July 1999, 34.

[7] Barbara A. Glanz, *Balancing Acts: More Than 250 Guiltfree, Creative Ideas to BLEND Your Work and Your Life* (Dearborn, MI: Dearborn Trade Publishing, 2003).

[8] Peter Drucker, *The Effective Executive* (New York: Harper & Row, 1966).

Alan Lakein, *How to Get Control of Your Time and Your Life* (New York: Signet, 1974).

Ann McGee-Cooper, *Time Management for Unmanageable People* (Dallas, TX: Ann McGee-Cooper & Associates, 1983).

[9] Linda J. Waite and Maggie Gallagher, *The Case for Marriage: Why Married People Are Happier, Healthier, and Better Off Financially* (New York: Doubleday, 2000).

[10] Clay, "Making Working Families Work," 54–56.

[11] Thomas F. Coleman, "Many Singles not Satisfied with Work-Life Balance," *Unmarried America*, www.unmarriedamerica.org/column-one/12-5-05-work-life-balance.htm.

Chapter 3

[1] Cited in Sarah Ban Breathnach, *Simple Abundance* (New York: Warner Books, 1995).

[2] Source: Robert P. Quinn and Grahm L. Staines, *Quality of Employment Survey* (Ann Arbor: University of Michigan, Institute for Social Research, 1979).

[3] Source: *Second Wind: Workers, Retirement, and Social Security* (John J. Heldrich Center for Workforce Development at Rutgers, the State University of New Jersey, and the Center for Survey Research and Analysis at the University of Connecticut, Fall 2000).

[4] Shari Missman Miller, "Workforce Solutions: Has Necessity Become the Mother of the Work Ethic?" www.bizsites.com/2003/september/article.asp?id=470, accessed 13 June 2006.

[5] Lynne Lamberg, "Impact of Long Working Hours Explored," *Journal of the American Medical Association* 292 (7 July 2004): 25–26.

[6] Robert Schlesinger, "Is There Life After Work?" *AARP Bulletin*, May 2005, 3.

[7] George Manning, Kent Curtis, and Steve McMillen, *Stress: Living and Working in a Changing World* (Duluth, MN: Whole Person Associates, 1999).

[8] "Stress Epidemic Wreaks Havoc in U.K. Businesses," *Management Issues News*, www.management-issues.com, 6 November 2002; accessed 16 January 2005.

[9] *Working Today: Exploring Employees' Emotional Connections to Their Jobs*, Towers Perrin study, www.towersperrin.com/tp/jsp/search.jsp, accessed 5 April 2006.

"Taking Stress Seriously," *Management Issues News*, www.management-issues.com, 3 November 2004; accessed 16 January 2005.

[10] Mihaly Csikszentmihalyi, *Finding Flow: The Psychology of Engagement with Everyday Life* (New York: Basic Books, 1997).

[11] Wayne M. Sotile and Mary O. Sotile, "Physicians' Wives Evaluate Their Marriages, Their Husbands, and Life in Medicine: Results of the AMA–Alliance Medical Marriage Survey," *Bulletin of the Menninger Clinic* 68 (2004): 31–51.

[12] Ellen Galinsky, *Ask the Children: The Breakthrough Study that Reveals How to Succeed at Work and Parenting* (New York: Quill, Harper Collins, 1999).

[13] Gallup Management Group, "Gallup Study: Unhappy Workers Are Unhealthy Too," http://gmj.gallup.com, 13 January 2005; accessed 6 June 2006.

[14] W. Schlotz et al., "Perceived Work Overload and Chronic Worrying Predict Weekend-Weekday Differences in the Cortisol Awakening Response," *Psychosomatic Medicine* 66 (2004): 207–14.

[15] Robert Karasek et al., "Job Decision Latitude, Job Demands and Cardiovascular Disease: A Prospective Study of Swedish Men," *American Journal of Public Health* 71 (1981): 694–705; Robert Karasek and Tores Theorell, *Healthy Work: Stress, Productivity, and the Reconstruction of Working Life* (New York: Basic Books, 1990).

[16] P. L. Schnall, P. A. Landsbergis, and D. Baker, "Job Strain and Cardiovascular Disease," *Annual Review of Public Health* 15 (1994): 381–411.

[17] Thomas J. Peters and Robert H. Waterman, Jr., *In Search of Excellence* (New York: Harper & Row, 1982), xxiii, xxiv.

[18] E. Herzberg, in W. E. Natemeyer, ed., *Classics of Organizational Behavior* (Oak Park, IL: Moore Publishing, 1978).

[19] Ibid.

[20] Manning, Curtis, and McMillen, *Stress*, 327.

[21] Adapted from Csikszentmihalyi, *Finding Flow*.

[22] John G. Miller, *Flipping the Switch* (New York: G. P. Putnam's Sons, 2006).

23 Working Today: The Towers Perrin 2003 Talent Report, www.towersperrin.com/tp/jsp/masterbrand_webcache_html.jsp?webc=HR_Services/United_States/Press_Releases/2003/20030528/2003_05_28.htm, accessed 23 May 2006.

24 Adapted from Manning, Curtis, and McMillen, *Stress*.

25 M. R. Frone, "Work-Family Conflict and Employee Psychiatric Disorders: The National Comorbidity Survey," *Journal of Applied Psychology* 85 (December 2000): 888–95.

26 Csikszentmihalyi, *Finding Flow*.

27 B. E. Robinson, *WorkAddiction:Hidden Legacies of Adult Children* (Deerfield Beach, FL: Health Communications, 1989).

28 T. A. Judge and S. Watanabe, "Another Look at the Job Satisfaction–Life Satisfaction Relationship," *Journal of Applied Psychology*, cited in "Well-Being and the Workplace," 392–412, in Daniel Kahnman, Ed Diener, and Norbert Schwarz, eds., *Well-Being: The Foundations of Hedonic Psychology* (New York: Russell Sage Foundation, 1993).

Chapter 4

1 D. C. Dollahite, A. J. Hawkins, and S. E. Brotherson, "Fatherwork: A Conceptual Ethic of Fathering as Generative Work," in Hawkins and Dollahite, eds., *Generative Fathering: Beyond Deficit Perspectives* (Thousand Oaks, CA: Sage Publications, 1997), 17–35.

Laura Hernandez-Guzman and Juan Jose Sanchez-Sosa, "Parent-Child Interactions Predict Anxiety in Mexican Adolescents," *Adolescence*, Winter 1996.

Jungmeen Kim and Dante Cicchetti, "A Longitudinal Study of Child Maltreatment, Mother–Child Relationship Quality and Maladjustment: The Role of Self-Exteem and Social Competence," *Journal of Abnormal Child Psychology*, August 2004.

E. E. Werner, E. E., "The Children of Kauai: Resiliency and Recovery in Adolescence and Adulthood," *Journal of Adolescent Health* 13 (1992): 262–68.

2 John Gottman and Nan Silver, *The Seven Principles for Making Marriage Work* (New York: Three Rivers Press, 1999).

3 John H. Fleming, Curt Coffman, and James K. Harter, "Manage Your Human Sigma," *Harvard Business Review* (July–August 2005): 107–14.

4 Scott Clark, "The Cost of Not Knowing Your Customers," *Biz Journals*,www.bizjournals.com/bizwomen/consultants/company_doctor/1999/12/13/column186.html, posted 13 December 1999; accessed 26 August 2005.

5 L. R. Murphy, "Organisational Interventions to Reduce Stress in Health Care Professionals," in J. Firth-Cozens and R. Payne, eds., *Stress in Health Professionals: Psychological and Organisational Causes and Interventions* (New York: John Wiley & Sons, 1999). 149–62.

Wayne M. Sotile and Mary O. Sotile, *The Resilient Physician: Effective Emotional Management for Doctors and Their Medical Organizations* (Chicago: American Medical Association Press, 2002).

6 Tom Rath and Donald O. Clifton, *How Full Is Your Bucket? Positive Strategies for Work and Life* (New York: Gallup Press, 2004).

7 A. J. Carter and M. A. West, "Sharing the Burden: Teamwork in Health Care Settings," in Firth-Cozens and Payne, *Stress in Health Professionals*, 191–202.

8 James M. Kouzes and Barry Z. Posner, *Encouraging the Heart: A Leader's Guide to Rewarding and Recognizing Others* (San Francisco: Jossey-Bass, 1999).

9 H. E. McIlvain et al., "Practical Steps to Smoking Cessation for Recovering Alcoholics," *American Family Physician*, 15 April 1998.

10 J. C. Barefoot et al., "Moderators of the Effect of Social Support on Depressive Symptoms in Cardiac Patients," *American Journal of Cardiology* 86 (15 August 2000): 438–42.

Dean Ornish, *Love and Survival: The Scientific Basis for the Healing Power of Intimacy* (New York: Harper Perennial, 1999).

11 James K. Harter . . . Jennifer Robison, "Your Job May Be Killing You," *The Gallup Management Journal* (13 April 2006), http://gmj.gallup.com. Harter is also coauthor of "Manage Your Human Sigma," *Harvard Business Review*, July–August 2005.

12 Rath and Clifton, *How Full Is Your Bucket?*

13 Peter Fraenkel, "Time and Couples, Part II: The Sixty-Second Pleasure Point," in T. S. Nelson and T. S. Trepper, eds., *101 More Interventions in Family Therapy* (New York: The Haworth Press, 1998), 145–49.

14 Gary Chapman, *The Five Love Languages: How to Express Heartfelt Commitment to Your Mate* (Chicago: Northfield Publishing, 1995).

15 www.fivelovelanguages.com/30sec.html#love, accessed 3 August 2006.

16 J. Levey and M. Levey, *Living in Balance—A Dynamic Approach for Creating Harmony and Wholeness in a Chaotic World* (Berkeley, CA: Conari Press, 1998).

17 Modified from Brian Tracy, *Goals! How to Get Everything You Want—Faster Than You Ever Thought Possible* (San Francisco: Berrett-Koehler, 2003).

Rath and Clifton, *How Full Is Your Bucket?*

18 Modified from Wendy Leebov, "How Do You Say Thanks?" *Hospitals and Health Networks*, www.hhnmag.com/hhnmag/jsp/articledisplay.jsp, 17 September 2005.

19 Wendy Leebov, "Less Turnover, Better Patient Care," *Hospitals and Health Networks*, 18 October 2005, www.hhnmag.com/hhnmag/jsp/articledisplay.jsp?dcrpath=HHNMAG/PubsNews Article/data/051018HHN_Online_Leebov&domain=HHNMAG, accessed 28 August 2006.

20 Lichtenstein, "Partner Behaviors that Support Quitting Smoking," *Journal of Consulting and Clinical Psychology* 58 (1990): 304–09; K. Ell and C. Dunkel-Schetter, "Social Support and Adjustment to Myocardial Infarction, Angioplasty, and Coronary Artery Bypass Surgery," in S. A. Shumaker and S. M. Czajkowski, eds., *Social Support and Cardiovascular Disease* (New York: Plenum Press, 1994).

21 Ibid.

22 Roger Fisher and William R. Ury, *Getting to Yes: Negotiating Agreement Without Giving In* (New York: Penguin, 1983).

John Gottman and Nan Silver, *The Seven Principles for Making Marriage Work* (New York: Three Rivers Press, 1999).

23 Daniel Goleman, *Emotional Intelligence* (New York: Bantam Books, 1995).

Right Management Consultants, *Lessons Learned from Mergers and Acquisitions: Best Practices in Workforce Integration* (Philadelphia: Right Management Consultants, 1999).

B. D. Wong, "Collegiality and Collaboration," workshop presented to American Hospital Association, New Orleans, LA, 1994.

K. D. Ryan and D. K. Oestreich, *Driving Fear Out of the Workplace*, 2nd ed. (San Francisco: Jossey-Bass, 1998).

R. Kelly and J. Caplan, "How Bell Labs Creates Star Performers," *Harvard Business Review*, July–August 1993.

Mihaly Csikszentmihalyi, *Finding Flow: The Psychology of Engagement with Everyday Life* (New York: Basic Books, 1997).

Quint Studor, *Hardwiring Excellence* (Gulf Breeze, FL: Fire Starter Publishing, 2003).

24 Rebecca A. Clay, "Making Working Families Work," *Monitor on Psychology* (December 2005): 54–56.

25 Barbara A. Glanz, *Balancing Acts: More Than 250 Guiltfree, Creative Ideas to BLEND Your Work and Your Life* (Dearborn, MI: Dearborn Trade Publishing, 2003).

26 Modified from a similar exercise recommended by Louise Hay, *You Can Heal Your Life* (Santa Monica, CA: Hay House, 1985).

Chapter 5

1 J. Polivy and C. P. Herman, "If at First You Don't Succeed: False Hopes of Self-Change," *American Psychologist* 57 (September 2002): 677–89.

2 Ray Pelletier, *Permission to Win* (Akron, OH: Oakhill Press, 1997).

3 Phillip C. McGraw, *Self Matters: Creating Your Life from the Inside Out* (New York: The Free Press, 2001).

4 The psychodynamic perspective was summarized by R. R. Kilburg in *Executive Coaching: Developing Managerial Wisdom in a World of Chaos* (Washington, DC: American Psychological Association, 2000).

5 C. M. Aldwin, *Stress, Coping, and Development: An Integrative Perspective* (New York: Guilford), 1994), 216.

6 C. A. Dolan, A. Sherwood, and K. C. Light, "Cognitive Coping Strategies and Blood Pressure Responses to Real-Life Stress in Healthy Young Men," *Health Psychology* 11 (1992): 233–42.

7 J. Mattlin, E. Wethington, and R. C. Kessler, "Situational Determinants of Coping and Coping Effectiveness," *Journal of Health and Social Behavior* 31 (1990): 103–22.

P. P. Vitaliano et al., "Appraisal Changeability of a Stressor as a Modifier of the Relationship between Coping and Depression: A Test of the Hypothesis of Fit," *Journal of Personality and Social Psychology* 59 (1990): 582–92.

[8] I. Stewart and V. Joines, *TA Today: A New Introduction to Transactional Analysis* (Nottingham, England, and Chapel Hill, NC: Lifespace Publishing, 1987).

[9] Wayne M. Sotile and Mary O. Sotile, *The Resilient Physician: Effective Emotional Management for Doctors and Their Medical Organizations* (Chicago: American Medical Association Press, 2002).

[10] James O. Prochaska, John C. Norcross, and Carlo C. DiClemente in *Changing for Good* (New York: Avon Books, 1994).

[11] G. A. Marlatt, "Relapse Prevention: Theoretical," in R. Gordon ed., *Relapse Prevention* (New York: Guilford Press, 1985).

Chapter 6

[1] Marianne Williamson, *A Return to Love: Reflections on the Principles of a Course in Miracles* (New York: Harper Collins, 1992), 190–91

[2] Muriel James and Dorthy Jongeward, *Born to Win: Transactional Analysis with Gestalt Experiments* (Reading, MA: Addison-Wesley, 1996).

[3] T. Ernst, "The OK Corral: The Grid for 'Get-On-With,'" *Transactional Analysis Journal* 1 (1971): 4.

[4] Adapted from Brian Tracy, *Goals! How to Get Everything You Want—Faster Than You Ever Thought Possible* (San Francisco: Berrett-Koehler, 2003); and Stephen R. Covey, *The 8th Habit: From Effectiveness to Greatness* (New York: The Free Press, 2004).

[5] Tracy, *Goals*.

[6] Ibid.

[7] This exercise is adapted from Wayne M. Sotile and Mary O. Sotile, *The Resilient Physician: Effective Emotional Management for Doctors and Their Medical Organizations* (Chicago: American Medical Association Press, 2002), 75–6, with thanks to Vann Joines, Ph.D., Southeast Institute, Chapel Hill, NC. See I. Stewart and V. Joines, *TA Today: A New Introduction to Transactional Analysis* (Nottingham, England, and Chapel Hill, NC: Lifespace Publishing, 1987).

Chapter 7

[1] E. E. Werner and R. S. Smith, *Overcoming the Odds* (Ithaca, NY: Cornell University Press, 1992).

N. Garmezy and A. S. Masten. "Stress, Competence, and Resilience: Common Frontiers for Therapist and Psychopathologist," *Behavior Therapy* 17 (1986): 500–521.

Steven J. and Sybil Wolin, *The Resilient Self: How Survivors of Troubled Families Rise Above Adversity* (New York: Villard Books, 1993).

G. E. Vaillant, *The Wisdom of the Ego* (Cambridge: Harvard University Press, 1993).

Nan Henderson, Bernard Bonnies, and Nancy Sharp-Light, eds., R*esiliency in Action: Practical Ideas for Overcoming Risks and Building Strengths in Youth, Families, and Communities* (Ojai, CA: Resiliency in Action, 1999).

Dennis Saleeby, *The Strengths Perspective in Social Work Practice*, www.resiliency.com.

[2] Anton Antonovsky, *Unraveling the Mystery of Health* (San Francisco: Jossey-Bass, 1987).

[3] Brian Tracy, *Goals! How to Get Everything You Want—Faster Than You Ever Thought Possible* (San Francisco: Berrett-Koehler, 2003).

[4] M. D. Boltwood et al., "Anger Report Predicts Coronary Artery Vasomotor Response to Mental Stress in Atherosclerotic Segments," *American Journal of Cardiology* 72 (1993), 1361–65.

[5] W. Tiller, R. McCraty, and M. Atkinson, "Cardiac Coherence: A Review of Non-Invasive Measure of Autonomic Nervous System Order," *Alternative Therapies in Health and Medicine 2* (1996): 52–65.

[6] C. D. Spielberger, S. S. Krasner, and E. P. Solomon, "The Experience, Expression and Control of Anger," in M. P. Janisse, ed., *Health Psychology: Individual Differences and Stress* (New York: Springer, 1988), 89–l08.

[7] P. E. Spector, "Individual Differences in the Job Stress Process of Health Care Professionals," in J Firth-Cozens and R. Payne, eds., *Stress in Health Professionals: Psychological and Organizational Causes and Interventions* (New York: John Wiley & Sons, 1999), 33–42.

[8] S. M. Jex and P. E. Spector, "The Impact of Negative Affectivity on Stressor-Strain Relationships: A Replication and Extension," *Work and Stress* 10 (1996): 36–45.

P. Moyle, "The Role of Negative Affectivity in the Stress Process: Tests of Alternative Models, *Journal of Organizational Behavior* 16 (1995): 647–68.

P. Y. Chen and P. E. Spector, "Negative Affectivity as the Underlying Cause of Correlations between Stressors and Strains," *Journal of Applied Psychology* 76 (1991): 398–407.

[9] Martin E.P. Seligman, *Learned Optimism* (New York: Simon & Schuster, 1998).

Martin E.P. Seligman, *Authentic Happiness: Using the New Positive Psychology to Realize your Potential for Lasting Fulfillment* (New York: The Free Press, 2002).

See also M. F. Scheier et al., "Dispositional Optimism and Recovery from Coronary Artery Bypass Surgery: The Beneficial Effects of Physical and Psychological Well-Being," *Journal of Personality and Social Psychology* 57 (1989): 1024–40.

[10] M. F. Scheier and C. S. Carver, "Optimism, Coping, and Health: Assessment and Implications of Generalized Outcome Expectancies," *Health Psychology 4* (1985): 219–47.

[11] R. Ornstein and D. Sobel, *Healthy Pleasures* (Reading, MA: Addison-Wesley, 1989).

[12] C. E. Thoresen and A.II.S. Harris, "Spirituality and Health: What's the Evidence and What's Needed?" *Annals of Behavioral Medicine 24* (2002): 3–13.

F. Luskin, "Review of the Effect of Spiritual and Religious Factors on Mortality and Morbidity with a Focus on Cardiovascular and Pulmonary Disease," *Journal of Cardiopulmonary Rehabilitation* 29 (2000): 8–15.

13 Ibid.

14 A. Mahoney et al., "Marriage and the Spiritual Realm: The Role of Proximal and Distal Religious Constructs in Marital Functioning," *Journal of Family Psychology* 13 (1999): 321–38.

15 L. G. Underwood and J. A. Teresi, "The Daily Spiritual Experience Scale: Development, Theoretical Description, Reliability, Explanatory Factor Analysis, and Preliminary Construct Validity Using Health-Related Data," *Annals of Behavioral Medicine* 24 (2000): 22–33.

A. H. Peterman et al., "Measuring Spiritual Well-Being in People with Cancer: The Functional Assessment of Chronic Illness Therapy—Spiritual Well-Being Scale (FACIT-Sp)," *Annals of Behavioral Medicine* 24 (2002): 49–58.

J. L. Shaffer, "Spiritual Distress and Critical Illness," *Critical Care Nurse* 11 (1991): 42–45.

Bruno Cortis, *Heart & Soul: A Psychological and Spiritual Guide to Preventing and Healing Heart Disease* (New York: Villard Books, 1995).

Chapter 8

1 Eknath Easwaran, *Gandhi the Man: The Story of His Transformation*, 2nd ed. (Tomales, CA: Nilgiri Press, 1978), 145.

2 A modification of this scale first appeared in Wayne Sotile and Mary Sotile, *The Medical Marriage* (Chicago: American Medical Association Press, 2002).

Chapter 9

1 Doc Childre and Deborah Rozman, *Transforming Stress: The HeartMath Solution for Relieving Worry, Fatigue, and Tension* (Oakland, CA: New Harbinger, 2005), 2.

2 Bruce McEwen with Elizabeth Norton Lasley, *The End of Stress As We Know It* (Washington, DC: Joseph Henry Press, 2002).

3 F. Luskin and K. R. Pelletier, *Stress Free for Good* (San Francisco: Harper San Francisco, 2005).

Chapter 10

1 Bruce McEwen with Elizabeth Norton Lasley, *The End of Stress As We Know It* (Washington, DC: Joseph Henry Press, 2002).

2 Jim Loehr and Tony Schwartz, *The Power of Full Engagement* (New York: The Free Press, 2003).

Deborah Rozman and Doc Childre, *Transforming Stress: The HeartMath Solution for Relieving Worry, Fatigue, and Tension* (Oakland, CA: New Harbinger, 2005).

3 Ann McGee-Cooper with Duane Trammell and Barbara Lau, *You Don't Have to Go Home from Work Exhausted! A Program to Bring Joy, Energy, and Balance to Your Life* (New York: Bantam, 1992).

David Allen, *Getting Things Done: The Art of Stress-Free Productivity* (New York: Penguin, 2001).

4 Adapted from McGee-Cooper, *You Don't Have to Go Home from Work Exhausted!*

[5] Robert Kubey and Mihaly Csikszentmihalyi, *Television and the Quality of Life: How Viewing Shapes Everyday Experience* (Hillsdale, NJ: Lawrence Erlbaum Associates, 1990).

[6] Wayne Sotile, "The Psychosocial Benefits of Exercising," in Roy J. Shephard and Henry S. Miller, Jr., eds., *Exercise and the Heart in Health and Disease*, 2nd ed. (New York: Marcel Dekker, 1999), 561–72.

[7] Loehr and Schwartz, *The Power of Full Engagement*, 65.

[8] JoAnn E. Manson et al., "Walking Compared with Vigorous Exercise for the Prevention of Cardiovascular Events in Women," *New England Journal of Medicine* 347 (2002): 716–25.

[9] Rozman and Childre, *Transforming Stress*.

[10] Joseph C. Piscatella and Barry A. Franklin, *Take a Load Off Your Heart* (New York: Workman Publishing, 2003).

[11] Hans Selye, *The Stress of Life*, rev. ed. (New York: McGraw-Hill, 1976).

[12] P. W. Linville, "Self-Complexity as a Cognitive Buffer against Stress-Related Illness and Depression," *Journal of Personality and Social Psychology* 52 (1987): 663–76.

[13] Donald Norfolk, *Executive Stress* (New York: Warner, 1986).

[14] Robert K. Cooper and Aywan Sawaf, *Executive EQ: Emotional Intelligence in Leadership and Organizations* (New York: Grosset/Putnam, 1997).

[15] Adapted from McGee-Cooper, *You Don't Have to Go Home from Work Exhausted!*

[16] D. C. Baldwin and S. R. Daugherty, "Sleep Deprivation and Fatigue in Residency Training: Results of a National Survey of First-and Second-Year Residents, Sleep 27 (2004): 217–23

[17] Used with permission from the Stanford Patient Education Research Center.

[18] Source: www.sims.berkeley.edu/courses/is206/f97/GroupE/infoglut.html, accessed 27 December 2005.

[19] "Do Filters Really Solve Information Overload?" *The Information Advisor* 9 (February 1997), reported on www.sims.berkeley.edu/courses/is206/f97/GroupE/infoglut.html.

[20] www.management-issues.com/display_page.asp?section=research&id=2071, accessed 27 December 2005.

[21] Source: 2003 E-Mail Rules, Policies and Practices Survey from the American Management Association, Clearswift, and the ePolicy Institute.

[22] Pamela Kristan, *The Spirit of Getting Organized: 12 Skills to Find Meaning and Power in Your Stuff* (York Beach, ME: Red Wheel/Weiser, 2003).

[23] www.breathingspace.com/content/view/65/84, accessed 27 December 2005.

[24] Jeff Davidson, *Breathing Space: Living and Working at a Comfortable Pace in a Sped-Up Society* (Portland, OR: MasterMedia, 1991).

[25] Jeff Davidson, *The Complete Idiot's Guide to Managing Stress*, 2nd ed. (New York: Alpha Books, 1999).

Chapter 11

[1] Ann McGee-Cooper with Duane Trammell and Barbara Lau, *You Don't Have to Go Home from Work Exhausted! A Program to Bring Joy, Energy, and Balance to Your Life* (New York: Bantam, 1992), 171.

[2] John Gottman, *Why Marriages Succeed or Fail: And How You Can Make Yours Last* (New York: Fireside, 1994).

[3] A. D. Kanner et al., "Comparison of Two Modes of Stress Measurement: Daily Hassles and Uplifts versus Major Life Events," *Journal of Behavioral Medicine* 4 (1981): 1–39.

[4] R. J. Larsen, E. Diener, and R. S. Cropanzano, "Cognitive Operations Associated with Individual Differences in Affect Intensity," *Journal of Personality and Social Psychology* 53 (October 1987): 767–74.

[5] E. Diener, "Subjective Well-Being: The Science of Happiness and a Proposal for a National Index," *American Psychologist* 55 (2000): 34–43.

Larsen, Diener, and Cropanzano, "Cognitive Operations Associated with Individual Differences in Affect Intensity."

[6] Ibid.

[7] J. W. Reich and A. Zatura, "Life Events and Personal Causation: Some Relationships with Satisfaction and Distress," *Journal of Personality and Social Psychology* 41 (1981): 1002–12.

[8] B. L. Fredrickson et al., "What Good Are Positive Emotions in Crises? A Prospective Study of Resilience and Emotions Following the Terrorist Attacks on the United States on September 11th, 2001," *Journal of Personality and Social Psychology* 84 (2003): 365–76.

[9] Boltwood et al., "Anger Report Predicts Coronary Artery Vasomotor Response to Mental Stress in Atherosclerotic Segments," *American Journal of Cardiology* 72 (1993): 1361–65.

[10] B. L. Fredrickson et al., "The Undoing Effect of Positive Emotions," *Motivation and Emotion* 24 (2000): 237–58.

[11] A. Steptoe, J. Wardle, and M. Marmot, "Positive Affect and Health-Related Neuroendocrine, Cardiovascular, and Inflammatory Response," *Proceedings of the National Academy of Sciences*, USA 102 (2005): 6508–12.

[12] S. Cohen et al., "Emotional Style and Susceptibility to the Common Cold," *Psychosomatic Medicine*. 65 (2003): 652¬57.

[13] R. J. Davidson et al., "Alterations in Brain and Immune Function Produced by Mindfulness Meditation," *Psychosomatic Medicine* 65 (2003): 564¬70.

[14] D. D. Danner, D. A. Snowdon, and W. V. Friesen, "Positive Emotions in Early Life and Longevity: Findings from the Nun Study," *Journal of Personality and Social Psychology*. 80 (2001): 804–13.

B. R. Levy et al., "Longevity Increased by Positive Self-Perceptions of Aging," *Journal of Personality and Social Psychology* 83 (2002): 261–70.

J. T. Moskowitz, "Positive Affect Predicts Lower Risk of AIDS Mortality," *Psychosomatic Medicine* 65 (2003): 620¬25.

G. V. Ostir et al., "Emotional Well-Being Predicts Subsequent Functional Independence and Survival, *Journal of the American Geriatrics Society* 48 (2000): 473–78.

[15] J. K. Harter, F. L. Schmidt, and E. A. Killham, *Employee Engagement, Satisfaction, and Business-Unit-Level Outcomes: A Meta-Analysis* (Washington, DC: The Gallup Organization, 2003).

[16] Tom Rath and Donald O. Clifton, Ph.D., *How Full Is Your Bucket? Positive Strategies for Work and Life* (New York: Gallup Press, 2004).

J. M. George, "Leader Positive Mood and Group Performance: The Case of Customer Service," *Journal of Applied Social Psychology* 25 (1995): 778–94

[17] B. L. Fredrickson, "What Good Are Positive Emotions?" *Review of General Psychology.* 2 (1998): 300–319.

[18] B. L. Fredrickson and C. A. Branigan, "Positive Emotions Broaden the Scope of Attention and Thought-Action Repertoires," *Cognition and Emotion* 19 (2005): 313–32.

[19] Ibid.

[20] A. Bolte, T. Goschkey, and J. Kuhl, "Emotion and Intuition: Effects of Positive and Negative Mood on Implicit Judgments of Semantic Coherence," *Psychological Science* 14 (2003): 416–21.

[21] Reported in Martin E.P. Seligman, *Authentic Happiness* (New York, The Free Press, 2002).

[22] Source: Adapted from Bethesda Hospitals: Stress Management Program (St. Louis, MO: Department of Health Promotions, St. Louis University Medical Center). Cited in: George Manning, Kent Curtis, Kent, and Steve McMillen, *Stress: Living and Working in a Changing World* (Duluth, MN: Whole Person Associates, 1999).

[23] Adapted from information summarized in: Nick Donovan and David Halpern with Richard Sargeant, "Life Satisfaction: The State of Knowledge and Implications for Government," December 2002, www.strategy.gov.uk/downloads/seminars/ls/paper.pdf, accessed 12 July 2006.

Martin E.P. Seligman and M. Csikszentmihalyi, eds., Special Issue on Happiness, Excellence, and Optimal Human Functioning, *American Psychologist.* 55 (2000): 5¬183.

Michael Argyle, *The Psychology of Happiness*, 3rd ed. (New York: Taylor & Francis, 2001), Chapter 6.

Ed Diener and Richard E. Lucas, "Personality and Subjective Well-Being," in Daniel Kahnemann, Ed Diener, and Norbert Schwarz, eds., *Well-Being: The Foundations of Hedonic Psychology* (New York: Russell Sage Foundation), 213–29.

[24] Rafael Di Tella, Robert J. MacCulloch, and Andrew J. Oswald, "The Macroeconomics of Happiness" (University of Warwick, 2001); Andrew Clark and Andrew Oswald, "A Simple Statistical Method For Measuring How Life Events Affect Happiness" (University of Warwick, 2002); John F Helliwell, "How's Life? Combining Individual and National Variables to Explain Subjective Well-Being" (Department of Economics, University of British Columbia).

[25] Andrew Oswald and Jonathan Gardner, "Does Money Buy Happiness? A Longitudinal Study Using Data on Windfalls," March 2001, University of Warwick mimeo.

26 Michael Argyle, "Causes and Correlates of Happiness," in Kahnemann, Diener, and Schwarz, *Well-Being: The Foundations of Hedonic Psychology*, 357–73.

27 R. A. Easterlin, "Explaining Happiness," *Proceedings of the National Academy of Sciences* 100 (2003): 11176–83.

R. E. Lucas et al., "Reexamining Adaptation and the Set Point Model of Happiness: Reactions to Changes in Marital Status," *Journal of Personality and Social Psychology* 84 (2003): 527–39.

28 J. L. Matjasko and A. F. Feldman, "Bringing Work Home: The Emotional Experiences of Mothers and Fathers, *Journal of Family Psychology*, 20 (2006): 47–55.

29 We presented this exercise originally in our book *Supercouple Syndrome: How Overworked Couples Can Beat Stress Together* (New York: John Wiley & Sons, 1998).

30 McGee-Cooper, *You Don't Have to Go Home from Work Exhausted!*

31 Ed Diener et al., "Subjective Well Being: Three Decades of Progress," *Psychological Bulletin* 125 (1999): 276–302.

32 L. S. Richman et al., "Positive Emotion and Health: Going Beyond the Negative," *Health Psychology* 24 (2005): 422–29.

33 Alan Lakein, *How to Get Control of Your Time and Your Life* (New York: Signet, 1974).

34 S. R. Maddi, "The Story of Hardiness: Twenty Years of Theorizing, Research and Practice," *Consulting Psychology Journal* 4 (2002): 173–85.

35 P. B. Sutker et al., "War Zone Stress, Personal Resources, and PTSD in Persian Gulf War returnees," *Journal of Abnormal Psychology* 104 (August 1995): 444–52.

36 J. C. Brunstein, "Personal Goals and Subjective Well-Being," *Journal of Personality and Social Psychology* 65 (1993): 1061¬70.

37 J. M. Mossey and E. Sapiro, "Self-Rated Health: A Predictor of Mortality among the Elderly," *American Journal of Public Health* 72 (1982): 800–807.

38 G. A. Kaplan and T. Camacho, "Perceived Health and Mortality: A Nine-Year Follow-up of the Human Population Laboratory Cohort," *American Journal of Epidemiology* 117 (1983): 292–304.

39 I. S. Breetvelt and F. S. van Dam, "Under-reporting by Cancer Patients: The Case of Response Shift," *Social Science and Medicine* 32 (1991): 981–87.

40 F. D. Wolinsky and R. J. Johnson, "Perceived Health Status and Mortality among Older Men and Women," *Journal of Gerontology: Social Sciences* 47 (1992): S304–12.

41 Stanford Chronic Disease Self-Management Study. Psychometrics reported in: K. Lorig et al., *Outcome Measures for Health Education and Other Health Care Interventions* (Thousand Oaks, CA: Sage Publications, 1996), 25.

42 H. Kimata, "Emotion with Tears Decreases Allergic Responses to Latex in Atopic Eczema Patients with Latex Allergy," *Journal of Psychosomatic Research* 61 (July 2006): 67–9.

43 L. S. Berk et al., "Neuroendocrine and Stress Hormone Changes during Mirthful Laughter," *American Journal of Medical Science* 298 (December 1989): 390–96.

[44] D. L. Mahony, W. J. Burroughs, and A. C. Hieatt, "The Effects of Laughter on Discomfort Thresholds: Does Expectation Become Reality?" *Journal of General Psychology* 128 (April 2001): 217–26.

[45] S. Ravicz, *High on Stress: A Woman's Guide to Optimizing the Stress in Her Life* (Oakland, CA: New Harbinger Press, 1998).

[46] Adapted from McGee-Cooper, *You Don't Have to Go Home from Work Exhausted!*

[47] R. M. Schwartz et al., "Optimal and Normal Affect Balance in Psychotherapy of Major Depression: Evaluation of the Balanced States of Mind Model," *Behavioural and Cognitive Psychotherapy*. 30 (2002): 439–50.

Barbara L. Fredrickson and M. F. Losada, "Positive Affect and the Complex Dynamics of Human Flourishing," *American Psychologist* 60 (2005): 678–86.

[48] John M. Gottman, What Predicts Divorce? *The Relationship between Marital Processes and Marital Outcomes* (Hillsdale, NJ: Erlbaum, 1994).

[49] P. Ekman, R. J. Davidson, and W. V. Friesen, "The Duchenne Smile: Emotional Expression and Brain Physiology II," *Journal of Personality and Social Psychology* 58 (1990): 342–53.

[50] E. L. Rosenberg et al., "Linkages between Facial Expressions of Anger and Transient Myocardial Ischemia in Men with Coronary Artery Disease," *Emotion* 1 (2001): 107–15.

MARY O. SOTILE, M.A., AND WAYNE M. SOTILE, PH.D., are among the most sought-after motivational speakers and workshop leaders today. They have delivered more than 5,000 invited addresses to a client list that includes Fortune 500 companies and health care organizations throughout the country. Their pioneering work is featured frequently in the national and international media.

Mary and Wayne co-direct Sotile Psychological Associates in Winston-Salem, North Carolina, where Mary also serves as President of Real Talk, Inc. Wayne serves as Director of Psychological Services for the Wake Forest University Healthy Exercise and Lifestyles Program and as special consultant in behavioral health for the Carolinas Medical Center, in Charlotte, North Caorlina.

For further information about the Sotiles and DVDs and CDs that feature their work, please visit their web site, www.sotile.com.

REAL TALK, INC.
1396 Old Mill Circle
Winston-Salem, NC 27103
PHONE 336-794-0230
EMAIL realtalk@triad.rr.com
WEB SITE www.sotile.com

❊ Other Books by Wayne and Mary Sotile ❊

Marriage Skills for Busy Couples: How to Avoid Supercouple Syndrome

The Medical Marriage: Sustaining Healthy Relationships for Physicians and Their Families

The Resilient Physician: Effective Emotional Management for Doctors and Their Medical Organizations

Thriving with Heart Disease: A Unique Program for You and Your Family
(by Wayne Sotile with Robin Cantor-Cooke)

LET GO